LUCIN
O'SULLIV

LITTLE BLACK BOOK

Great Places to Stay and Eat
2008

IRELAND

Enchanting Houses, Inns
Castles, Hotels and Spas

TSAR PRESS

This book is published by

TSAR PRESS

Post Office Box No. 9647
Glenageary, Co. Dublin.

www.lucindaosullivan.com
www.wheretostayinireland.com

Written and collated by Lucinda O'Sullivan
Publishing Editor Brendan O'Sullivan

Regional Editors
Margaret Browne
Bayveen O'Connell
Carmel O'Neill

Maps and Mapping Joe Morris
Technical Support Ian O'Sullivan
Cover Design Aidan & Ian O'Sullivan
Layout Susan Waine, Ashfield Press

Lucinda O'Sullivan has asserted her right to be identified
as author of this book

Although every effort is made to ensure that the information given in this book is
accurate at the time of going to press, the publishers and authors do not accept
responsibility for any errors or omissions, or for any change which may arise in the
circumstances of the entries. They cannot either accept responsibility for any loss,
injury, or inconvenience resulting from the use of information contained therein.
All prices are per room for 2 people with breakfast unless otherwise stated.

ISBN 978-0-9547256-3-1

Printed in Ireland

A word from Lucinda

My first Little Black Book of Great Places to Stay came about by virtue of reader's letters and emails. People are always writing to me asking about places to stay, knowing that, in my role as the Restaurant Critic of the Sunday Independent I travel the country and, as well as eating, I also have to find a bed for the night! This has given me an unequalled opportunity each week to experience the good, the bad, and the ugly, of accommodation in Ireland. Tourism is a subject close to my heart, as I started out my career in the industry. But, my goodness, how things have changed over the intervening years. Even since my first Little Black Book 2004 there have been leaps and bounds – its like the change in the aero industry from piston powered engines to jet propelled!

What we have also seen in Ireland is the demise of the B & B with nylon sheets, watery smiles, "you don't want the full Irish do ye", and give me the money attitudes. People have a much better standard of living nowadays – interiors and food are a passion – and nobody will tolerate that type of miserable "welcome" anymore. What has taken over in that area are slick Guesthouses with all the facilities and comforts. There are cracking designer boutique hotels and the country is now awash with gorgeous Spas and de-stress destinations. Traditional family hotels have also seen the light and been progressing with the times, embarking on stunning makeovers. 2007 also saw the opening of some fab new hip Country House Hotels and gorgeous Country Estates to while away your time Grace Kelly "High Society" style – quite a number in the North West alone.

I have stayed in countless places over the years and I have learned that the most expensive lauded or grand establishment is not necessarily the greatest or the most enjoyable place to be a guest. They can be carried away with their own importance, be chilly, uncaring and offhand. Country Houses of the variety popular in the 80's, of the affected grand accents, threadbare rugs and watery tomato soup, who ever so delicately charge top dollar, are not standing up well to today's hip historic houses with all the comforts, less starch in all directions, good food and fun.

The Castles, Inns, Country and City Houses, Spas and special Hotels included in my Little Black Book for 2008 are rich in their thinking and attitude towards the guest and the tourists. Some are lavish and luxurious, some are simple, quirky, and sincere, some are creative and humorous, but you can expect, at all different levels, the greatest of what Ireland has to offer by way of hospitality, friendship, helpfulness and value for money in each category.

Don't forget to use my website www.lucindaosullivan.com through which you can contact me, share your experiences, and let me know if you have any wonderful discoveries.

As always, get out there and enjoy!

Lucinda

Ireland

reland, perceived as the Emerald Isle, Land of the Shamrock, the Leprechaun, the Blarney Stone, Thatched and White Washed Cottages, and the attitude of "as God made time he made plenty of it" has changed dramatically in recent years. It is now a thriving progressive country holding its head high as a member of the European Union but City traffic is bumper to bumper from early morning as workers head for their places of employment to keep the wheels of progress turning. However, underneath all the hustle and bustle, people haven't changed all that much. They still like to meet and talk, share a story, have a laugh and generally enjoy life.

Sport is a major interest here. Our bloodstock industry, both racing and show jumping is respected world-wide. Irish golf courses are a match for any in the World and our golfers, of the standing of Padraig Harrington, Darren Clarke, Paul McGinley, regularly contest major competitions internationally. Rugby and soccer both have a solid following but the major football game is Gaelic football with interest reaching its climax at the end of September when the all Ireland Final between the two leading Counties is played. For visitors possibly the most fascinating sport is traditional hurling, which is probably the fastest field game in the world, requiring speed, fitness, physical strength, great skill and application.

The open countryside, from the pleasant valleys and rounded mountains of the East to the rugged features of the West, provide ample scope and pleasant diversity of scenery for the walker or cyclist. For the motorist there are limitless places of interest from ancient ruins, fine buildings and museums, breathtaking scenery and even a Fairy Tree on the Comeragh drive near Dungarvan. The gourmet is well catered for as each and every county provides some excellent Restaurants to please even the most demanding palate.

Most pubs and bars provide good value lunches during the day and, in the evenings, many of them have traditional musicians and singers and, as we say in Ireland, the craic.

Most of all, apart from the sport, scenery, food, drink, craic, music the main attraction must be the people themselves, generally warm friendly and welcoming.

Ireland – you won't be disappointed.

EXPLANATION OF SYMBOLS

The symbols are a guide to facilities rather that a positive statement, and may change, so check important points when booking.

Working Farm

Children welcome, no age limits, but cots, high chairs etc are not necessarily available.

Credit Cards accepted – generally Visa/MC

T.V. in bedrooms

Swimming pool on premises

P Parking

Wine License – Hotels have full licenses

Disabled Facilities – check level with establishment.

Non-Smoking House

Pets welcome but may have to sleep in outbuilding or car. Check.

Pets accommodated in house.

Bikes on loan or for hire.

Tennis Court on premises

H Helipad

NET Internet access

Spa Spa

9h 9 Hole Golf Course on Site

18h 18 Hole Golf Course on Site

Contents

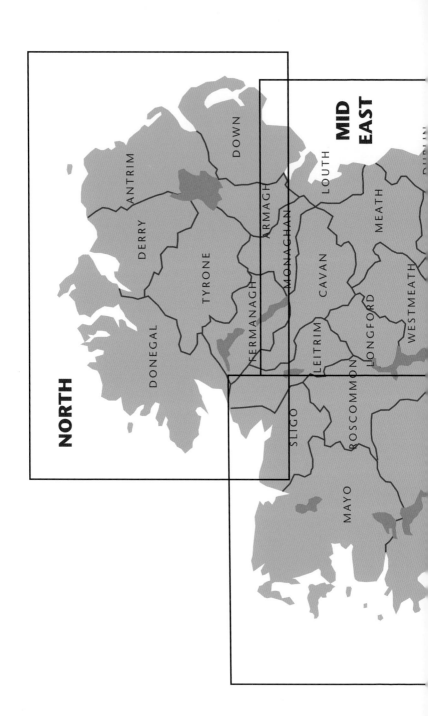

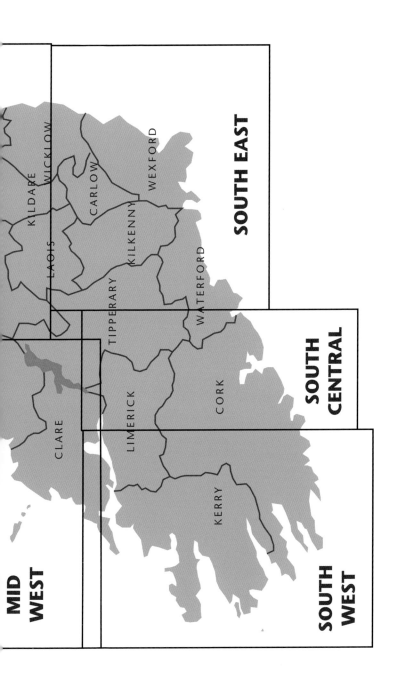

MID WEST

SOUTH EAST

SOUTH CENTRAL

SOUTH WEST

CLARE

KILDARE

WICKLOW

LAOIS

CARLOW

WEXFORD

KILKENNY

TIPPERARY

WATERFORD

LIMERICK

CORK

KERRY

North

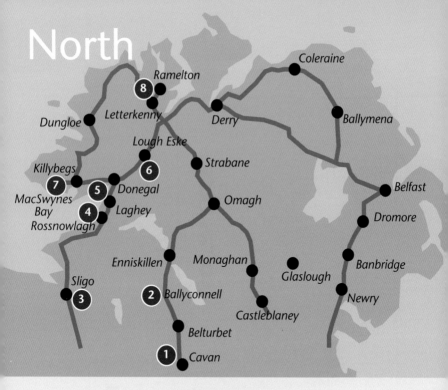

1. Cavan Crystal Hotel & Spa
2. Slieve Russell Hotel Golf Country Club
3. The Glass House Hotel
4. Sandhouse Hotel & Marine Spa
5. Donegal Manor Guest House
6. Harvey's Point Country House Hotel
7. Castle Murray House Hotel & Restaurant
8. Frewin Country House

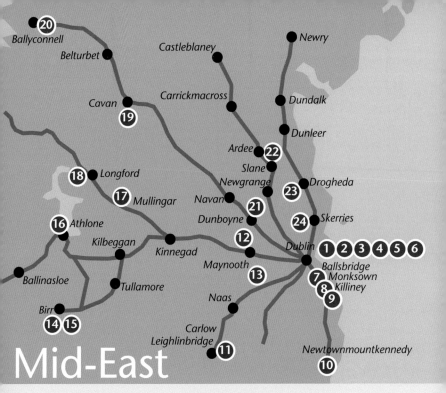

Mid-East

1. Clarence Hotel
2. Dylan Hotel
3. Fitzwilliam Hotel
4. Hotel Isaacs
5. Merrion Hotel
6. Shelbourne Hotel
7. Aberdeen Lodge Guest House
8. Drummond Mews S.C
9. Fitzpatrick Castle Killiney
10. Marriott Druids Glen Hotel
11. Lord Bagenal Inn
12. Carton House Hotel
13. Westgrove Hotel
14. County Arms Hotel & Leisure Club
15. Dooly's Hotel
16. Shamrock Lodge Country House Hotel
17. Mullingar Park Hotel
18. Viewmount House
19. Cavan Crystal Hotel
20. Slieve Russell Hotel Golf Country Club & Spa
21. Dunboyne Castle Hotel
22. Tankardstown House .
23. D Hotel
24. Redbank Guest House & Restaurant

South-East

South-Central

1. Lismore Country House Hotel
2. Ballymakeigh Country House
3. Capella Castlemartyr
4. Garryvoe Hotel
5. Bayview Hotel
6. Sheraton Fota Island Hotel & Spa
7. Radisson SAS Cork
8. Hotel Isaac's
9. Hayfield Manor
10. Crawford House
11. Kingsley Hotel
12. Cork International Airport Hotel
13. Blue Haven Hotel
14. Friar's Lodge
15. Harbour Lodge
16. Old Bank House
17. Shearwater S.C.
18. Woodlands House
19. Dunmore House Hotel
20. Bansha Castle
21. Bailey's of Cashel Hotel
22. Inch House
23. County Arms Hotel & Leisure Club
24. Dooly's Hotel
25. Coolbawn Quay Lakeshore Spa
26. Ashley Park House
27. AbsoluteHotel.com
28. Dunraven Arms Hotel
29. Old Ground Hotel

South-West

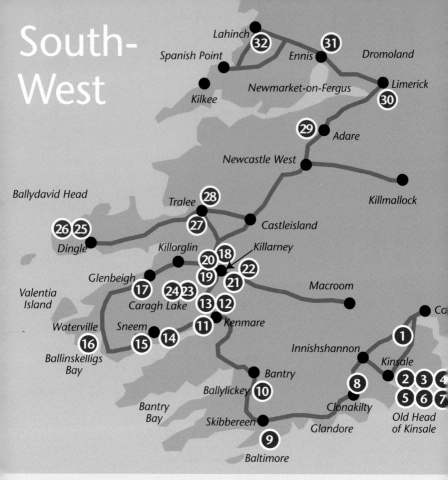

1. Cork International Airport Hotel
2. Blue Haven Hotel
3. Friar's Lodge
4. Harbour Lodge
5. Old Bank House
6. Shearwater S.C.
7. Woodlands House
8. Dunmore House Hotel
9. Waterfront Guesthouse
10. Seaview House Hotel
11. Brooklane Hotel
12. Muxnaw Lodge
13. Virginia's Guesthouse
14. Parknasilla Hotel
15. Sneem Hotel
16. Butler Arms Hotel
17. Carrig Country House
18. Aghadoe Heights Hotel & Spa
19. Cahernane House Hotel
20. Hotel Europe
21. The Ross Hotel
22. Killarney Royal Hotel & Spa
23. Muckross Park Hotel & Spa
24. 19th Green Guesthouse
25. Heaton's Guest House
26. Castlewood House
27. Manor West Hotel
28. Meadowlands Hotel
29. Dunraven Arms Hotel
30. AbsoluteHotel.com
31. Old Ground Hotel
32. Vaughan Lodge

Mid-West

1	Coolbawn Quay Lakeshore Spa	15	Dan O'Hara's Farmhouse
2	Ashley Park House	16	Ardmore Country House Hotel
3	AbsoluteHotel.com	17	Knockranny House Hotel & Spa
4	Old Ground Hotel	18	Lisloughry Lodge
5	Vaughan Lodge	19	Ashford Castle Estate
6	Cliffs of Moher Hotel	20	JJ Gannon's Hotel
7	Ballyvara House	21	Kelly's Gateway Hotel
8	Ballinalacken Country House Hotel	22	The Ice House
9	Tir Gan Ean Hotel	23	Mount Falcon Country House Hotel
10	Burren Coast Hotel	24	Shamrock Lodge Hotel
11	Radisson SAS, Galway	25	Viewmont House Guesthouse & Restaurant
12	The House Hotel	26	The Glass House Hotel
13	Ross Lake House Hotel		
14	Renvyle House Hotel		

County Carlow

Carlow is a low-rise busy midlands Town, on the River Barrow, and was an Anglo Norman stronghold at the edge of a very Gaelic county. Its present calm and serene atmosphere belies its turbulent past. At its heart is a beautiful classical Courthouse with the portico modelled on the Parthenon. Also worth seeing in Carlow is the controversial Regency Gothic Cathedral designed by Pugin. For those interested in Irish brew the Celtic Brewing Company, beside the Railway Station, is worth a tour. The beers brewed there are based on traditional Celtic recipes including a wheat beer, red ale and stout. Carlow has become a commuter town from Dublin and is developing rapidly, hence a plethora of new boutiques, restaurants, bars and cafes. Lennons and La Strada on Tullow Street are good buzzy spots with decent food. Teach Dolmen, also in Tullow Street, has impromptu traditional Irish music

sessions. Two miles east of town on the R726 is Browneshill Dolmen, possibly the largest Neolithic stone formation in Europe dating from 2500 BC. Seven miles south of Carlow on the N 9 is Leighlinbridge, the birthplace of Cardinal Cullen. Altamont Gardens near Tullow and Ballon are beautiful and attract many visitors. Borris, St. Mullins and the South Leinster Way are very popular with walkers and cyclists, and are a great weekend destination. Carlow is mainly a farming county, which accounts for its easy going and generous atmosphere.

"You'll never plough a field by turning it over in your mind"
(Irish Proverb)

LEIGHLINBRIDGE

As a child my mother regaled me with stories of how she and her younger brother went to school by pony and trap. Their daily adventures took them along by the River Barrow through the historic waterside village of Leighlinbridge. Consequently, being family stamping ground, I know the area very well. With its fine valerian stone bridge and Norman castle ruins, Leighlinbridge is totally underexplored, and perfect for a break. Located on The Barrow Way, one can follow the towpath and nature trail to St. Mullins – where I was married – and to Graiguenamanagh.

THE LORD BAGENAL INN

At the heart of Leighlinbridge is James Kehoe's Lord Bagenal Inn, which had it's beginnings in 1979 in a small olde worlde pub. Keeping apace with the times it has moved on to being the uber smart Lord Bagenal Inn of today with 39 state of the art luxurious bedrooms, reached by a sweeping glass staircase with silk lined steps. Many of the rooms overlook the River Barrow, lending an unbeatable air of relaxation and serenity. They have kingsize beds, black and gold furnishings, and crocodile embossed seating, mixing with panne velvet. So it's a long way from pony and trap time! The Lord Bagenal has all the modern conveniences from WIFI to HiFi. There is a fab new deck overlooking the river, so you can sit there sipping Champagne or a snazzy cocktail under chic white canopies – perhaps after a cruise on the river.

James Kehoe is a foodie, and a wine buff with an unbeatable wine cellar, so this is a destination too for the very serious wino, who will be in heaven trawling through the wine list. Combined with James' love of good food, fine wines and Cuban cigars, is his love of art, and you will feast your eyes on contemporary works by Irish and British Artists such as Peter Collis and Tony O'Malley.

There are two restaurants, the longstanding very popular Peter Collis Room, and the superb new gastronomic Waterfront Restaurant, with James' son, George, firmly at the helm. George has a distinguished culinary pedigree, having worked in Dublin's Michelin starred restaurants, including L'Ecrivain and Chapter One. It is a fab room overlooking the decking and you can indulge in a superb tasting menu or dine a la carte. George does wonderful pan-fried scallops paired with home made crubeen pudding with apple and fennel salad – really innovative food. I also love the grilled Dover Sole with mussels, fresh linguini and asparagus – oh yes – and dark chocolate fondant with milk chocolate sauce, mandarin sorbet and sherry syrup.....

Follow me down to Carlow lads – it is fantastic.

Owner	James Kehoe
Address	Main Street, Leighlinbridge, Co. Carlow.
Tel	+353 (0)59-97-74000
No of Rooms	39
Price	
Suites	€160 - €240
Double/Twin	€110 - €190
Single Rate	€ 75 - €120
Family	On request
Dinner	Yes – 2 Restaurants and Bar Food
Open	All Year save 25th/26th December
Credit Cards	Yes
Directions	From Dublin take N7. Join N9 Dublin – Carlow/Waterford Road. Shortly after Carlow, on road to Kilkenny, follow signs for Leighlinbridge.
Email	info@lordbagenal.com
Web	www.lucindaosullivan.com/lordbagenal

County Cavan

County Cavan, for years rather neglected as a holiday and leisure area, is becoming more popular as people discover what the county has to offer. A factor in this has been the opening of the Shannon-Erne waterway linking streams, rivers and lakes through almost forty miles of beautiful unspoiled countryside and making an attractive destination for pleasure boat users. The county is also a popular venue for anglers from both home and abroad.

Cavan town is the ideal centre for exploring the many lakes and rivers of the county. Quiet and friendly, the town's many shops provide all the goodies any tourist might require. The Lough Oughter area in the north of the county is a major focus of scenic interest. Belturbet on the River Erne is a popular angling and boating centre with a marina and cruiser centre and boats available for rental. Killeshandra is a good place if your interest is in

traditional music and, eleven miles south of Cavan town, is Ballyjamesduff, the home of the County Cavan Museum with an impressive collection which covers all aspects of the county's history. The town was made famous by the beautiful Percy French song – "Come Back Paddy Reilly to Ballyjamesduff". The county is also unique in that its Gaelic football team won the All Ireland Title in 1947, the only time it was ever played outside of Ireland. It was played that year in the Polo Grounds in New York, in commeration of the 100th anniversary of the Great Famine.

"All you need to be a fisherman is patience and a worm"
(Herb Shriner)

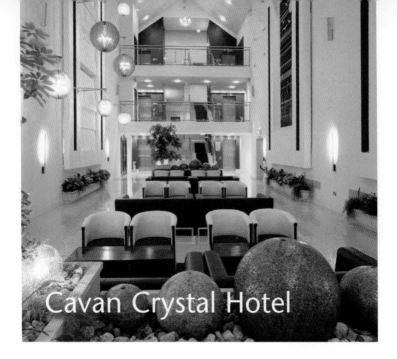

Cavan Crystal Hotel

If you want a destination where you can dine well, be pampered in a Health and Beauty Clinic, and shop 'til you drop, well it has to be the Cavan Crystal Hotel. It is a Hotel with a difference – funky bright beautiful – fabulous contemporary design showcased in a Hotel that has the Cavan Crystal Showrooms under the one roof for it is under the same ownership.

Cavan is a beautiful county, full of romantic lakes and forests, plenty of golf courses, but it really needed a special hotel and this gap has now been filled. The white and stone walled enormously high Atrium, filled with light and magnificent chandeliers, is stunning and you realize immediately this place has been done with style.

There are 85 gorgeous bedrooms fitted out to very high specifications with lovely crisp bedlinen, beautiful covers and throws, fluffy bathrobes, remote control television, bottled water, ironing facilities, so there is everything you could possibly want. If you really want to push out the boat there is always the Presidential Suite. Need a lift after the journey? Book yourself into the Utopia Health & Beauty Clinic for an Express Facial or maybe a Hydro-Active Mineral Salt Scrub - while he heads for the bar – you won't know yourself – he won't either. There is also the Azuma Hair Salon.

Cavan Crystal are very keen on sourcing local producers – indeed they host an Annual Awards for the best Irish small producers - so you can be sure what you are eating is good. Their Opus One Restaurant is sleek and bright and the food is cracking. Think maybe of kicking off with foie gras terrine, mango jelly, crisp ginger bread and a sharp raspberry reduction or baked goats cheese and pumpkin seed tartlet, white onion mousseline and beetroot

ice. Follow up maybe with panfried fillet of seabass and scallop with baby fennel, millefeuille of tomato and fennel icecream. They also do delicious roasted scallops on Asian vegetables with a fig and loganberry dressing. Wow.

You will certainly enjoy your visit to the Lake County if you make the Cavan Crystal Hotel your destination.

Owners	Siobhan Smyth, General Manager.
Address	Dublin Road, Cavan.
Tel:	+353 (0)49 4360600
No of Rooms	85
Price	
Suite	€230
Double/twin	€180
Family	€200
Single	From €110
Dinner	Yes - Restaurant
Open	All year save Christmas Day
Credit Cards	Yes
Directions	Located on the Dublin Road on the outskirts of Cavan Town, just off the N3. A location map can be downloaded from their website.
Email	info@cavancrystalhotel.com
Web	www.lucindaosullivan.com/cavancrystalhotel

NET Spa H P

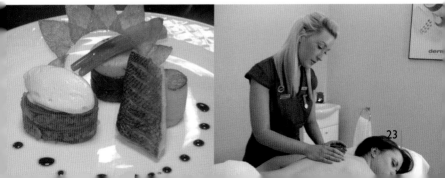

Slieve Russell Hotel Golf Country Club

When the Slieve Russell Hotel opened in Cavan a few years ago, there was a huge fanfare and talk about this palatial place. A well known lady journalist went up on a press trip and her very camp walker friend said afterwards; "you won't believe it Darling, she wanted floating ashtrays in the pool"!! Well I don't imagine she got her floating ashtrays but she had a whale of a weekend. Meanwhile the Slieve Russell survived her visit and has just got better and better.

Famed for hosting prestigious golfing tournaments such as the Irish PGA Championship and set amongst 300 acres of lush greenery and lakes, the Slieve Russell Hotel offers luxurious style set in tranquil surroundings in the lush heart of Co. Cavan.

There are rooms to suit all space requirements and budgets, all lavishly and beautifully fitted out. Options include standard, deluxe and superior rooms, a choice of two suite styles and the piece de resistance, the Presidential Suite. Numerous rooms have views of the golf course, while many of the corner rooms boast balconies. All rooms have Internet access

and TV with digital in-room entertainment and many offer minibar, in-room safe, bathrobes and slippers and separate bath and shower facilities.

In terms of dining, I was spoilt for choice! There are three very different restaurants in a variety of styles. For light meals, with fabulous views of the impressive golf course, the Summit Restaurant is spacious yet cosy. The Setanta Restaurant is light, airy and modern and offers modern European/Asian cuisine. Start with Tagliatelle of Lobster and then go for the Roast Moroccan Spiced Lamb for a beautiful blend of flavours. For award-winning, traditional fine dining, there is the Conall Cearnach Restaurant – the succulent Roast Breast of Thornhill Duck with potato, sage and Brambly apples from this extensive menu goes down a treat.

The superb 18 hole Golf Course sets a challenge even for the pros – and for the inexperienced but eager golfer there is a professional Golf Teaching Academy. The course is open to residents (at a good rate) and also to Day Visitors (for a slightly more expensive rate). Waterbabies take note of the decadent 20 metre swimming pool and Jacuzzi, which can be followed by a visit to the steamroom or sauna.

Be pampered in the Ciuin Spa and Wellness Centre – I recommend the Hammam Turkish Bath in the Hydro Area – nothing like it to wind you down and perk you up again. The Yon-Ka treatments offered incorporate botanical extracts to provide face and body treatments for men and women including a wide selection of facials and massages. Molton Brown, tanning and hand and foot therapy treatments are also available. There is more than enough to occupy the ladies while their other halves are out chasing after balls!

So if you are looking for a destination which offers more satisfaction than a hole in one – the Slieve Russell hits the spot.

Owner	Quinn Hotel Group
Address	Ballyconnell, Co. Cavan.
Tel	+353 (0) 49 952 6444
No of Rooms	222
Price	
Suites	From €330
Double/Twin	From €175
Single	From €117.50
Family	Children sharing parent's room €45 per child B&B per night
Dinner	Yes three restaurants
Open	All year
Credit cards	Yes
Directions	Take N3 from Dublin, follow road to Enniskillen and at rn'abt after Belturbet take left for Balllyconnell town. Hotel 5 miles from Belturbet on left.
Email	slieve-russell@quinn-hotels.com
Web	www.lucindaosullivan.com/slieverussell

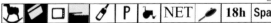

County Clare

County Clare is bordered by Galway to the north – the Atlantic to the west and the River Shannon on the east and south. Renowned as a stronghold of traditional music, it also offers many other attractions to the visitor. The Burren is a stark expanse of moonlike grey limestone and shale which is home to the most extraordinary flora and fauna and is a must visit. Kilkee is a seaside resort popular with families and scuba divers and has plenty of restaurants and pubs. Lahinch with its fabulous broad beach attracts surfers and boasts a magnificent golf

course. The Cliffs of Moher attract a number of visitors as does the town of Doolin, four miles from the Cliffs. Doolin is for many the music centre of the west and you are sure to find some kind of merriment in one of the town's pubs (O'Connor's, McCann's and McDermott's). If you are unmarried and visit Lisdoonvarna in the month of September you may well find yourself "Spoken For" before you leave, for the town is famous for its month long Matchmaking Festival which comes after the Harvest has been saved.

Wedlock – "the deep, deep peace
of the double bed
after the hurly burly of the chaise
longue"
(Mrs. Patrick Campbell)

Ballinalacken Castle Country House Hotel

E ven the name sounds romantic – you just couldn't invent it. It smacks of history and romance – crashing waves, lusty thighs, flowing hair - young men and beautiful girls out on the wild stormy cliffs of Clare. What a field day novelist Daphne du Maurier could have had down here writing about her pirates a la Frenchman's Creek.

The historic Ballinalacken House is located in one of the most stunning situations on the western seaboard with spectacular views of the Aran Islands, the Cliffs of Moher, just ten minutes away, and Galway Bay. In the shadow of the ruins of the O'Brien Clan's 15th c Ballinalacken Castle, the house was built by Lord O'Brien in 1840 as his family home and remained as such for 99 years until, in 1939, it was bought by the present family. The beautiful rooms have been restored to their original grandeur, antiques, lovely cornice work, light fittings, and splendid marble mantelpieces on which to rest your glass of port. All of the bedrooms are lovely. Some have four-poster beds for that really romantic visit and there are four superior rooms and two beautiful suites.

If you have been out playing golf all day, or touring, or visiting the Burren – for which Ballinalacken could not be better placed – you want to be

able to dump the car when you get back and crash out with really good food and wines. They have a cute little rustic "pub" bar where you can have a pint of Guinness before or after dinner, or both, as you go over the day and the "near misses" on the golf course. The dining room is rich and lush and there is an emphasis at Ballinalacken on really good food with plenty of

fish on the menu, as well as the County Clare specialty of Burren Lamb. Think maybe of enjoying cannelloni of fresh Doolin crabmeat in a light salmon mousse with a shellfish jus. Sounds good, doesn't it? It gets better. At Ballinalacken pan seared fillets of John Dory are served French style with a barigole of artichokes and port whilst supreme of Barbary duck is served on a celeriac puree complemented by Guinness and Fresh honey sauce – now that's a talking point.

   Grab your cailin by the waist and go … it might change your life.

Owner	Denis O'Callaghan
Address	Coast Road, Doolin, Co. Clare.
Tel:	+353 (0)65 7074025
No of Rooms	12
Price	
Suite	€200
Double/twin	€160 (DBB packages available – April and October specials)
Family	Enquire
Dinner	Yes - Restaurant
Open	Early April – End October
Credit Cards	Yes
Directions	Take R476 north of Doolin. 2 miles at junction R476 + R477 is hotel. From Lisdoonvarna take R477 coast road – 3 miles from town.
Email	ballinalackencastle@eircom.net
Web	www.lucindaosullivan.com/ballinalackencastle

Ballyvara House

D oolin is a pretty and popular village, in a dramatic setting, just four miles north of the Cliffs of Moher, close to the Burren, and ten minutes from Lahinch if you are a golfer! Doolin is also a take off point for the Aran Islands, it makes an ideal place in which to base oneself. Visit the sights during the day and enjoy the pubs and seisiuns at night. You want somewhere nice to stay that is where the Ballyvara House comes in to play.

Ballyvara was once a charming farm cottage which John Flanagan inherited and which he turned into a B & B. However, John, a joiner and builder, took the idea much further and, retaining the stone and timber of the old cottage, has transformed the place into the spanking new Guest House it is today. Bedrooms are large and all have queen beds, spa or Jacuzzi baths, some even have balconies with stunning views. There are a couple of suites complete with a large lounge with big T.V, mini-bar, mini plasma flat screen T.V. and safes if you don't want to carry around your valuables while sightseeing.

Located on 20 acres, there is a pretty courtyard garden but also plenty of room to romp around. Children will love to go out and visit the donkey

duo, Shetland and Welsh ponies, and dogs, as well as enjoy the new Play Area. They have also added a multi purpose astro turf playing court. Ballyvara is a fun place with a little residents' bar where you can meet other visitors, have a drink and a bit of craic, and not worry about having to drive home. Excellent reasonably priced food is available in their new adjoining Tir gan Ean House Hotel. It might be crab claws; Burren smoked salmon roulade. Follow up then with the fish dish of the evening or maybe Barbary duck breast or steak. They always do a vegetarian dish and they have an extensive wine list. Breakfasts are brilliant – you can have the Full Irish or the Empty Irish and that, in case you didn't know, is eggs, bacon and tomato, without the sausage, pudding and beans! They also do delicious omelettes and luscious pancakes with syrup ... If you so desire, instead of making a breakfast deadline ... you can even have your breakfast in bed...most unusual for a Guest House.

John and Becky are welcoming hosts – you will be glad you discovered Ballyvara – I was.

Owners:	John and Becky Flanagan
Address:	Ballyvara, Doolin, Co. Clare.
Tel	+ 353 (0)65 7074467
No. Of Rooms	11
Price	
Suite	€150 - €350
Double/Twin	€100 - €200
Family	€140 - €240
Dinner	Yes – in next-door hotel under same ownership.
Open	May – September
Credit Cards	Yes
Directions.	Once in Doolin village – from Roadford take the first Left after Cullinan's Restaurant (on right); Ballyvara is half mile up hill on left.
Email:	info@ballyvarahouse.ie
Web:	www.lucindaosullivan.com/ballyvarahouse

 NET P

The Burren Coast Hotel & Halcyon Spa

You couldn't get closer to the splendid and stormy Atlantic if you tried, as this hotel is situated right on the water in Ballyvaughan, Co. Clare, the self-proclaimed capital of the Burren. This recently opened establishment makes the most of its stunning location by incorporating a bar and restaurant with sea vistas. Come rain or shine these features provide an excellent opportunity to sit, gaze out and imagine the ships of the Armada Fleet battling the elements or Granuaile's pirate ship moving along the horizon, such is the rich nautical history of the West coast of Ireland.

The hotel's 20 bedrooms are comfy and tastefully decorated, all offer en suite bathrooms, T.V. and internet access. The hotel provides access for those in wheelchairs and is child friendly.

The dining area in the Hazelwood Restaurant is presented in an open, warm and homely traditional style with bare wooden beams running across the ceiling, dark wooden floors and stone-façade fireplace. The cosy Limestone Bar is ideal for popping in to quench an afternoon thirst, for that pre/post dinner drink, or even a liquid lunch if you fancy it!

There are myriad historical and scenic attractions to take advantage of in the area, not least the limestone-rich, cavernous Burren landscape with its unique ecosystem, the pre- historic Polnabrone Dolmen and the famed Cliffs of Moher (where scenes from the hilarious "Princess Bride" motion picture were filmed in the 1980s). Also of interest is the nearby Ballyvaughan Bird Sanctuary which is an idyll for birdwatchers. Horse riding can be arranged locally and other possible leisure activities include tennis, hill walking, cycling, swimming (al fresco!) and surfing.

Although, if you prefer to recharge your energy rather than expend it, the on site Spa will be the best place to chill out. Alas it hadn't yet opened

when I was there, late in 2007, but I've been given good guidance that this eagerly awaited pamper parlour is set to be fabulous when it is launched late Feb/March 2008. Experience Facials, Body wraps, Swedish, Aromatherapy, Indian Head and Sports massages, Reflexology, Manicures, Pedicures, Professional Make up application and Hot Stone therapy. Hedonism here we go! (Masochists not forgotten – catered for with Gym!)

There are also 24 Holiday Homes nearby, sleeping 5, 7 or 9 people, which will be available from March.

Owner	Atlantis Holiday Group
Address	Coast Road, Ballyvaughan, Co. Clare.
Tel	+353 (0) 65 708 3000
No of Rooms	20
Price	
Suites	€160-€240
Double/Twin	€140-€220
Single	€100-€150
Family	2 interconnecting rooms available
Dinner	Yes Restaurant
Open	All year save for 25th & 26th December
Credit cards	Yes
Directions	From Ennis take N85 to Ennistymon, R476 to Ballyvaughan. Go through Corrofin, Killnaboy and Ballyvaughan village. Hotel on left overlooking Galway Bay.
Email	info@burrencoast.ie
Web	www.lucindaosullivan.com/burrencoast

Cliffs of Moher Hotel

Situated on the edge of the Burren in Co. Clare, Liscannor village is home to the charming new Cliffs of Moher Hotel, which is 4 star, equipped with 23 bedrooms and lies within a stone's throw of one of Ireland's most famous tourist attractions – the cliffs themselves and the fascinating nearby visitor's centre.

The cliffs, a mere 10 minute drive away, stand at 214 m above sea level at their highest point and continue for 8km. On a clear day, along the Clare coastline, the spectacular Aran Islands can be seen from the cliffs. They are home to Ireland's largest bird colony and are therefore a great place for birdwatchers and nature lovers alike. Lahinch Golf Club is also easily accessible from the hotel, as is Lahinch beach which is heaven for surfing enthusiasts. Pitch and Putt is also offered nearby as are fishing tours of Liscannor Harbour. If you feel brave enough to use your sea legs, you could take a cruise to the Aran Islands or view the Cliffs of Moher from below on a boat tour.

Bedrooms are simple, restful and modern with most displaying views of the roaring Atlantic in Liscannor Bay and Lahinch. All are en suite, have direct dial telephone lines, hairdryer, safe, satellite television and ironing facilities.

If you don't have any luck spotting puffins on the Cliffs, take solace in dining on succulent fresh fish in the Puffin restaurant on site at the Hotel. The menu is extensive and reasonable – just what you need to satisfy the hunger horrors after a long day's sightseeing.

It is a little known fact, but the man who developed the first submarine vessel prototype in the mid to late 1800s was a Mr. John P. Holland – proud scientist and republican who was born in Liscannor, in 1841. His memory was honoured when Castle St. in Liscannor was renamed Holland St. and is also preserved inside the Hotel through their specially sub aqua themed bar, The Submarine, where you can avail of the bar food menu. The apt bronze statue of Holland and his masterpiece outside provides a great photo opportunity.

If you are looking for somewhere small, intimate and friendly, superbly located for exploring the delights of the West of Ireland, and also excellent value, the Cliffs of Moher Hotel is the place for you.

Owner	Atlantis Holiday Group
Address	Liscannor, Co. Clare.
Tel	+353 (0)65 708-6770
No of Rooms	23
Price	
Double/Twin	€130 – €200
Single	€ 95 – €130
Dinner	Yes – Restaurant and Bar food
Open	March to November – weekends in Winter – Check.
Credit Cards	Yes
Directions	From Lahinch follow road to Cliffs of Moher, on entering Liscannor hotel is on left.

Email
info@cliffsofmoherhotel.ie
Web
www.lucindaosullivan.com/cliffsofmoher

35

Old Ground Hotel

The Gardening Editor of the up market American magazine, Traditional Home, was visiting Ireland last year and what, of course, would be a gardens tour of Ireland if it did not incorporate the Burren. We then worked our way further down through County Clare and found ourselves in Ennis. "Let"s go to the Old Ground." I said. She was flying out of Shannon next day. Well, was I ever in for a surprise. I had been there a few years earlier and I hardly recognized the place. It was, and is, just amazingly beautiful now - like a thoroughbred gorgeous Country House with all the modern conveniences of a Hotel.

The Old Ground was a former manor house built in the 18th c as a private residence. In 1946 with the advent of transatlantic flights into Shannon Airport an extension was built onto the house. Meals were served throughout the night for TWA and Pan Am crews. Next door was the Town Hall, which incorporated a jail and this became part of the Old Ground Hotel.

The Old Ground was bought by Allen Flynn of the Flynn Hotel Group and, oh boy, has it ever had a makeover. It is hard to know where to start for the public areas, drawingrooms, resident's library, bars are all beautifully draped and furnished. There is a magnificent private contemporary art collection throughout and details like this make such a difference. The bedrooms are beautifully equipped with crisp white linen. the softest squishy duvets and pillows, all mod cons, and cracking bathrooms. Rooms with air-conditioning, seating areas, sound systems and Wireless Internet access are also available. There are plenty of places to eat. We loved their Town Hall Bistro with its stone walls, cool décor, where we had sesame crusted seabass with dill scented couscous which came with an unusual lime and chardonnay butter, and roast rack of Clare lamb with a balsamic and port reduction. You can pop in here all day and have morning coffee and scones or afternoon tea. There is also the more formal red and gold themed O'Brien Room where the food is superb.

"I'm going to come back here next year" my guest said. "The whole place just has a magical feel." I felt really good showing off such a beautiful establishment.

Owners	Mary Gleeson (General Manager)
Address	O'Connell Street, Ennis, Co. Clare.
Tel:	+353 (0)65 682 8127
No of Rooms	110
Price	
Suite	€180 - €295
Double/twin	€125 - €190
Family	€150 - €190
Single	€ 95 - €125
Dinner	Yes – Restaurant, Bistro and Bar Food
Open	All year Save Christmas Day
Credit Cards	Yes
Directions	From Limerick, follow signs for Galway/Shannon Airport N1
Email	reservations@oldground.ie
Web	www.lucindaosullivan.com/flynnhotels

Tir gan Ean House Hotel

S ister Hotel to Ballyvara House, Tir Gan Ean, meaning " birdless land", is a luxury boutique style hotel with partial stone façade near the village of Doolin in North West Co. Clare. Doolin itself is said to be the throbbing heart of Irish traditional music, where mighty craic and ceol is to be had by all who visit, all year 'round. It has a rich history of music, folklore, storytelling, dancing and the Gaelic language which attracts flocks of tourists annually.

The hotel's décor is modern and minimalist with a funky combination of metal and wood finishes throughout, the design is light infused and spacious in the dining and lobby areas. Abstract paintings in muted browns and yellows adorn the walls in the lounge area. Furnishings are in warm colours and varied textures. This subtle attention to detail contributed to the general sensation of peacefulness and relaxation I felt while I was there.

An t'Oilean, the dining room, offers the best of modern Irish cuisine specialising in local local meat and seafood. Watch out for the treats the new chef has in store for you! Corcomroe, the resident's bar, provides drinks by a roaring fire, where no doubt you will make new friends and meet lots of new people from around the world.

The tranquil atmosphere flows into its 12 bedrooms, which receive lots of natural light. Bedrooms are spacious with ample storage space and flat screen TV Wheelchair facilities are provided and Internet access is available.

The prime leisure activity in the surrounding area is golf due to the hotel's close proximity to Lahinch, a town famed for its championship golf courses. Swimming pool and tennis facilities are available nearby and other popular pastimes include surfing, scuba diving, fishing, horse riding and cycling. Those tempted by sight seeing can visit the Cliffs of Moher, just 8km away, and the legendry karst Burren landscape is also within driving distance. Don't forget to visit Doolin Cave - the town's other claim to fame!

Owner	Atlantis Holiday Group
Address	Coast Road, Doolin, Co. Clare.
Tel	+353 (0) 65 7075726
No of Rooms	12
Price	
Double/Twin	€130 - €200
Single	€95
Family	
Dinner	Yes – Dining room
Open	All Year – save Christmas
Credit cards	Yes
Directions	On entering Doolin village, turn right at t-junction, hotel on right.
Email	info@tirganean.ie
Web	www.lucindaosullivan.com/tirganean

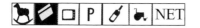

Vaughan Lodge

There are certain counties that are always on the visitor's list when they come to Ireland and Clare is one of them. It is one of the most "away from it all" places you could possibly be in – the Real Ireland of both yesterday and today. It remains untouched and splendiferous and, in so many ways, is quite heartbreakingly beautiful and nostalgic. They come to visit the amazing Cliffs of Moher; to play golf and feel the breeze of the Atlantic; to visit the natural phenomenon that is the Burren.

You can take in all that County Clare has to offer and indulge in absolutely delicious food as well if you stat at Vaughan Lodge at Lahinch. They say that good hoteliers aren't made they are bred and that can certainly be said of Michael Vaughan who is fourth generation of his family of hoteliers who has grasped with vigour and enthusiasm what is required by today's discerning guest and, by gosh, Michael and his wife Maria are providing it. Vaughan Lodge is a new Boutique style Hotel and my interest in it was first attracted when I heard how good their food was and how serious they were about that end of their operation. Specialising in seafood their Chef trained at Dromoland Castle so you can expect some seriously good food.

Bedrooms are done in contemporary style with state of the art facilities so what you really have here is country house ambience with all of the comforts and facilities of a sleek state of the art hotel. Have a cocktail or a "ball of malt" in the evenings in the cocktail club lounge and replay your golf round before dinner. The Vaughan's modestly suggest in their

promotional brochure that you book dinner one evening in the restaurant during your stay. I would respectfully suggest that you book dinner in their restaurant every evening of your stay … you will not find better in Lahinch. Think maybe of pan seared scallops, lentils, scallion and spinach salad with a Balsamic reduction or maybe roasted fillet of halibut, lemon and olive potato, parsley coulis and vin blanc. Puddings are scrumptious – classic chocolate fondant, apple filled crepes, bread and butter pudding … .and you will get a complementary half bottle of House Champagne and chocolates if you mention the Little Black Book on making your booking …

   Vaughan Lodge is a serious addition to the County Clare gourmet golfer's repertoire….

Owners	Michael Vaughan
Address	Vaughan Lodge, Ennistymon Road, Lahinch, Co. Clare.
Tel:	+353 (0)65 708 1111
No of Rooms	22
Price	
Double/twin	€170 - €200
Single	€ 95 - €155
Dinner	Yes - Restaurant
Open	Mid March – 31st October
Credit Cards	Yes
Directions	Situated on the eastern side of the village of Lahinch on the N67
	Just inside the 50 KMP sign.
Email	info@vaughanlodge.ie
Web	www.lucindaosullivan.com/vaughanlodge

County Cork

Known as the Rebel County, for past deeds and the fact that Michael Collins was a native, Cork is the largest county in Ireland. An area of lush fertile farming land, and of fabulously indented coastline, it is also site of Ireland's second City. On the eastern side of the county there is the impressive little fishing port of Ballycotton. Close by is Shanagarry Pottery which is well worth a visit. Further along the coast is the historic town of Cobh, the harbour from which thousands of Irish emigrants departed for the U.S. and Australia, and was the last port of call of the ill fated Titanic. Close by Cobh is Fota Wildlife Park and, not far away, is a spot close to the heart of most Irish men – Midleton – the home of Jameson's Irish whiskey. Travel further west and visit Blarney Castle where you can kiss the famed Blarney Stone, said to endow one with the gift of the gab. Kinsale with its impressive Forts, narrow streets, and yachting marina is a picturesque town, and known as the gourmet capital of Ireland. Moving on west through Clonakilty you come to Rosscarbery, with its lovely Continental type village square, but swing left off the main road and wend your way to magnificent Glandore. Stop, take a seat by the wall, overlooking the water and have lunch. Take it easy and enjoy the peace. Further West is the nautically inclined very popular Baltimore. Travel on to Bantry Town which overlooks the famous bay of the same name and you can visit magnificent Bantry House, home of many art treasures. Move on then to the lushness and splendour of Ballylicky and Glengarriff, the last stop before entering the Kingdom of Kerry. And what about Cork City you might ask, for we Dubliners know that Cork is the "real" capital of Ireland. It is a major port on the estuary of the River Lee and this both lively and relaxed City is one of the most pleasurable urban areas in Ireland and is the south's self proclaimed cultural capital. This fantastic county with its rich pastoral land and its rugged coastline of beautiful bays and inlets has many places of historic and cultural interest and the natives are very friendly.

"Culture is roughly anything we do and monkeys don't"

(Lord Raglan)

Ballymakeigh Country House

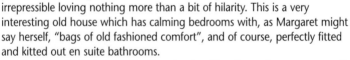

A s if on cue, 200 glorious Friesian cows trundled from the fields, in what seemed like a never-ending line for milking, as we arrived at Ballymakeigh House. Margaret and Michael Browne's lovely 300-year-old Farmhouse has won every award in the book and continues to do so. Not just has the house won awards but Margaret, who is Cork's answer to Superwoman, has been Housewife of the Year, T.V. Chef and published her own best selling cookery book "Through My Kitchen Window". Ballymakeigh is a fun place because Margaret and Mike are absolutely irrepressible loving nothing more than a bit of hilarity. This is a very interesting old house which has calming bedrooms with, as Margaret might say herself, "bags of old fashioned comfort", and of course, perfectly fitted and kitted out en suite bathrooms.

If you are feeling energetic, there is a hard tennis court, or you can walk the land, see the milking parlour, or merely sit down in the lovely big conservatory for the day with a glass in hand – nobody will bat an eyelid. Americans love to visit "real Irish" homes and this I can tell you is a "real Irish" home, but with everything running to perfection down to the ice machine. A spanking dinner is served in the lovely old world diningroom. Breakfasts are hearty with fresh pressed apple juice, fruits and yoghurts, traditional grainy porridge with spices, cereals, kippers with thyme, and a super "Full Irish" including rashers, sausages, Clonakilty pudding tomatoes and eggs. Preserves, of course, are homemade as are the breads – traditional Irish soda bread and leek and onion savoury scones are to die for. Mark my words, like me, you will go back again and again to Ballymakeigh.

Owners:	Michael and Margaret Browne
Address:	Killeagh, Co. Cork.
Tel	+353 (0)24 95184
No. Of Rooms	6
Price	
Double/Twin	€130
Single	€75
Family	On request
Dinner	Yes
Open	All Year
Credit Cards	Visa MC Amex
Directions	Located 1 mile of N25. 22 miles east of Cork City. Signposted in Killeagh village at Old Thatch Pub.

Email:
ballymakeigh@eircom.net
Web:
www.lucindaosullivan.com/ballymakeigh house

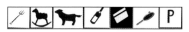

Bayview Hotel

allycotton is a completely unspoiled Fishing Village in East Cork dating back to 1250 AD. Not only is it completely unspoiled but it is also largely undiscovered save by those in the know, for people tend to dash on further west to the overblown more high profile villages. Once you turn down at Castlemartyr you whirl around the back roads amongst high hedges and fertile fields which are eons away from the modern world – and yet so near. Ballycotton is an ideal base for visiting Cork, if you prefer to stay out of a City, or for taking a leisurely tour of Stephen Pearce's Pottery and for visiting Ballymaloe, and the Jameson Irish Whiskey Centre at Midleton, after which you might need to be careful on the Ballycotton Cliff Walk!!

BAYVIEW HOTEL BALLYCOTTON

I have had a problem for a number of years with Hotels and Restaurants a problem which can spoil one's entire visit – namely – the "back room" and the "table beside the toilet door respectively. I have been offered a far from romantic attic in Paris, a box in London beside a lift shaft with pneumatic drills working in it, no sea view all over the place, a room over the rubbish exit in Palma, and even rooms with no view at all save the sidewall of the next building. The Bayview Hotel in my eyes is just perfectly designed for all the rooms have magnificent sea views. As you look out it feels more like a "visual tour" because you are just over the sheer drop onto the rocks, gazing out into infinity, broken only by the old world little quaint Ballycotton Harbour. Not only does the newly revamped Bayview have 35 perfect rooms, a comfortable library style bar and lounge, it has excellent food provided by Head Chef, Ciaran Scully, who cooks up the best of luscious French style food in The Capricho Restaurant in this special little gourmet Hotel. Think prawns the size of your thumb and silky foie gras …

There are six golf courses within 30 minutes drive, as well as some of the best sea angling in Europe. Stephen Belton provides a 5 star service at the 4 star Bayview. Go and discover it for yourself.

Owners	John & Carmel O'Brien
	Stephen Belton (General Manager)
Address	Ballycotton, Co. Cork.
Tel	+353(0)21 464 6746
No. Of Rooms	35
Price	
Suites	From €189 Room Only
Double/Twin	From €129 Room Only
Single	From €129 Room Only
Family	From €129 Room Only
Dinner	Yes - Restaurant
Open	Mid April to end October
Credit Cards	All Major Cards
Directions	Located in Ballycotton Village
Email	res@thebayviewhotel.com
Web	www.lucindaosullivan.com/bayviewhotel

The Blue Haven Hotel

I was at the very first Kinsale Gourmet Festival in the mid 70's when it was a fledgling event but, like Topsy, it just growed and growed, along with it Kinsale's reputation worldwide on the foodie scene. A pivotal part of this foodie arena has always been the Blue Haven Hotel, which was run like a very tight ship and into which everybody seemed to report at some part of the day. We have had great nights there with people from all over the world in Kinsale for shark fishing, the food, sailing or just the fun of the whole place. In fact on one occasion we had such an hilarious stay it took us three days to leave! We got up each morning with the best of intentions but, we would meet someone we knew, and after a couple of "farewell" jars couldn't set off to drive to Dublin so, back we would have to go to Reception, and beg for our room, or any room!

Local guy, Ciaran Fitzgerald, is now at the helm of the Blue Haven and has spent the past two years revamping and restoring it into a very fine atmospheric and welcoming Boutique Hotel. All of the very stylish bedrooms have had a major face lift to bring them in line with the requirements of today's discerning traveller - flat screen TV's, those really expensive beds, pillow menus, wild wood furniture, wireless broadband and spanking newly fitted bathrooms.

There is a new relaxed yacht like bistro off the sleek recently revamped bar, which is like a luxury liner, as well as the Blue Haven Restaurant, where I have spent many a good night including ringing in the New Year with gusto! The food is modern, well executed and just what is wanted nowadays. You can think perhaps of lobster, scallops, or prawns, partnered with good Mediterranean vegetables, asparagus, artichokes, aubergines and followed by scrumptious puds. Really good food is available all day so if you want to be at the hub in Kinsale – The Blue Haven is the place to be – you never know if you are lucky like me it might take you 3 days to check out!

Owners:	Ciaran Fitzgerald
Address:	Pearse Street, Kinsale, Co. Cork.
Tel	+353 (0)21 477 2209
No. Of Rooms	17
Price	
Double/Twin	€195 - €240
Single	From €140
Dinner	Yes – 2 Restaurants and Cafe
Open	All Year
Credit Cards	Visa MC Amex Laser
Directions.	Follow signs for the South Link and the airport and you will join the R27. After passing Cork Airport, three miles further on at the Five-Mile-Bridge take the R600 to Kinsale Town.

Email:	info@bluehavenkinsale.com
Web	
www.lucindaosullivan.com/bluehaven	

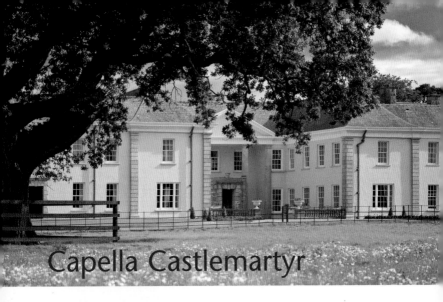

Capella Castlemartyr

Singapore, Austria, Mexico, Colorado, Dusseldorf, Castlemartyr and Castletownbere don't appear to have much in common but they are locations for the new luxury Capella Hotels and Resorts brand just launched by former Ritz Carlton President, Horst Schulze. Aimed at the discerning, luxury seeking traveller, many of the estates, which form this new hotel group, have had interesting previous owners from sex kitten, Bridgette Bardot's ex husband, Gunther Sachs, at Schloss Velden in Austria, to the swashbuckling explorer Sir Walter Raleigh at Castlemartyr, who was awarded the estate by the British Crown after the rebellion of 1578 when seized from the Earl of Desmond. The Castlemartyr Estate later passed to the Earls of Cork who built the present manor house, which in recent years was a Carmelite Friary

Approaching through 220 acres of lush greenery and waters with swans gliding by says it all. The entrance hall is quite beautiful but pales into insignificance when faced with the Knights Bar - the former church - with it's quite gloriously restored high ornate Rococo ceiling. Off the hall are two serenely elegant dining rooms, the Bell Tower and the Garden Room, overlooking the formal lawns where you can relax on big cushions sipping chilled Pimms. There is also a 2,400 square metre Auriga Spa with ten

treatment rooms for pampering oneself while he is out on the Ron Kirby designed 18 hole Championship Golf Course.

All of the bedrooms at various levels from standard, deluxe, through to the Grand Suites and Presidential Suites have all the de rigueur luxurious comfort and technologies of today, so whichever you choose, you will be in the lap of luxury.

We had a romantic carriage ride around the estate before coming back to dinner, which was superb. The food reflects the whole ambiance of the Estate - elegantly understated with extravagant gestures concealed within - such as lobster in light colcannon with Ballycotton cod and lemon parsley foam. Rosscarbery black pudding was paired with baby beet root, Cooleeny cheese and truffle whilst Jerusalem artichoke soup had tea smoked girolles and Gubeen smokehouse bacon. A very vibrant verdant green risotto of periwinkles, parsley, garlic and cured lemon, was perfectly executed, not a minute more, not a minute less, simple in its structure but so appetising and fresh tasting.

Chocoholics will die for the scrumptious Hot Chocolate Caca macaroon, Irish Coffee ice cream and stuffed raspberries and more. I opted for cheese – a perfect board with Durrus, Stilton, Camembert and an Italian Goat's cheese with grapes, baby plums, date chutney and onion marmalade, put together by the very charming attentive Maitre d'

You won't forget your visit to Castlemartyr – as long as you don't lose your head as well as your heart – like poor old Walter Raleigh!!

Owner	Capella Hotels	
Address	Castlemartyr, Co. Cork.	
Tel	+353 (0)21 464-4050	
No of Rooms	103	
Price		
Suites	€750 - €2750	
Double/Twin	From €320	
Dinner	Yes - Restaurants	
Open	All Year	
Credit Cards	Yes	
Directions	Located on N25 between Midleton and Youghal in village of Castlemartyr	
Email	reservations.castlemartyr@capellahotels.com	
Web	www.lucindaosullivan.com/capellacastlemartyr	

Cork International Airport Hotel

"Fasten Your Seatbelts it's going to be a bumpy night" – a quote from the 1950's movie "All About Eve" – is emblazoned on the new Cork International Airport Hotel's brochure. One of my Kinsale friends had sent me a text while having dinner saying; "you've got to come here, you will love it". She was right – it is really wild. The ground floor is a cross between the cult TV series "The Prisoner" where Patrick McGoohan dashed from place to place - each madder than the other - and couldn't escape – and maybe Austin Powers had a hand in the décor!

"Portmerion" style topiary lead to the whacky lobby. Aviation is the theme, complete not just with an enormous Aircraft Simulator on a hoist, but an aeroplane fuselage, seats and all, siding on to the Strata Restaurant. As for the loos – they are amazing – go see – lozenge coloured washstands and Dyson handdryers that look as if they will swallow you up!!

A fab in-house bakery faces the "departure lounge" – the O Bar – where we knocked back a cocktail before dinner. The O Bar does very good casual food. There is also the Pullman Lounge where, if your flight is delayed, you can buy a pass and relax on loungers with WIFI, bath and shower facilities, complimentary coffee, snacks, and free shuttle bus to the airport. Now that is a little secret worth knowing about! They also have Park and Fly packages which are cheaper than parking at the actual airport car park.

Is it airplane food? Most certainly not! I had a delicious layered Smoked Salmon terrine with pickled cucumber, followed by a cracking chargrilled 10oz fillet of beef with sauteed mushrooms, sumo chips and a tarragon jus. They are very good with fish – roast haddock was atop Puy lentils, confit tomatoes, with a garlic foam, and pan-fried sea bream with mussels on creamed cabbage, cherry tomatoes, with a pesto dressing – excellent. If you want to impress your guests, you can entertain them in a plush private

dining space, the Wine Vault, around a big 10 seater round table – now that is First Class!

After dinner we went up to the Star Wars Section – Reception on the 1st Floor with its planet shaped desks! However, the bedrooms are very grounded – if you will forgive the pun – contemporary comfort – just beautiful – with great views. In true aeronautical speak there three classes – Economy, Business and First Class – translated that means Standard, Executive with more space, or a Suite with a living area and even more space! All fab. WIFI is free throughout the Hotel. There is 24 hour room service plus breakfast from 7 a.m. or a ready to go breakfast available from 3.30 a.m. Continental breakfast is available 24 hours and all have those delicious breads from their own bakery.

"As God is my witness I'll never be hungry again" said Scarlet O'Hara. You certainly won't be at CIAH. It's fun, it's different. Children, Trekkies, and Escapists alike will love it. We did.

Owner	New Great Southern Hotel Group
Address	Cork Airport, Cork City, County Cork.
Tel	+353 (0)21 454-9800
No of Rooms	150
Price	
Suites	€300
Double/Twin	€180
Family	€205
Dinner	Yes – Restaurant and Bar Food
Open	All Year
Credit Cards	Yes
Directions	At Cork Apt r'abt take 2nd exit. Turn right at Gate 2 Cork Airport Business Park which leads directly to the hotel.

Email
info@corkinternationalairporthotel.com
Web
www.lucindaosullivan.com/corkairporthotel

Crawford House

I don't know about you but I have ended up in foreign cities wishing I knew of some gorgeous place to rest my head. I ended up one time in an attic in Paris in a street lined with prostitutes and I was absolutely petrified. On another occasion I ended up in London in a dreary hotel with a bedroom beside the lift shaft – that wasn't too bad save that the lift was out of order and being repaired with pneumatic drills going 24/7. If you are in bad accommodation you are not only miserable but it completely colours your view of the City you are in.

My Cork City gem is Crawford House which has it all – quality – distinction – style – contemporary ambience. On top of that it has a location that is second to none being in the City's University area – in fact it is just across from the College. Two Gothic revival style tall imperious Victorian houses have been converted into a slick modern home away from home by Cork girl Cecilia O'Leary and her husband Hossayn providing all the facilities the modern day traveller wants.

There are 12 beautiful bedrooms with oakwood furniture custom made by the same crafts people who furnished U2's uber chic Clarence Hotel in Dublin. There are superking orthopaedic beds, even for single occupancy,

cool crisp bedlinen, all modern facilities, satellite television, and modem and fax points for the business traveller. The bathrooms are pristine and elegant with Jacuzzi baths and power showers,

There is a comfortable serene lounge in which to relax and breakfast next morning is served in the cool diningroom and conservatory. You can of course have the de rigueur Full Irish but there is also a lavish buffet of cereals, fruit, compotes, breads as well as pancakes, omelettes, confitures. Hossayn is a great cook with a light hand and everybody just loves his breakfasts. Most importantly, if you have a dietary requirement, they will, with advance notice of course, be more than happy to cater for you.

Crash out at Crawford House … you will have found your new base in Cork.

Owners	Cecilia O'Leary Kareem
Address	Western Road, Cork.
Tel:	+353 (0)21 427 9000
No of Rooms	12
Price	
Double/twin	€110-€120
Single	€80
Family	
Dinner	No
Open	January 15 – December 15
Credit Cards	Yes
Directions	From central Cork follow signs for Western Road. Facing UCC.
Email	info@crawfordhouse.ie
Web	www.lucindaosullivan.com/crawfordhouse

55

Dunmore House Hotel

Clonakilty in West Cork is definitely worth exploring. With its colourfully painted houses and Georgian Squares, it is lovely little town to stroll through, bursting with blooming flower baskets in the spring and summer. It was the hometown of the "Big Fella" Michael Collins, who grew up in the picturesque Georgian neighbourhood of Emmet Square. Those of you with a gra for Irish history can visit The National Michael Collins Memorial Statue, which was unveiled by actor Liam Neeson in 2002. Rumour has it that Eamon De Valera himself spoke to an audience from the second floor window of No. 4 Emmet Square. The Model village, nostalgically representing the 1940s, is an ideal place to take the children for an afternoon's entertainment. You can also climb on board the "Tschu Tschu" Road Train which runs from the Model Village to the town centre daily during the summer and at weekends during the winter.

Just 4 kms outside Clon – as it is affectionately known – is Dunmore House – a family run gem situated in the heart of the West Cork countryside. This is a friendly place where you will quickly settle in and relax as you only can in West Cork. It boasts a beautiful Atlantic sea view from almost every bedroom and also offers a 9 Hole golf course on site with green fees free for guests. Not only that, but Dunmore has a private shoreline which makes it an ideal place for the guest who enjoys fishing and

watersports. If you fancy yourself as a bit of a John Wayne, there are Horse riding facilities offered close to the hotel and the surrounding area provides an excellent backdrop for walking and trekking. We found the staff were more than happy to provide a packed lunch, upon request, for you for your day's adventure or sightseeing activities.

The homey, traditional, old world bar provides a cosy nook to sit and relax beside the stone fireplace and revel in the laid back atmosphere. The restaurant, which overlooks the sea and greets its guests with an open and airy appeal, specialises in the best of local Irish surf 'n turf. The bedrooms have been individually decorated and have en suite bathrooms, satellite television and direct line phones. Children are welcome and babysitting services are available.

A lovely place for an informal and relaxing holiday break.

Owner:	Mary & Jeremiah O'Donovan and family
Address:	Clonakilty, Co. Cork
Tel:	+ 353 (0) 23 33352
No of Rooms:	29
Price:	
Double/Twin:	€190 - €210
Single:	€ 95 - €105
Family:	Prices vary depending on age of children. U 4s FOC.
Dinner:	Yes – Restaurant
Open:	March to January (Closed February)
Credit cards:	Yes
Directions:	Take N7 Route to West Cork. 4km from Clonakilty
Email:	enq@dunmorehousehotel.ie
Web:	www.lucindaosullivan.com/dunmorehousehotel

Friar's Lodge

The first time I met Maureen Tierney we had arrived with two small boys in the car, hot, tired and ratty. Jack Charlton was the Irish Soccer Team Manager, it was "Ole Ole Year"- 1990 when Ireland took the summer off to support the Irish Team in the World Cup. We were renting a self-catering house from her. She strolled up the street smiling and cool, immediately lowering our stress levels – nothing seemed to faze her and nothing was a problem

Maureen Tierney has always been ahead of the game. In recent years, various luxury B & Bs and Guesthouses have come on stream in Kinsale and they may well be very excellent but some are also very expensive, catering for wealthy golfers coming to play at the Old Head. Maureen said to herself "what about providing luxury accommodation but at reasonable prices" and Friar's Lodge was born.

In the centre of town, nothing is lacking for Maureen's specifications were meticulous for her new venture which is proving a real winner. Friar's Lodge is built over and around a central archway, leading to ample private parking and three self-catering houses. The rooms and suites are like good hotel rooms, spacious, with all creature comforts, turn down service, choccies on your pillow – a pillow menu – telephone, TV, DVD, radio, internet connection, safe, ironing centre, mini bar available, and of course an elevator. You can also bring your pet – but do enquire first cos that doesn't include elephants or alligators!

There are lovely relaxing lounge areas where you can sit and chat with other guests or read the magazines. Maureen and her staff provide that extra

4 Star Service and will make any reservations you wish or arrange tee times –
there is also a drying room for golfers. There is a compact wine menu
available to residents and complimentary sherry sits in the decanter just
waiting for you to have that aperitif before you toddle out to one of the
many famous Kinsale restaurants. Breakfasts are delicious – help yourself to
the cereals, fruits, and juices and then have a hot breakfast. "Would you like
some fish," said Maureen, "we just run down to the local fish shop – which is
particularly good – and bring it in fresh........."

Nothing is ever too much trouble for Maureen Tierney – she is still
smiling and unflappable – outstanding – loves horses and is definitely in the
winner's enclosure.

Owners	Maureen Tierney
Address	Friar's Street, Kinsale, Co. Cork.
Tel	021 4777384
No. Of Rooms	18
Price	
Suite/Family	€140 Children under 5 free.
Double/Twin	€120
Single	€80
Dinner	No – Kinsale is awash with restaurants.
Open	All Year – Closed 22nd – 28th December.
Credit Cards	Visa MC Amex Laser
Directions.	Follow signs for the South Link and the airport and you will join the R27. After passing Cork Airport, three miles further on at the Five-Mile-Bridge take the R600 to Kinsale Town.
Email:	mtierney@indigo.ie
Web:	www.lucindaosullivan.com/friarslodge

Garryvoe Hotel

Garryvoe in East Cork is to scores of Corkonians what Skerries is to Dubliners, and maybe what Long Island was to New Yorkers– where the childhood holidays were spent. Long innocent days on the beach, simple fun in rented summer houses or caravans, sand in the banana sandwiches and romps through the rough grass with Fido, beach balls, rounders and windbreakers, it was not in any way sophisticated. Fond memories.

For Irish people along with those memories of Skerries, Garryvoe, and sand filled sandwiches, is the taste of those wonderful Dublin Bay Prawns - which we took for granted – great big bruisers that our parents used to buy straight from the Fishing boats, pop in the boiling water for a flash and eat with salt and mayonnaise. They are nearly a thing of the past on Irish menus now, replaced by every old excuse of a prawn from distant shores, but I can let you in on a secret – at the Garryvoe Hotel you will also find them on the menu in bucket loads – Prawn Cocktail – the real thing – Prawns with Garlic Butter – the real thing – Prawn Scampi – the real thing – Prawns Mornay – you haven't seen that in a while have you?

The Garryvoe Hotel used to be a country hotel but has been transformed into a magnificent new establishment with superb bedrooms and suites overlooking the beach. It has a swish new diningroom complete with twinkling ceiling, and smart new bar. We were in a glorious Junior Suite with a wonderful high cathedral ceiling - I could have stayed in that room for a week without leaving it – and lived on room service. It was so cool and calming with a giant sized bed, beautiful big brown sofas, clear white walls, blue curtains and a view of the sea that seemed never ending. We left the balcony doors open all night to hear the lapping of the waves – it was just bliss.

There is a generosity of spirit too in The Garryvoe both with Stephen Belton, the General Manager, and proprietors, John and Carmel O'Brien, who also own the Bayview Hotel in Ballycotton. Garryvoe is just beside Ballymaloe and Shanagarry and is a superb place to stay

Owners:	Stephen Belton, General Manager.
Address:	Garryvoe, Castlemartyr, East Cork.
Tel	+ 353 (0)21 464 6718
No. Of Rooms	48
Price	
Suite	From €249 Room Only
Family	From € 99 Room Only (2 adults + 2/3 children up to 12 years)
Double/Twin	From €99 Room Only
Dinner	Yes – Restaurant and Bar Food.
Open	All Year
Credit Cards	Yes
Directions	In the heart of Garryvoe village facing the beach
Email:	res@garryvoehotel.com

Web: www.lucindaosullivan.com/garryvoehotel

Harbour Lodge

Apart from actually being in a yacht, you are not going to get much closer to the water than when staying at Harbour Lodge. Stunningly located, sitting proud right on the waterfront at Scilly, the appropriately named Harbour Lodge looks out over the fabulous Kinsale Harbour and Marina and is just a magical place to absorb the charm and fascination that is Kinsale.

A 4 Star luxurious Guest House, there are nine exclusive and serene bedrooms, including a beautiful two room suite, if you want to push the boat out. Just imagine chilling out with a nice glass of complementary champagne on arrival and gazing out from your balcony over the shimmering water. I spend a lot of time in Kinsale in the winter and I know that any time of the year in Harbour Lodge would be just sheer bliss, and get you totally into relax mode.

Not only will you be staying in a unique location at Harbour Lodge, where you will be pampered and spoiled, but owner Siun Tiernan is also a Chef whose speciality is handmade chocolates – now you won't find many other Guesthouses anywhere with that attribute. Your very own chocolate supply literally on tap … and you do know of course that chocolate is good for you!

Dinner is served each evening in the Orangerie Conservatory with its 180 degree views out over the water. Siun's food combines classic French influences with modern Irish flare. She is big into locally sourced, seasonal produce, using her own individualistic recipes. Her fish is caught fresh from the Atlantic Ocean and her lamb and beef are the very best quality and, of course, from traceable sources. Just think of sitting looking out at the yachts and fishing boats gliding by as you have the freshest prawns just tossed in butter, followed up maybe with succulent roast rack of West Cork lamb. Make sure to leave space for puddings … it might homemade hot blackberry pie … or mouthwatering strawberries and cream … and then a

glass of Port as the sun goes down....

Breakfast will set you up for the day, whether it is touring West Cork or playing golf, you will be well fortified with a choice of porridge with fresh fruit and cream, or gourmet muesli, or a plate of organic smoked salmon, or maybe even crepes....

Ask Siun about her cookery weekends, they are great fun as well as being illuminating. Great too for a girls weekend away. Oh yes, as well as all those choccies and goodies, you can bring the significant other half, and the mutt as well … the well behaved canine that is.

Owner	Siun Tiernan
Address	Scilly, Kinsale, Co. Cork.
Tel	+ 353 (0)21 477 2376
No of Rooms	9
Price	
Suites	€220
Double/Twin	€165
Single	€130
Dinner	Yes
Open	All Year
Credit Cards	Yes
Directions	On entering Kinsale, take first left turn. At Spaniard Bar follow sign for Harbour Lodge. Right turn.
Email	relax@harbourlodge.com
Web	www.lucindaosullivan.com/harbourlodge

Hayfield Manor

"Thelma and Louise" said the General Manager, of the 5 Star Hayfield Manor Hotel welcoming and helping the windblown disheveled pair scramble out of the low open topped car with their bags. It is not very often that the General Manager of any Hotel is at the door to greet one – they are usually hiding away in their Offices leaving the front of house stuff to their minions. I must say it was very impressive and this hands on approach clearly results in a very high standard of performance all round. Hayfield Manor, a member of the Small Luxury Hotels of the World, is where the Legal fraternity rest their briefs when in Cork – and believe me they like their comforts. A red bricked neo-Georgian building set in two acres of ground with mature trees and surrounded by a 15-foot wall. Located beside the University it has a magnificent new Spa, along with shimmering Pool and Beauty Salon just for residents' use. The first impression is "oh, it's so pretty" – like a Connecticut Mansion in an American movie – everything perfect with a lovely old picturesque tree right outside the front door, topiary planters, carriage lights, and a liveried doorman. The bedrooms are beautifully draped and lavishly furnished and I got to stay in the Master Suite

immediately following on Pierce Brosnan and his wife! I felt like I never wanted to leave it. This is where anyone who is anyone stays when they come to Cork. There is an air of being cushioned away from the real world at Hayfield and, although it is 5 star, it is absolutely unpretentious. Fabulous gourmet food is served in Orchids Restaurant – foie gras parfait, scallops, turbot, lamb, organic duck breast and so on whilst in the lovely new light and airy conservatory style fashionable Perrott's Bistro there is a superb a la carte selection of modern food at very reasonable prices. There is of course further pampering available at The Beautique at Hayfield Manor, which offers superb Elemis Spa Therapy in male and female treatment rooms. It is the ultimate urban retreat. Hayfield, a wonderful luxurious oasis in Cork, only a mile from Patrick Street and is the perfect place for business or pleasure. Enquire too about their special breaks. I just want to live permanently in the picture postcard world of Hayfield Manor. Special Offers are available throughout the year so do check the website and contact the hotel re those rates.

Owners	Joe and Margaret Scally
Address	Perrott Avenue, College Road, Cork.
Tel	+353 (0)21 484-5900
No. Of Rooms	88
Price	
Suites	From €590
Double/ Twin	From €220
Family	From €285
Dinner	Yes – 2 Restaurants
Open	All Year
Credit Cards	Visa MC Amex Diners Laser
Directions	Signed off College Road
Email	reservations@hayfieldmanor.ie
Web	www.lucindaosullivan.com/hayfieldmanor

The idea for Hotel Isaac's was inspired. A vast, red bricked, Victorian landmark building on Cork's MacCurtain Street, used by Nat Ross Removals, was converted into Hotel Isaac's, offering great value accommodation in excellent surroundings.

While the Hotel itself is an oasis of calm its Bar and Greene's Restaurant are very popular with those in the know seeking good food. But more of that later. The bedrooms are extremely comfortable, bright and airy, and ideal for the technophile and modern day traveller requiring Internet access, safes, minibars, transcontinental built in adaptors, airconditioning, trouser press, iron and ironing boards. The location is brilliant, for Hotel Isaacs is a few minutes from Cork's Kent Station, is surrounded by restaurants, clubs, pubs, boutiques and antique and décor shops.

Greene's, the Hotel's own Brasserie Restaurant, is under the baton of French chef, Frederic Deformeau. It overlooks a floodlit cascading feature waterfall so you are ideally placed for a fun gourmet weekend. The food is excellent and you can think perhaps of lovely fresh timbale of crab with avocado, lemon and chive mayonnaise, topped with toasted brioche or French Chavignol goat's cheese stuffed with semi-dried tomato and black olives, wrapped in Parma ham and served on spicy red onion bruschetta drizzled with balsamic and olive oil. One of my favourite dishes there is a parcel of Savoy cabbage, filled with an excellent duck confit and vegetable brunoise served on spicy Puy lentils with a rich deep red wine jus. That always

makes my trip to Greene's worth while – a little bit of rustic France in the Rebel County. Mains include excellent shellfish, shank of lamb on confit roast potatoes and much much more.

There are also 11 excellent two and three bedroomed apartments adjacent to the Hotel which are very popular and suitable for small groups, families and business people who like a bit more space and freedom.

At Hotel Isaacs you are in the heart of Cork.

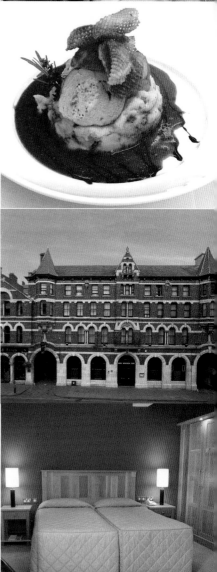

Owners	Paula Lynch (General Manager)
Address	48 MacCurtain Street, Cork.
Tel:	+353 (0)21 450 0011
No of Rooms	61
Price	
Double/twin	€90 - €250 Room Only
Single	€70 - €200 Room Only
2/3 Bed Apts	€750 - €1200 per week
Dinner	Yes – Restaurant and Barfood
Open	All year save Christmas
Credit Cards	Yes
Directions	From Patrick Street follow directions to Cork Railway Station. Hotel on left in one-way traffic system.
Email	cork@isaacs.ie
Web	www.lucindaosullivan.com/hotelisaacscork

Kingsley Hotel

I was out to lunch with a T.V. producer friend of mine recently and we were talking about a presenter we both knew and loved who travels quite a bit. "I hope he doesn't get too spoiled...." My friend said. "I remember when we used to rough it around the country and crash in and out of places ... now he only likes the best Spas ... and all the luxuries". I thought, I must tell him about the Kingsley in Cork – he will absolutely love it!! Having roughed it in many places myself over the years, I have reached the stage where I want my comforts too!!

The 5 Star Kingsley Hotel on the Banks of the famous River Lee in Cork City has recently undergone a €30 million refurbishment programme. It has everything that my by now very discerning presenter friend would love, from superb Health and Fitness Facilities, to the holistic Yauvana Spa with an in-house Ayurvedic practitioner Doctor Anu and her highly trained therapists. Yauvana Spa is the only Spa in Ireland to offer Sodashi treatments. I am convinced too that my permanently tanned friend also gets Botoxed but we'll say nothing!

There are different categories of rooms. Superior rooms, some overlooking the River Lee, have lots of features such as mini-bar, satellite television and music system, air conditioning and so on. De Luxe rooms are decorated in rich lush warm hues and have a workstation, voice mail, complimentary internet access, flat screen TV naturally, and DVD player with surround sound, mini bar, sleep easy beds, choice of pillows and all the other 5 star accoutrements. Executive Suites are everything the others have plus and a fine sitting room to entertain clients or friends. They also have a lovely view of the weir on the river. The 750 sq metres penthouse Presidential Suite – on two floors – is all singing all dancing with handcrafted walnut featuring throughout – as well as an outdoor Hot Tub on the balcony. There are two bedrooms, fully serviced kitchen, security office, living room, library, cinema screen and open fire and my TV pal could have 14 of his "very closest friends" to dinner around the dining table – and of course a personal Butler is available during your stay. Oh dear God, Mr. Presenter will be really carried away with himself.

The staff are very friendly throughout the hotel and the same can be said for the hotel's restaurant, Otter's, where you might be enjoying the likes of beetroot tartlet, goats cheese quenelles with a balsamic reduction followed maybe by pan seared seabass, citrus and fennel salad with a passionfruit dressing or a really decent sirloin with mushroom ragout and peppercorn jus. After that you can take yourself into the Sabrona Lounge for a nightcap but don't end up singing "On De Banks Of My Own Lovely Lee"... or maybe do ... it will cause a stir!

... and if you see a tanned TV presenter...

Owner	Seamus Heaney – General Manager
Address	Victoria Cross, Cork.
Tel	+353 (0)21 480-0500
No of Rooms	131
Price	
Suites	From €400
Double/Twin	From €280
Single	On request
Family	On request
Dinner	Yes – Restaurant and Bar Food
Open	All Year
Credit Cards	Yes
Directions	On the N22 "Western Road"
Email	resv@kingsleyhotel.com
Web	

www.lucindaosullivan.com/kingsleyhotel

Old Bank House

KINSALE

My favourite place in the whole world is undoubtedly Kinsale. The first time I went away from home with a group of friends on a Bank Holiday skite it was to Kinsale. I spent my honeymoon in Kinsale, my eldest son took his first steps in Kinsale, I will probably end up in Kinsale. The pretty narrow streets are lined historic old houses, colourful shops and galleries, great bars, and great places to eat. Stroll down Pier Road by the new marina, take a trip out on the water. You just won't find another Kinsale anywhere else in the world.

During the years I have seen many of the good people who put Kinsale firmly on the world map retire and take life a little more easily. A town to be vibrant and maintain its good reputation has to have fresh blood in its arteries who will bring it forward – as far as Kinsale is now concerned – local chap Ciaran Fitzgerald is one such person. Ciaran has recently embraced the beautiful Old Bank House as part of his group, The Blue Haven Collection, which also owns the nearby super Blue Haven Hotel.

The Old Bank House is a magnificent Georgian House right smack in the middle of all the activity in Kinsale. It has been lavishly revamped from top to toe with the most magnificent fabrics, drapes, throws, bedcovers, fine antiques and original paintings. Most of the individually designed bedrooms have views of the harbour and town and they really are superb so if you want lush plush luxury – and who doesn't – the Old Bank House is for you …and me.

What I like about the Old Bank House too is that after you have meandered around the shops and the bars, you can just stroll back in and crash out in a squishy sofa in the lovely drawingroom, read the paper, have

a glass of wine, relax, you are on your holidays. After a great nights sleep in those big comfortable beds, you will be ready for the beautifully set out Breakfast Room. There is a lavish buffet selection with probiotic Greek yogurt, a platter of freshly cut seasonal fruit and berries, local cheeses, fruit compotes, traditional oatmeal porridge, scrambled eggs with smoked salmon, omelettes.......

The Old Bank House is "doing Kinsale" in style

Owners	Ciaran Fitzgerald
Address	10/11 Pearse Street, Kinsale, Co. Cork.
Tel:	+353 (0)21 477 4075
No of Rooms	17
Price	
Suite	From €280
Double/Twin	From €210-€250
Family	From €230
Dinner	No – but sister hotel Blue Haven just beside it.
Open	All Year
Credit Cards	Yes
Directions	On arrival into Kinsale, there is a junction. The Old Bank House is directly on the right, on the main street.
Email	info@oldbankhousekinsale.com
Web	www.lucindaosullivan.com/oldbankhouse

Radisson SAS Hotel & Spa, Cork

When I read "Sensual Chocolate Wrap", I immediately thought, that sounds tasty. Well, it is, but not in an edible way. The wrap, made with real cocoa, is a luxurious chocolate body wrap – every woman's dream - and is one of the many treatments available in the luxurious Retreat Spa and Fitness Centre in the Radisson SAS Hotel and Spa at Little Island , which uses Elemis products and also has a unique Hydrotherapy Treatment Pool. Ditchley House, a 19th C listed building, has been lavishly restored and the Radisson was built adjacent to the victorian house and opened its welcoming doors to the public on the 21st June 2005.

Just beside Cork City, and conveniently located to Cork International Airport, the Hotel is everything one would expect from a Radisson SAS operation. There are 129 ensuite rooms – deluxe suites, business class rooms, and family rooms, all beautifully styled and luxuriously furnished in Urban and Ocean style. All rooms have 24 hour room service, one touch direct dial telephones, plasma screen TVs, in house movie channels, mini-bar, tea or coffee hospitality tray, in room safe, trouser press incorporating iron and ironing board, and free WIFI internet access. With all such accessories you may never wish to leave your room.

But there is more. The Banks Bar is the destination after a long business meeting or an afternoon in the Spa. Relax and enjoy one of the creative cocktails on offer – after a couple of sassy Bahama Mamas or Margaritas. They have

a very good bar menu and also for dining, just off the bar, is the Island Grill Room which does things like a really decent fish pie as well as warm cracked crab claws, confit duck leg with Lyonnaise potates or maybe ravioli filled with asparagus and ricotta cheese at good prices. They really push out the boat for breakfast with a superb super buffet with up to 63 mouth watering items to choose from.

The hotel's conference and meeting facilites are second to none – up to date in-room equipment and services and anything else required, and their detailed information packs mean you can select and dictate what you want and expect, and you won't be disappointed.

Whether it is business, a spa break, or a weekend in Cork, the new Radisson SAS is fab.

Owners	Ruairi O'Connor (General Manager)
Address	Ditchley House, Little Island, Cork.
Tel:	+353 (0)21 429 7000
No of Rooms	129
Price	
Executive Suite	€260
Double/twin	€130/€140
Single	€130€140
Family	€250
Dinner	Yes – Restaurant and Bar food
Open	All Year
Credit Cards	Yes

Directions	East of Cork City. From Dunkettle Interchange roundabout, take 3rd exit signed Rosslare/Waterford. 1 mile on, take slip road for Little Island. Cross flyover, take 3rd exit off roundabout. Hotel is 1st entrance on right.
Email	info@radissonsas.com
Web	www.lucindaosullivan.com/corkradissonsas

Seaview House Hotel

"Yes, we do breakfast in bed … if necessary," said the wonderful Miss Kathleen O'Sullivan, Proprietress of the Seaview House Hotel at Ballylickey, in response to my timorous enquiry on the telephone the night before. We felt like two naughty schoolgirls – but yes, they did breakfast in bed all right and, as one would expect under Kathleen O'Sullivan's eagle eye, it arrived on the button of 8 a.m. and was just perfect. It is no wonder that this much loved haven of hospitality won the AA Courtesy and Care Award. A new wing was added not so long ago to the Seaview House, along with a magnificent French classical style round

"conservatory" to the dining room, and it is just a fab place to stay. All of the rooms are splendid with larger rooms being absolutely divine – some opening out to the gardens – beautifully furnished with antiques, French Armoires and headboards, wonderful paintings – each different and each special We had arrived like two exhausted rats into the hall of the Seaview, having driven in and out of every peninsula from Cork to Ballylickey. Make no mistake this takes hours, but I don't feel I have had my fix of West Cork each summer without doing it. Having showered and dickied ourselves up we went down the corridor past Kathleen O'Sullivan's "Command Centre". "You look very nice", she said to my companion – "go through that door there and you can have a drink". Having passed muster we went into a cocktail bar and armed ourselves with suitable sherries and set down to peruse the menus. The food is excellent – think Sauté Lamb kidneys Madeira sauce, whisper light Scampi or avocado with real Dublin Bay Prawns, Rack of Lamb or lemon sole all perfectly produced and served. "Do we get both Puddings and Cheese?" asked a young Englishman sitting across from us with his wife. His eyes lighting up like a child's when given the affirmative answer. We all looked together at a Victor Meldrew look-alike who passed by us and the young man said "we feel very young" – "so do we", we chimed sharply" to this mere fresh faced youth. The Seaview House Hotel is brilliant – you will absolutely love it.

Owners:	Kathleen O'Sullivan
Address:	Ballylickey, Bantry, Co. Cork.
Tel	+353 (0)27 50462/50073
No. Of Rooms	25
Mini Suite	€185
Double/Twin	€140 - €165
Family	€175
Dinner	Yes
Open	Mid March to Mid November
Credit Cards	All Major Cards
Directions.	Located on main Bantry to Glengarriff road.
Email:	info@seaviewhousehotel.com
Web:	www.lucindaosullivan.com/seaviewhousehotel

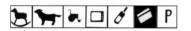

Shearwater

Without a doubt, Kinsale is on the itinerary of pretty well every tourist who comes to our shores, be they foodies or yachtties, or just plain wanting to visit this pretty town, which has achieved world wide fame. We went on our honeymoon to Kinsale and have been up and down a few times every year since to this gorgeous romantic town with its narrow colourful streets and myriad of restaurants. There is always a buzz in Kinsale – be it winter or summer – in fact we like it even better out of season.

Right on the marina, just beside Kinsale Yacht Club, is Shearwater, a new development of exclusive magnificent apartments and duplexes in what is probably the most stunning location in Ireland, never mind Kinsale, unrivalled and unprecedented.

Available for short-term letting in Shearwater is a magnificent duplex,

which very comfortably sleeps up to four people. The steps up to the front entrance bring you into your own little world that is so modern and airy that it has the feel and panache of a New York loft. The first floor has two bedrooms. The very spacious master bedroom, which is ensuite, has a super kingsize bed, which can convert to two singles. The guest bedroom has two single beds and both have views of the harbour.

Upstairs leads you to the most amazing enormous room with high Cathedral ceiling and velux windows. There is a bay window at one end with views of the boats and out over the roof tops of Kinsale. It is very stylishly furnished with eclectic Franco Chinese furnishings. The kitchen area is beautifully constructed and fitted with everything anyone could possibly want. There is private secure car parking and on the ground level is Vista a coffee/wine bar so you just nip downstairs and pick up your croissants for breakfast. Live the dream – you won't want to leave.

Owners	Mary Morris
Address	Shearwater, Kinsale, Co. Cork.
Tel	087 2513249
No of Rooms	Sleeps 4
Price	€695 – €995 per week
Dinner	Self-Catering
Open	All Year
Credit Cards	Yes
Directions	On Marina
Email	tsar@eircom.net
Web	www.lucindaosullivan.com/shearwater

P ☐ NET ◪

Sheraton Fota Island Hotel & Spa

FOTA ISLAND

Fota Island just east of Cork City is one of the most beautiful places in Ireland. It is best known for its Wildlife Park, which is a joint project between the Zoological Society of Ireland and University College Cork. It is a wonderful opportunity to see many endangered species from lemurs to zebras up close and personal with very little restriction.

SHERATON FOTA ISLAND HOTEL & SPA

Last year saw the opening of the stunning new Sheraton Fota Island Hotel & Spa. The location is fab, right beside this wonderful nature reserve, only 10 minutes to Cork City, close to Cobh and the Titanic trail. Nip on the little car-ferry across the bay, and you are into West Cork and Kinsale in half an hour. The Hotel itself is a low rise building sitting at the top of a hill overlooking parklands and the golf course and there is just that wonderful

feel of being away from it all … and somewhere special. There is an almost Hispanic feeling to the large lobby with its beamed ceiling, stone columns, marble floors and oak furnishings. Off the lobby is a beautiful Amber lounge leading to the Fota restaurant which serves excellent food. Tucked away at the other side of the lobby, beside the wine cellar, is a fabulous fine dining seafood grillroom, The Cove. The food here is really special but you do need to book this in advance as it is very popular with local foodies and it is "small and beautiful". We dined on slivers of Pata Negra filled with fig puree and topped with Parmesan shavings. We followed up with divine scallops on sautéed foie gras and braised pork belly … and the best ever sole on the bone filled with a Nicoise dressing … and the puddings – seriously good.

The bedrooms are very stylish with all the de rigueur requirements of today's up market hotels … great big comfortable beds, lovely bedlinen, mini bar stocked with goodies, plasma TV, internet access, extra large dressing area with his and hers hanging spaces, and a stunning bathroom with big walk in wet room style shower and a big bath as well.

The Fota Island Spa is amazing set in this natural habitat. There are 18 treatment rooms and the whole place is just beautiful. There is a 16 metre Hydrotherapy Suite with a unique walking river … the only one in Ireland.

Actually I could stay in the Sheraton Fota Island Hotel & Spa for a week and never move out.

Owners	John O'Flynn (General Manager)
Address	Fota Island, Cork.
Tel:	+ 353 (0)21 467 3000
No of Rooms	131
Price	
Double/twin	From €129 Room Only
Single	From €129 Room Only
Family	From €129 Room Only
Dinner	Yes – 2 Restaurants and Barfood
Open	All Year
Credit Cards	Yes
Directions	Located off the N25 east of Cork City. Take slip road signposted Carrigtohill/Cobh R624. At roundabout take 4th exit. At next roundabout take 1st exit.
Email	reservations.fota@sheraton.com
Web	www.lucindaosullivan.com/sheraton/cork

The Waterfront Guest House

I t's many a long year now since the legendary Youen Jacob Snr set sail from his native Brittany and landed on the shores of Ireland. He married and opened his Chez Youen restaurant in the little fishing village of Baltimore, West Cork, concentrating on shellfish served the simple way that it is in France. The rest, as they say, is history. He has continued to enthrall diners with big platters of jumbo Galley Head prawns, Sherkin Island Oysters and lobster for years and has played host to hundreds of well-known names from here and abroad.

Baltimore is an enchanting village straight out of the Pirates of Penzance or the Caribbean – but it is just more beautiful in West Cork. Really magic, it has to be experienced. The village attracts such a diverse and colourful cross section of visitors that it has a unique atmosphere. Baltimore is your oyster whether you want to swim, dive, fish, sail, whale watch, dolphin watch, island-hop or simply sit in the square and watch the sun go down in splendour over the harbour and Mount Gabriel.

Youen's family are now grown and actively involved in the business. Youen Jnr opened a fab casual continental style café on The Square called La Jolie Brise and has now, not only married the lovely Kate, but has bought the next door pub, knocked it and done a major redevelopment. On the ground floor is a big bar called Jacobs with over that a lovely restaurant with a 25 foot panoramic glass window – can you imagine that for a view over Baltimore Harbour. What was formerly the Youen's Baltimore Bay Guest House has been incorporated and enlarged and they now have 13 spankingly great bedrooms.

Understated chic is the theme, furnished in a contemporary classy style

with well-chosen antique pieces, which intermingle charmingly with the cool modern furniture and feel of this boutique guesthouse. Walls are cool cream, the rooms are a good size, bed linen is crisp and fresh, there are televisions with videos, direct dial phones, and you are right smack in the middle of things. Sit down outside the door, and take in the sun and the atmosphere whilst you have your cappuccino, or later in the day delicious pizzas and pastas, grilled fish or vegetarian dishes, chill out in the Bar and finish the evening with a fab dinner in the restaurant.

Breakfast can be continental or the Full Irish - whatever is your choice – they also offer fish plus delicious hot chocolate. You can bring the family – they have family rooms and you can also bring Fido.

It's cool.

Owner	Youen & Kate Jacob
Address	The Square, Baltimore, Co. Cork.
Tel:	+353 (0)28 20600
No of Rooms	13
Price	
Double/twin	€80 -€120
Single	€60 - €80
Family	Enquire (children under 4 sharing room free)
Dinner	La Jolie Brise or Chez Youen
Open	All Year
Credit Cards	Yes
Directions	Take the N71 from Cork to Skibbereen and follow the R595 to Baltimore.
Email:	res@youenjacob.com
Web	www.lucindaosullivan.com/waterfrontguesthouse

Woodlands House

Kinsale is virtually a second home to me so I know every stone on the streets and what is good and what is bad.

Woodlands House is a pretty house perched on a hill with scenic views of Kinsale town and harbour, just seven minutes stroll from the centre of the town. Its charming façade blooms with vibrant flowers in the Spring and Summer seasons and its roof is trimmed with snow white, Austrian style, filigree facias giving it a cosy, romantic feel. It is perfectly located in a quiet area for enjoying all the famous port of Kinsale has to offer, not forgetting its famous restaurants.

There are three great golf courses on your doorstep here: Kinsale Golf Club, Old Head Golf Links and Farrangalway Golf Course, not to mention all the other exciting outdoor activities to choose from in the area like sea angling, yachting and Whale and Dolphin spotting boat trips. Fota Wildlife Park is an hour's short spin away on the eastern side of Cork city and is definitely worth a visit for all age groups – keep an eye out for the playful lemurs and the cheeky squirrel monkeys!

Valerie and Brian are extremely friendly and hospitable and have created a perfect restful serene haven in their new Bed and Breakfast at Woodlands. Bedrooms are spacious and comfortable, some have harbour views, furnished with warm, antique style dark wood floors, lockers and bedsteads and are punctuated by luxurious king-sized beds. Rooms are en suite and feature a safe, tea/coffee making facilities, hairdryer, TV, direct dial telephone service and iron with ironing board. WIFI access is also available. There is an inviting sitting room, decorated in a traditional style, in keeping with the bedrooms, whose focal point is the ornate, black marble fireplace. The rich, striking wall colours contrast beautifully with the floors and furniture and create a subtly sophisticated yet relaxed feel to the house. There is great care and attention to detail here and it adds to the enjoyment of your stay. Look out for the cute little lamps dotted about!

Breakfasts are scrumptious and generous – there is a wide selection from the decent orange juice – to the lavish Full Irish or scrambled eggs – oh and the French Toast – definitely something to write home about.

The real thing about staying away from home in a B & B is that you want to feel it is almost a home from home – Valerie and Brian are so welcoming and warm – you will relax and be most reluctant to leave.

Owner:	Valerie & Brian Hosford
Address:	Bandon Rd., Kinsale, Co. Cork
Tel:	+353 (0) 21 4772633
No of Rooms:	6
Price	
Double/Twin:	€80-€100
Single:	€80
Family:	€120 - €140
Dinner:	No
Open:	1st March to 12th November
Credit cards:	Yes
Directions:	Take R600 from Cork to Kinsale. Drive through Kinsale town and turn left at White House. Continue until you see St Multose Church and follow sign for Bandon until you see sign for Woodlands House.
Email:	info@woodlandskinsale.com
Web:	www.woodlandskinsale.com

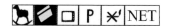

County Donegal

From the Inishowen peninsula in the north, to the sweeping beaches of the south, Donegal with its two hundred mile coastline has scenery that is unsurpassed throughout the country and is well worth a tour. Enter Donegal from the south through the popular bucket and spade holiday resort of Bundoran and travel north through Laghey before reaching Donegal Town where you may visit O'Donnell Castle. Continue around to Dunkineely with its fabulous St. John's Point and then on to Killybegs, Ireland's most successful fishing village. Onwards and upwards will bring you to Glencolumbcille and its numerous megalithic remains and nearby folk village and museum. Rejoin the N56 which winds its way northwards through Ardara, Glenties, Dungloe, and the Irish speaking Gweedore and Gortahork. The road turns southwards at Dunfanaghy, leave the N56 and go further east to the sweeping Lough Swilly and southwards through Rathmullan, to the pretty Ramelton on the banks of the salmon rich River Leannan. Continue on to Letterkenny, the county's largest town, and site of St. Eunan's Cathedral and onwards to Lifford the county town close to the Northern Ireland border town of Strabane. I should mention that Donegal has the highest seacliffs in Europe at Slieve League. Don't forget the Rosses, an area which includes Kincaslough from whence Ireland's most popular balladeer comes, and where hundreds of people flock every year to his home for the annual tea party with Daniel O'Donnell and his mother.

"A folk singer is someone who sings through his nose by ear"
(ANON)

Castle Murray House Hotel and Restaurant

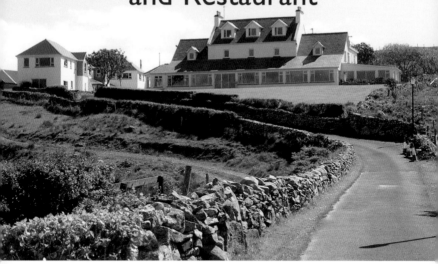

astle Murray House Hotel is fabulously located on a cliff top, with spectacular sea and stunning coastal views out over McSwyne's Bay, in one of the most dramatic counties in Ireland. Dunkineely has Mountcharles to the east with its sea angling centre and boats available for hire and, to the west, Killybegs, probably Ireland's busiest fishing village. The ruins of McSwyne's Castle are owned by the Hotel and are floodlit at night which adds to an already wonderful inherently brilliant atmosphere. The word Hotel conjures up Modern 4 Star with Leisure Centre but CastleMurray is far more intimate than that – more inns and havens feel – which are not words used very much in Ireland but do describe very well a good Restaurant with excellent accommodation and atmosphere. The ten bedrooms are all en-suite, furnished individually, and have digital T.V. and all facilities. The bathrooms are beautiful having just been recently refurbished. One room is done in African style with black African carved face masks, giraffe cushions with leopard skin lampshades – you can fantasise you are on Safari though I would prefer to be here in Donegal. Another room has a pretty window seat and is beautifully decorated in colorful coral. CastleMurray is a very comfortable and relaxing spot. Have a jar in the newly refurbished bar before and after dinner – you can relax as you are not going to have to drive anywhere. Meals can be served outside on the verandah in the Summer. The

food is wonderful – pick your own lobster out of a tank – prawns, scallops, crab and don't forget to finish up with the Prune and Armagnac parfait … it is to die for. Castle Murray is a strictly non-smoking house.

Owners:	Marguerite Howley
Address:	St. John's Point, Dunkineely, Co. Donegal.
Tel	+353 (0)74 9737022
No. Of Rooms	10
Price	
Double/Twin	From €130
Family	€162.50
Dinner	Yes – Restaurant
Open	Mid February – Mid January.
Credit Cards	Yes
Directions.	2 kms from Dunkineely Village
Email:	castlemurray@eircom.net
Web:	www.lucindaosullivan.com/castlemurray

89

Donegal Manor

The mere mention of Donegal Town leads my husband into a reverie of remeniscences about his time spent there in the days of his childhood. He talks of Dan McBrearty's forge where he spent many an hour pumping the bellows.

He mentions the central Diamond, the O'Donnell Castle on the bank of the river Eske, and the particularly lovely "Church of the Four Masters" where women prayed on one side of the central aisle, and men on the other. That was all in the 40's and 50's and, like all over the country, things have changed.

Donegal Town is a very busy commercial centre, and probably one of the most friendly and welcoming places in the country, gateway to many places of historical and current interest in the county, and now boasts the exceptional Donegal Manor. This is not your run of the mill B & B but one of the new breed of boutique 4 Star Guest House accommodations.

The Manor, which was custom built in 2004, is run by Sian and Michael Breslin who fall over backwards to make your stay pleasant and enjoyable. All the bedrooms are spacious and are furnished to the highest possible standard with ensuite facilities. There is interesting original artwork on the walls, and very welcoming turf fires. Oh how I love the smell of burning turf and there is Nana Murphy's tearooms too to supply needed sustenance all day. Each bedroom is also provided with a refreshment tray, TV, and for the business person there is Broadband connection in each room. The Manor also boasts a business centre where you can fax, print, scan, or copy documents at reasonable rates.

Donegal Manor is also more than family friendly. Children sharing with parents are free up to age 12 and, from 13-18 years cost just €15 each. Breakfasts are excellent with each morning a fruit dish, maybe rhubarb and raspberry compote, apricots and prunes poached in a spicey juice, fresh fruit salad in summer, all served with Greek yoghurt. Their coarse brown bread is superb and they also do a super Porter Cake. Their local prize winning butcher supplies great sausages for the Full Irish … you won't go wrong at Donegal Manor – it is a place with a warm Donegal heart and great value.

Owners	Sian and Michael Breslin
Address	Letterkenny Road, Donegal Town, Co. Donegal.
Tel:	+353 (0)74 972 5222
No of Rooms	9
Price	
Double/twin	From €110
Single	€55 - €70
Family	From €120. 0-12 Stay Free BB. 13- 18 years sharing room with with parents €15
Dinner	No
Open	1st March – 2nd January
Credit Cards	Yes
Directions	At 1st roundabout for Donegal Town, take 2nd exit onto bypass. At 2nd Roundabout, take last exit. Continue on N15, and take 2nd round to right.
Email	info@donegalmanor.com
Web	www.lucindaosullivan.com/donegalmanor

 NET P

Frewin

RAMELTON

Ramelton is an old plantation town with beautiful Georgian buildings sited on the River Lennan that flows into Lough Swilly. In times past the river was navigable by ocean going vessels and Ramelton was an important town for trade. The town itself was prosperous and homes were furnished with many exotic imported items. The Fishhouse, on the Quayside, has a town map listing a number of important buildings worth seeing. Eateries are plentiful and superb fresh fish is widely available.

FREWIN

Whether in winter or summer, Thomas and Regina Coyle's picture postcard pretty former rectory, Frewin, is a magnificent place to visit. Everything about the house, bedrooms, suites, and gardens, have been lovingly restored by the owners. Thomas hails from the area and has a knowledge of the countryside which would enthrall and keep visitors listening to local folklore for many an hour. Many of the bedrooms are decorated in white, with white painted furniture, and white muslin curtains. One of the bedrooms is just perfect for honeymooners or a romantic stay, a bridal suite complete with lace drapes over the bed, delicately carved mirrors, and beautiful ornaments adorn the room. Throughout, the house has retained its original character but with all modern facilites of course. Thomas and Regina have a great interest in antiques and restoration and there is a little antique shop and self catering cottage in the the grounds. The gardens are beautiful. Dinner is available with advance notice and you can bring your own wine if you wish. The diningroom is special, no electric

lighting, but a really splendid atmosphere under a real candle lit chandelier. You can relax after dinner in the lovely library. Thomas and Regina are warm and entertaining hosts who genuinely enjoy meeting their guests. Frewin is a place one doesn't want to leave. The house is not suitable for young children.

Owners	The Coyle Family
Address	Ramelton, Co. Donegal.
Tel:	+353 (0)74 915 1246
No of Rooms	4 (3 En Suite)
Price	
Suite	€180
Double	€130 - €180
Twin	€170 - €180
Single	€ 75 - €95
	1 bed self catering cottage €500-€550 per week
Dinner	Yes – Enquire on booking
Open	All year save Christmas
Credit Cards	Yes
Directions	Turn right at speed limits to Ramelton (driving from Letterkenny). Frewin 300 metres on right.
Email	flaxmill@indigo.ie
Web	

wwww.lucindaosullivan.com/frewin

 P

Harvey's Point Country Hotel

I n 1983 whilst on holidays from Switzerland, Jody Gysling, attracted by the stunning Swiss like snow capped Blue Stack Mountains, bought an old cottage on a swamp on the shores of Lough Eske, from two brothers by the name of Harvey. Jody gradually renovated the cottage, painstakingly drawing stones by tractor ten miles in the process. Six years later, escaping the pressures of Swiss business life, Jody and his brother Marc opened a small Guest House. A young local girl, Deirdre, took a summer job with them, romance blossomed between Deirdre and Marc and the rest, as they say, is history.

2004 was the turning point with major development and investment in Harvey's Point and what was once a tiny cottage is now a fabulous destination Hotel, nestling on the shores of shimmering Lough Eske. 42 fab new bedrooms and suites were added in keeping with the beauty and integrity of the area. From traditional Swiss designs, the bright airy rooms feature classically comfortable wooden furniture complimented with every conceivable modern convenience. There are four categories of accommodation from which to choose, each absolutely fantastic with amazing facilities. Executive rooms have a separate foyer, kingsize beds, mini bars, Broadband Internet access. De Luxe rooms are a larger version of the Executive category. Premium suites offer all of the above along with a private dressing room, whirlpool baths and lake views and then you have the fab Penthouse Suites double the size of the Executive Suites with bedroom, living room, bar area, lounge, dressing room, guest wc, whirlpool and bath king size bed. Latest additions to the luxury of Harvey's Point include new Beauty Treatment and Hairdressings Facilities as well as a new Boardroom with a capacity of 25 for corporate groups.

Food too is a major feature at Harvey's Point. The restaurant sweeps down to the water and there is a French slant to the delicious cuisine – Donegal Bay oysters or maybe a terrine of duck foie gras flavoured with Irish Mist liqueur whilst shellfish and prawn bisque comes with a puff pastry lid. Follow up then maybe with black sole or duo of Donegal lamb, scallops or monkfish but leave room for the luscious puds.

The scenery is spectacular in Donegal and the friendliness of the people well known whether you land on the helicopter pad or by car – get yourself to Harvey's Point – it is different and it is beautiful.

Owners:	Deirdre McGlone & Marc Gysling
Address:	Lough Eske, Donegal Town, Co. Donegal.
Tel	+353 (0)74 972 2208
No. Of Rooms	62
Price	
Penthouse Suite	€640
Double/Twin	From €320
Single	From €195
Dinner	Yes
Open	All Year (Nov – March closed Sun evening/ Mon/Tues)
Credit Cards	Yes
Directions.	6km from Donegal Town. Follow signs for Lough Eske.
Email:	info@harveyspoint.com
Web:	www.lucindaosullivan.com/harveyspoint

Sandhouse Hotel & Marine Spa

Just off the main road, between Bundoran and Donegal Town, is the magnificent sweeping beach at Rosnowlagh, on the Atlantic Coast of Donegal, where stands the lovely Sandhouse Hotel and Marine Spa. Virtually on the beach, you simply could not get any closer to sun, sea and sand!

Originally a Fishing Lodge it was transformed by the Britton family into the fine hotel it is today. Most of its bedrooms, furnished in lavish country house style, have spectacular views over Donegal Bay and its proximity to the Ocean, and its food, have always been star points. Seafood is a speciality at the aptly named Seashell Restaurant and oysters, crab, scallops, lobster, sourced from local unpolluted waters, are regularly on the menu, as well as delicious Donegal lamb, prime beef and veal, and game in season. During the day locally smoked salmon, fresh Donegal Bay oysters and mussels are also served in the cosy bar

I think we've come to realise how important it is to be able to switch off,

walk the beach, and take the sea air. The Victorians used to take the waters and visit Spa towns, as did the Germans and Austrians, and way back the Romans. We are now only realising, but realising in a big way, how important water therapy is. At the Spa Suite at the Sandhouse they offer the very best in Marine Body and Skin Care with Thalgo Marine, which uses 100% pure seaweed from the coast of Northern France. The richness of the sea oligo elements, proteins, amino acids and vitamins are captured within the Thalgo philosophy and are vital to health and well being, and ensure soft supple revitalised skin. Try the Balneotherapy, a high-powered bath with 200 water jets massaging all those tender spots like lower back and neck. Think of it, aromatic oils, mineral salts, dried seaweed. Sure, after all that toning and rejuvenation you will be running up and down the beach every day, and knocking back the champagne in the bar each evening.

Apart from walking, surfing or just relaxing the Sandhouse is within easy reach of many championship standard golf courses and Rosnowlagh is an ideal centre from which to explore places of historical and cultural interest.

The Sandhouse Hotel is one of those great places to which you feel you are coming home each time you arrive. Feel the sand between your toes.

Owners:	The Britton Family
	Paul Diver - Manager
Address:	Rossnowlagh Beach, Rossnowlagh,
	Donegal Bay,
	Co. Donegal.
Tel	+353 (0)71 9851777
No. Of Rooms	55
Price	
Suite	€300
Double/Twin	€240
Dinner	Yes
Open	February - December
Credit Cards	All Major Cards
Directions	From Ballyshannon take the Coast Road to Rosnowlagh.
Email:	info@sandhouse.ie
Web:	www.lucindaosullivan.com/sandhouse

County Dublin

ounty Dublin is dominated by Ireland's Capital City, Dublin. The city exudes the style and confidence of any European Capital but its citizens still know how to party and enjoy themselves like there was no tomorrow. Set on the fine sweep of Dublin Bay, the city is divided by the River Liffey, which flows from west to east. South of the river are the fine examples of Dublin's Georgian past with the lovely Fitzwilliam and Merrion Squares, and the beautiful St. Stephen's Green with its rich and colourful flowerbeds, green lawns, dreamy ponds and shaded walkways. North of the river is the Municipal Art Gallery, the Writers Museum, as well as the Phoenix Park, one of the largest enclosed parks in the world and the residence of the Country's President and the U.S. Ambassador – a favourite haunt of Dubliners. The city abounds with places and buildings that remind us of Ireland's historic and troubled past. The General Post Office was the scene of violent fighting in 1916. Dublin Castle was seat of the British Occupation Control, and Kilmainham Jail has many shadows of the past. Round the Bay to the South the road leads through fashionable Monkstown with its crescent of lively restaurants, on to the town of Dun Laoire with its harbour and yacht clubs, to Sandycove and its association with James Joyce. Further South is the magnificent sweep of Killiney Beach and the homes of many rich and famous. North of the city are some lovely and friendly seaside towns and villages – the very fashionable Malahide, the busy fishing town of Howth, the fine sandy beach of Portmarnock with its famous Golf Links and Skerries, a favourite spot for Dubliners and visitors alike. As the song says … Dublin can be Heaven.

"Other people have a nationality, the Irish and the Jews have a psychosis"

(Brendan Behan)

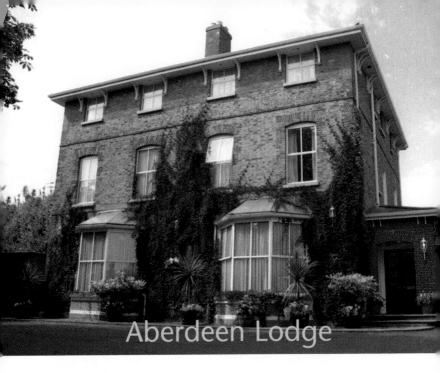

Aberdeen Lodge

You won't find any "Basil Fawlty's" at Pat Halpin's Aberdeen Lodge, in the heart of Dublin's leafy embassy belt, Ballsbridge. Pat, the ultimate Hotelier, quietly misses nothing, is supremely helpful and efficient whilst, seemingly effortlessly, running four small private Hotels. Nothing is too much trouble for the staff at Aberdeen who are motivated to provide the 5 star standard of friendliness and helpfulness expected by the Head Man. Aberdeen Lodge is a large Edwardian Villa on its own grounds expertly converted to provide accommodation of the very highest standard. Fine bedrooms, some with four-posters and whirlpool spa baths, have Satellite T.V. Mineral Water, trouser press, all the little details. There is an elegant drawingroom with plenty to read and you can order from their substantial Drawingroom and Room Service Menu. They also have a wine list. Breakfast is brilliant – a lavish buffet displayed in pretty Nicholas Mosse pottery followed by a hot selection. Breakfast is included in the room rate but if you want to have a business meeting over breakfast you can invite a guest to join you. There is also complimentary wireless Internet access for guests. Ballsbridge is where the Royal Dublin Society have their magnificent Showgrounds and is the venue of the famous Dublin Horse Show. Down the road is Lansdowne Road – the headquarters of Irish rugby. If you are a resident and your address is "Dublin 4" that says it all about you – money – class - although nowadays there is a fair scattering of nouveaux Celtic Tiger money types infiltrating the red bricked roads. Location, location, location is the story at Ballsbridge, for you can walk into the centre of Town in 15 minutes, the DART station is nearby at Sydney Parade or taxis will be reasonable as it is so close to Town. The Blue Airport Coach also stops at two

Hotels in Ballsbridge so transport is a dream. Cap that all with lots of nearby Restaurants, Thai, Indian, Chinese, French, Mediterranean and you can see what I mean about location. Not suitable for Children under 5. In Dublin for Shopping, Theatre, Rugby Matches, Business or just a break – Aberdeen Lodge is where it is at.

Owners:	Pat Halpin
Address:	53 Park Avenue, Ballsbridge, Dublin. 4.
Tel	+353 (0)1 283 8155
No. Of Rooms	19
Price	
Suite	From €200
Double/Twin	€130 - €160
Family	€160 - €190
Single	€ 90 - €129
Dinner	Drawingroom Menu
Open	All Year
Credit Cards	Yes
Directions	Down the road from Sydney Parade DART Station. Park Avenue runs parallel with Merrion Road and Strand Road close to RDS.
Email:	aberdeen@iol.ie
Web:	www.lucindaosullivan.com/aberdeenlodge

 □ ✎ ▬ NET P

Dylan Hotel

"It was the White Rabbit, trotting slowly …looking anxiously… The Duchess! The Duchess! Oh my dear paws! Oh my fur and whiskers!" Maybe I did see the White Rabbit in the new "dylan Hotel" on Eastmoreland Place, or was I dreaming, for it is like waking up in Alice's Wonderland? Quite amazing.

The Dylan is the hot Boutique Hotel which hit the ground running last year. The décor is funky and wild and there is a London-ish feel to the little cul de sac where it is located. Just five minutes from St. Stephen's Green and Grafton Street, it is perfectly placed in the up market side of town. Outside is a lovely big terrace, which is a social scene on balmy summer evenings. In the hallway is a padded purple button backed designer chair shaped like a languishing lady, just one of the many feature pieces throughout. The bar is a hive of activity doing great cocktails.

The bedrooms are stunning with fabulous French headboards, Frette bedlinen, magnificent drapes, lush brocade covered chairs, big plump pillows, plasma screen TV's and MP3 players, Internet access, mini bars and twice-daily housekeeping. The bathrooms are to die for with underfloor heating, Etro toiletries – just pure heaven – one room is more fabulous than the next.

Don't even think of going out to a restaurant before you have been to their Still Restaurant - which is like a Fairy Queen's Ice Palace – white white white. It only seats 44 people so book in advance. Down the centre of the room are 18 little crystal chandeliers, lots of silver gilt furnishings, great big White Queen's pearlised giant high backed thrones mixing with

virtually backless chairs. Lots of white button-backed leatherette banquette details, wild mirrors, crisp white napery and white porcelain.

The food is fabulous .... serious food in frothy surroundings. We had Foie Gras served with confit pork belly on a cep puree with Puy lentil jus and Seared rare Blue Fin tuna with a citrus dressing, sorrel aioli and radish. To follow we had absolutely glorious roasted venison – three little towers on a root vegetable terrine, parsnip puree and black trompettes and exquisite turbot with a little pot of incredibly intense crab soufflé into which was poured prawn bisque.... The puddings are out of this world so don't pass and, for wine buffs, the list is like a bible – but prices to suit all pockets.

The Dylan is a real wonderland.

Owner	The Fylan Group
	Siobhan Delaney
	– General Manager
Address	Eastmoreland Place,
	Dublin. 2.
Tel:	+353 (0)1 6603000
No of Rooms	44
Price	
Suites	From €690 – Room Only
Double/twin	From €395 – Room Only
Dinner	Yes – Restaurant
Open	All Year – save 24th – 26th
December	
Credit Cards	Yes
Directions	From St. Stephen's Green, go down Baggot Street. Cross Grand Canal and take left after Searson's Pub on to Eastmoreland Place.
Email	justask@dylan.ie

Web
www.lucindaosullivan.com/dylanhotel

Fitzpatrick Castle Hotel

The first time I was ever in Fitzpatrick Castle Hotel I was very very young! I was there with my parents to meet the visiting American cousins who naturally, having good taste, came to stay at Fitzpatrick Castle Hotel. Nowadays, I live just a couple of miles away and have always been a frequent visitor at the Castle for dinner, drinks, celebrations, weddings, and meeting visitors. It is just a fantastic place which I know very well and is very much part of the local scene.

Fitzpatrick Castle Hotel is located in the very much up-market area of Killiney, on the south County Dublin coastline overlooking Dublin Bay. Located majestically on a height close to Killiney Hill and nearby Dalkey village, I suppose you could say it is the Beverley Hills of Dublin! There is enough Botox in the area anyway!! During your stay at Fitzpatrick Castle you will have Bono and Ali, amongst others, as your neighbour for Killiney and Dalkey are magnets for Ireland's glitterati. Go up the nearby Vico Road and you could be in Sorrento. Sit out at many of the Cafes and bars of Dalkey village and you will feel you are on the Meditteranean.

Fitzpatrick Castle Hotel was started by Paddy and Eithne Fitzpatrick who were spectacularly good hosts and renowned hoteliers. Hospitality is a quality you cannot buy and they passed this gift on to their children who

now each run terrific hotels in Ireland and New York. Their daughter Eithne Fitzpatrick Scott Lennon, and her family, are at the helm of this 18th century Irish Castle which started out this hotel dynasty, and she always moves forward keeping ahead of the times.

Furnished with exquisite taste, nothing is left to chance in the pursuit of excellence and attending to your comforts. Bedrooms are equipped to suit every type of guest be it leisure or on a business trip. There are suites with spectacular views over Dublin Bay, and executive rooms with desks allowing plenty of workspace, as well as Front Deluxe Rooms with balconies, allowing you bask outside and take in the spectacular views.

There are three excellent dining options – PJ's Restaurant – styled in keeping with the traditional Castle environment; the Dungeon Bar & Grill – in the oldest part of the Castle – now a sleek hip minimalist spot doing excellent modern food. The third option is The Library Bar which boasts Killiney's best frozen Daiquiris – there is also an evening bar menu here offering a wide selection of snacks and light meals such as a Parma Ham, Chorizo and Buffalo Mozzarella platter or maybe a plate of oak smoked salmon. Whichever option you choose, the food and craic is always cracking.

As well as all that there is a Leisure Centre with a 22 metre indoor pool, a fully equipped gym and an on deck whirlpool spa and Scandanavian wood sauna and steam room, plus a beauty salon providing aromatherapy, reflexology or a soothing massage. Oh, and there are great shops and galleries nearby plus Golf Clubs galore.

Owner	Eithne Scott Lennon Fitzpatrick
Address	Killiney Hill Road, Killiney, Co. Dublin.
Tel:	+353 (0)1 230-5400
No. of Rooms	113
Price	
Suites	From €350
Double/Twin	From €160
Single	From €140
Family	From €220
Dinner	Yes – 2 Restaurants + Bar Food
Open	All Year
Credit Cards	Visa MC Amex Diners Laser
Directions	Pass Shell Garage on entering Dalkey Village. At T-junction turn right and take sharp left onto Dalkey Avenue. Drive to top of hill. Hotel is on left. Further directions emailed on request. Phone Lisa on 01 2305570
Email	info@fitzpatricks.com
Web	www.lucindaosullivan.com/fitzpatrickhotels

The Fitzwilliam Hotel

Some might think I am a bit of a foodie but they haven't met my English cousin who always plans his very frequent trips around Michelin starred restaurants. He swears it is the only way to travel if you want the best of everything and no awful foodie disasters. He looks well on it!

If that is what you like to do, and even if you don't, then you have to stay at the uber hip Fitzwilliam Hotel for it is also home to one of Ireland's best known, and always in the news, Michelin starred restaurant, Thornton's.

The Fitzwilliam Hotel opened to tremenduous and deserved acclaim a few years ago quite taking Dublin by storm. It is undoubtedly the ultimate in contemporary hip for it was designed by the master of visionary design and style, Sir Terence Conran. Conran's take on contemporary tradition is just wonderful, it is illuminating, and sets this superb Dublin hotel apart from the norm. That apart, the location is just the best there is. Facing the hotel is the superb St. Stephen's Green with its ponds and wildlife whilst, turn left, and you are straight down onto Grafton Street, Dublin's most exclusive shopping area.

The minute you walk through the door of The Fitzwilliam, into the vast cool modern baronial lobby, you are struck by the enormous really beautiful "modern ancestral" paintings hanging over the marble fireplace and contemporary sofas. It is just brilliant. Keep walking and you are into one of Dublin's hippest bars, The Inn on the Green which, believe me, does a deadly cocktail as well as great informal bar food. The mezzanine level above, where you can see all the comings and goings in the lobby, houses their informal Citron Café which does very reasonably priced modern cuisine in chic surroundings. So you have three cracking dining options without putting your foot outside the door. Oh, by the way, you don't have to go

outside to have your hair or beauty treatments, they are all available in house too, along with a gym, if you want to work off the lbs of indulgence!!

The bedrooms are fabulous. Cool, stylish. There are varying levels, Executive, Superior, Deluxe, all of which are stunning, having minibars, in-room safes, unlimited free broadband, fully air-conditioned, CD players, Interactive TV's. Superior and Deluxe rooms overlook St. Stephen's Green, whilst the Executive rooms overlook their garden to the rear. But, if you really want Life at the Top, there is the out of this world Penthouse Suite. An 1800 square foot playground of sophisticated style with glorious Italian furnishings, computer controlled lighting, a grand piano, a leather clad wall which retracts to reveal your own home cinema. There is 24 hour Butler Service and you can entertain your guests in privacy to Michelin starred food.

This is the place for a fab and fun stay in Dublin. You won't find anything cooler....

Owner	John Kavangh - General Manager
Address	St. Stephen's Green, Dublin. 2.
Tel	+353 (0)1 478-7000
No of Rooms	139
Price	
Suites	From €520
Double/Twin	From €220 Room Only
Single	From €220 Room Only
Dinner	Yes – 2 Restaurants + Bar Food
Open	All Year
Credit Cards	Yes
Directions	Located on the west side of St. Stephen's Green. At the top of Grafton Street.
Email	enq@fitzwilliamhotel.com
Web	www.lucindaosullivan.com/fitzwilliamhotel

Hotel Isaacs

The owners of Hotel Isaacs showed great foresight in 1979 when they first opened up their Isaacs Hostel in the city centre for this was not even on the cusp of the Celtic Tiger boom. Eleven years ago they opened Hotel Isaacs, which at that stage had only 25 rooms, and they followed up the following year with their very successful Il Vignardo restaurant. Hotel Isaacs, which provides very good value hotel accommodation, right in the heart of the City, was so successful it just grew and grew. Close to the Financial Services Centre, the Central Bus Station, the DART, the LUAS, it is perfect for brilliant value city breaks. A short walk brings you to Trinity College, O'Connell Street, or if you go the other direction you can take in the concerts at the Point.

There are now 90 bedrooms designated 3 Star. All are very comfortably furnished, both standard and superior rooms. They have TV, tea and coffee making facilities, trouser press, iron and board, safe, room service, air conditioning in some, and the now de rigueur facility of WIFI Internet access, which is just brilliant.

However, ever on the upwards move, The Isaacs Group late last year bought No 2 Beresford Place, a wonderful Gandon designed Georgian House, which overlooks The Custom House – what a spectacular outlook.

There are fifteen beautiful rooms in this glorious building which will serve, in conjunction with No. 1 Beresford Place, which is their meeting and conference centre, as their executive accommodation and conference wing. This magnificent house can also be rented for private and corporate parties and they will provide a delicious buffet menu which you can tailor to suit your own pocket and requirements.

Originally a wine warehouse, their light hearted and fun Restaurant Il Vignardo, which also has a courtyard garden, is located in a beautiful Italianate room with marbled columns and curved vaulted style ceilings, doing popular Italian food – pastas, pizzas, chicken and beef dishes. They have a great early bird a la carte at €8.90 for any pizza or pasta dish. Try the Amatriciana with smoked bacon, onions, chili and tomato – yum. They also have Le Monde Café Bar which is a very attractive space too – reminiscent of a middle European brasserie – where they also do light lunches as well as specialty coffees and wines.

There are limited private parking spaces which must be pre-booked. Check the website for Internet Specials.

Owners	Justin Lowry (General Manager)
Address	Store Street, Dublin 1.
Tel:	+353 (0)1 813 4700
No of Rooms	104
Price	
Suite	€150 – €350
Double/twin	€ 79 – €250
Single	€ 70 – €250
Dinner	Yes – Restaurant
Open	All Year save 23rd – 26th December
Credit Cards	Yes
Directions	Opposite Busaras and the Custom House
Email	hotel@isaacs.ie
Web	www.lucindaosullivan.com/hotelisaacs

 NET P

109

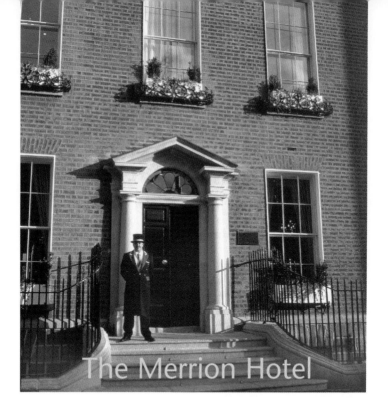

The Merrion Hotel

uring the 18th century, Dublin was transformed from a mediaeval town into one of the finest Georgian cities in Europe. The 5 Star Merrion Hotel, which opened in 1997, is set in the heart of Georgian Dublin, opposite Government Buildings and comprises four meticulously restored Grade 1 Georgian townhouses and a specially commissioned garden wing around private period gardens. Built in 1760 the most important of these houses is Morning ton House, birthplace of the 1st Duke of Wellington. Quite magnificently structured, the doors, architraves, the intricate delicate fanlights, heavy staircases, and amazing rococo plasterwork are just a pleasure to absorb.

Dubliners have clasped The Merrion to their bosom for a splendidly gracious atmosphere has been maintained whilst being elegantly unstuffy. The interior is designed using Irish fabrics and antiques reflecting the original interiors. The public rooms are welcoming and serene – particularly the Drawingrooms and terrace – where one can sit and have afternoon tea or a drink in the most civilized of surroundings, whilst also enjoying one of the finest private collections of 19th and 20th century Art for works by Mary Swanzy, Roderic O'Conor, Sir John Lavery, Paul Henry, and many more, are set against this beautiful backdrop.

There are two in-house restaurants - the beautiful Cellar Restaurant, with its cool uplit vault style columns and pale tiled floor. Here too the food is sublime under the baton of Executive Chef, Ed Cooney, and very reasonably priced apart at all from the fact that you are sitting in one of the finest 5 star hotels in Ireland. Patrick Guilbaud's, the superb 2 Michelin starred establishment is also situated in The Merrion.

The restoration of The Merrion demanded the highest standards and the designers' brief was both simple and clear – "To create a space with sensitivity to the 18th century heritage of the building with light and airy bedrooms". As a result, the guest rooms and suites are the epitome of elegance and also supremely inviting and comfortable, not to mention the most spectacular Penthouse Suite in Dublin.

There is also the beautiful Tethra Spa which offers a comprehensive choice of bodycare and beauty treatments using exclusive E'SPA products so this is just the place to relax after a hard day shopping in nearby Grafton Street or visiting the National Gallery and Museums just across the way.

The Merrion Hotel is Heaven on Earth – nothing more, nothing less.

Owners:	Peter McCann
	General Manager
Address:	Upper Merrion Street,
	Dublin 2.
Tel	+353 (0)1 6030600
No. Of Rooms	143
Price	
Suite	From €950
Double/Twin	From €505
Single	From €450
Dinner	Yes – 2 Restaurants
	Bar Food and
	Drawingroom menu.
Open	All Year
Credit Cards	Yes
Directions	From the top of Grafton
	Street, turn left, continue on
	straight and take the third
	turn left on to Upper
	Merrion Street.

Email:info@merrionhotel.com
Web:
www.lucindaosullivan.com/merrionhotel

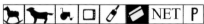

The Clarence Hotel

Bono and The Edge, of rock group U2, not only had an ear for music, they also had an eye for a good hotel – well why not? I suppose they spent so much time flying around the world that they really knew what they were at. They knew what they wanted of a hotel, and so decided to bring a super Boutique Hotel to Dublin.

The Clarence was a legendary longstanding Dublin Hotel in a great location beside the River Liffey, close to the Four Courts, City Hall, Temple Bar, IFSC, Trinity College, and the prime shopping areas. It used to be the slightly countrified haunt of the Irish clergy and the solicitor and legal eagle who fancied the odd tipple...

Along came U2 and it is now a hip, fantastic boutique hotel. The Bedrooms are cool, no two rooms are the same, and they are decorated in one of the hotel's five signature colours, crimson, royal blue, amethyst, gold and chocolate. There is specially crafted Shaker style furniture, Egyptian cotton linens, fully interactive TV and entertainment system, high-speed Internet access with keyboard, and of course the suites have all that and more … plus the finest views of Dublin City as Dubliners see it. On top of that there is the coolest two bedroomed Penthouse Suite complete with a Baby Grand Piano....

The Clarence is a one off with its Arts and Crafts style atmosphere. I would suggest you get into Jet Set mode by kicking off with a cocktail in the Octagon Bar – they make fabulous ones – how's about a Blue Champ – Bombay Sapphire Gin, Blue Curacao, lemon and sugar syrup topped up with Champagne. You might also like to try a glass of the black stuff. They do excellent casual food too in the Octagon including Sushi. We had a glorious dinner in the exquisite Tea Room – the food is always fab there. Red Leg Partridge was with smoked sausage, Savoy Cabbage and juniper jus and superb Roasted Loin of Veal with homemade tagliolini, carbonara and truffle sauce. Produce is meticulously sourced – fish and seafood locally, beef, lamb and chicken always EU accredited, Irish vegetables and fruits are prioritised, breads and chutneys homemade and cheese sourced through a local Farmers Market supplier. Fairtrade and Organic items are available. As one American also reported back to me, his food was "absolutely faultless". Well you couldn't countenance Bono and The Edge getting a bad dinner – could you?

As well as the rack rates, they very often have super 1 and 2-night package breaks so do check. There is also valet parking for hotel and Tea Room guests.

Bono and The Edge's Clarence Hotel really reflects the Ireland of the 21st Century. Perhaps they've found what they were lookin for….

Owner	Bono and The Edge
Address	6-8 Wellington Quay, Dublin. 2.
Tel:	+353 (0)1 407 0800
No of Rooms	49
Price	
Suites	From €499
Double/Twin	From €230
Family	From €499
Dinner	Yes – Restaurant and Bar Food
Open	All Year – Save Christmas 24th, 25th, 26th December inclusive.
Credit Cards	Yes
Directions	From O'Connell Bridge, go down Aston Quay, continue on to Wellington Quay, hotel is on the left.

Email
reservations@theclarence.ie
Web
www.lucindaosullivan.com/theclarence

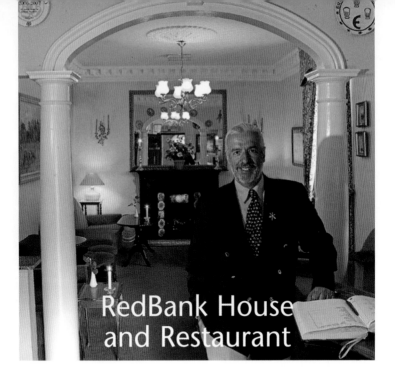

RedBank House and Restaurant

SKERRIES, CO. DUBLIN

Skerries is a fishing village north of Dublin which is forever in my heart as I spent summers there as a child. It all now seems so simple and real. We would swim on the sandy shore of the south beach be it rain or shine. I still remember being enveloped in a big soft towel and dried off on a wet day whilst the aroma of the frying chips and salt were blown down the beach. My mother would buy prawns from the fishermen while my father slipped into the Stoop Your Head or Joe May's for a pint and a half one, which is the colloquialism for a Pint of Guinness and a whiskey. Daddy would then have a smile on his chops as Mother and I would drop the live prawns into the boiling pot for a whisker of a second, take them out and eat them with salt. The local Cinema heralded the delights of Lilac Time with Anna Neagle warbling "we'll gather lilacs in the spring again" … it was a hundred years old then and it seems like a thousand years old now … but Skerries at its heart still retains a wonderful untouched sense of the real Ireland for it is largely undiscovered by tourists.

REDBANK HOUSE AND RESTAURANT

The RedBank House and Restaurant is owned and run by one of Ireland's best-known Chefs, Terry McCoy, with the addition now of Terry's son, Ross, in the business. Terry is a familiar figure on the Irish foodie scene, not just because he is a striking figure who sports a ponytail and beard but because he wins awards all round him for his handling of very fine seafood caught off the Fingal coast. Whilst the Red Bank Restaurant has been a destination

Restaurant for the past 20 years or so it is only in the last few years that Terry added 18 rooms by way of the Old Bank House beside the Restaurant and nearby The RedBank Lodge. Now a 4 Star Guest House the bedrooms are lovely. There are Corporate as well as Double, Twin and Family Rooms, all beautifully furnished with all mod cons and comforts in cool nautical colours, blues, yellows and cream, but with a warmth of feeling. All have T.V. and Internet access. "Revive yourself with a lungful of Skerries air", Terry says, and if you wish you can have your dinner "a la Tray" in your room. This is a house too for the Gourmet Golfer, for there are forty golf courses within "a driver and a sand wedge" of Skerries and what is better after a quick one at the 19th hole than to come back to enjoy Terry's hospitality and fabulous treatment of our wonderful Dublin Bay Prawns and other seafood. Try the Razor fish, caught locally, which are mainly exported to Japan and also ask the see the wine cellar in the old Bank Vault. The Red Bank's long Sunday lunches are legendary. St. Patrick who drove the snakes out of Ireland lived on Church Island off Skerries and fed himself on goat's milk and goats' cheese so you see chevre was popular in Skerries before anywhere else in Ireland! Skerries is only 18 miles from Dublin, easily commutable by train, and is only 20 minutes drive from Dublin Airport.

Walk the beaches, feel the sea breeze in your hair and the sand between your toes, chill out, this is the place.

Owners:	Terry McCoy
Address:	5-7 Church Street, Skerries, Co. Dublin.
Tel	+353 (0)1 849 1005
No. Of Rooms	18
Price	
Double/Twin	€120
Single	€75
Family	€145 for 3 + €25 per extra person including breakfast
Dinner	Yes - Restaurant
Open	All Year – Restaurant closed for dinner Sunday nights, and also 24th, 25th and 26th December.
Credit Cards	All major cards
Directions	Opposite AIB Skerries
Email:	info@redbank.ie
Web:	www.lucindaosullivan.com/redbankhouse

The Shelbourne Dublin

There were a lot of lost sheep wandering around Dublin for the year or so as The Shelbourne Hotel was closed undergoing total refurbishment, before re-opening last year as a shining light – a Renaissance Hotel – the elite Marriott branding. Arguably Ireland's most famous hotel, it is regarded as a national treasure and very much part of the fabric of Dublin social life. It's famous Horseshoe Bar has been party to many a State secret, not to mention many a grand affair. Everybody who is anybody has walked through the Shelbourne doors from Princess Grace to Pearse Brosnan, but then it's the sort of place that movies are made of. The Irish Constitution was drafted here … there is just so much history and style within its four walls. Naturally over the years, it has had a series of ownerships – some good – some not great – but now our national treasure is owned by a group of Irish Businessmen and Hoteliers with a wealth of experience and, even more importantly, an understanding of what The Shelbourne is all about in the fabric of Irish life.

Built in 1824, The Shelbourne, is located right on St. Stephen's Green, in the heart of all the upmarket City activity, the best shops, wine bars, restaurants, that is if you can bear to drag yourself out of the Shelbourne at all in case you miss anything! Millions have been spent on what is now, The Shelbourne Dublin A Renaissance Hotel, bringing it up to date yet retaining all the graciousness and elegance of past times – luxurious fabrics – marble bathrooms – it's a joy.

When you have dropped off your luggage and been wowed by your bedroom, head straight down to the new No. 27 Bar and after a pint of Arthur Guinness or a glass of champagne, you will begin to feel like one of us! They also do a great value casual menu in the No. 27 – lots of Irish staples like Bacon and Cabbage or Irish Stew. Back in the 70's one of the most popular places to eat in Dublin was The Saddle Room at the Shelbourne and I am delighted to say that the new Saddle Room and Oyster Bar is even better. A steak and seafood menu, just think of chomping your way through a delicious Seafood Platter with lobster, jumbo prawns, oysters and Seviche. I have had the Oysters

Rockefeller and the crab cakes, as well as the grilled black sole with caper, lemon and dill, not to mention the 10 oz tenderloins whilst my better half would kill for their 18oz T'bones. Do make your dinner reservation when booking because this is a busy place.

As for breakfast at the Saddle Room with its open kitchen … there is an enormous buffet selection or you can just order from the a la carte breakfast menu … if you are really hungry you can even have Eggs Shelbourne … farm fresh organic poached eggs and grilled Irish fillet of beef on sourdough muffin with sauce Bearnaise and potato hash … now that should keep you going for a while.

The Shelbourne … it's the ultimate Grand City Hotel - a one off.

Owner	Liam Doyle – General Manager
Address	27 St. Stephen's Green, Dublin 2.
Tel	+353 (0)1 663-4500
No of Rooms	265
Price	
Suites	From €450 room only
Luxury Guestrooms	From €255 room only
Dinner	Yes – Restaurant and Bar Food
Open	All Year
Credit Cards	Yes
Directions	Left at Trinity College, right at Kildare Street. Hotel at top of street on left onto St. Stephen's Green.

Email
rhi.dubbr.res.supv@renaissancehotels.com
Web
www.lucindaosullivan.com/theshelbourne

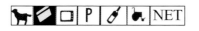

Drummond Mews

DUBLIN'S RIVIERA

The south coast of Dublin is an upmarket suburban area on the DART line with very pretty villages stretching out from Sandymount, through Blackrock, Monkstown, the port town of Dun Laoghaire, and on to Dalkey and Killiney. Known as Dublin's Riviera, the area is awash with clusters of restaurants, pubs and interesting galleries and boutiques. It is a perfect base, with lots to explore, and the DART whisks you into central Dublin in 10/20 minutes.

DRUMMOND MEWS

Looking for that perfect little *pied a terre* hideaway for a stay in Dublin? Well Drummond Mews is it. Located in Dublin's exclusive suburb of Monkstown, close to the sea, yacht clubs, the fashionable restaurants of Monkstown, Blackrock, Dun Laoire and Dalkey, Drummond Mews is the original coach house mews to a large Victorian house. It is not a shiny modern apartment, more quirky hideaway for independent minded people who like to do their own thing and appreciate mews houses and old buildings. It has the advantage of being totally independent and secluded, with its own private high-walled secure drive in courtyard, where one can dine al fresco, take the sun, or just sit and hear the birds sing. Close too to many Golf Clubs it is also the perfect golfer's hideaway. The bedroom is simply but comfortably furnished and decorated with Farrow & Ball colours, bathroom en suite (wash-basin, w.c. and bath – no shower).

Downstairs has a large Mediterranean tiled living cum dining area with small, but well fitted, new galley kitchen, fully equipped with microwave, washer-dryer, and everything you might require to cook up a banquet. There is also satellite T.V. and all bed linen and towels are supplied free of charge.

Dublin Tourism 3 Star graded. 10 minutes walk to the DART station, which whisks you into central Dublin in 15 minutes. The 46A bus also runs from the top of the road serving U.C.D and the city centre. Drummond Mews is also very convenient for the Sandyford/Stillorgan Industrial Estate for people on temporary assignments to Dublin and has easy access to the M50.

Owners	Mary O'Sullivan
Address	Monkstown, Co. Dublin
Tel/Fax	+ 353 (0)1 2800419
No. Of Rooms	Mews House sleeps 2
Price	€595 - €795 per week
Dinner	Self Catering
Open	All Year
Credit Cards	Visa MC
Directions	Phone above
Email	info@dublin-accommodation.net
Web	www.lucindaosullivan.com/drummondmews

County Galway

As a county, Galway encompasses a University City, the wild splendour and magnificence of Connemara and the Twelve Bens then, to cap it all, you have the Aran Islands. Galway City has a vibrancy all of its own and straddles the Corrib river which thunders down under the Salmon Weir Bridge and winds itself around the City to the lively pedestrianised Quay Street at Wolfe Tone Bridge, where the river enters the famous Galway Bay. Worth seeing is the Spanish Arch, a 16th century structure used to protect galleons unloading wine and rum – most important - and the Collegiate Church of St. Nicholas of Myra, the largest mediaeval church in Ireland, built in 1320 dedicated to the patron saint of sailors. It is almost impossible to find a bed in Galway during Race Week, the Arts Festival, and the Oyster Festival at Clarinbridge so book early. The City abounds with Art Galleries and here you can also visit the home of Nora Barnacle, wife of James Joyce, which is now a small museum. Beyond the Claddagh village from which originated the Claddagh ring – is Salthill – the more honky tonk holiday area with amusement arcades. Moving west around the coast road you come to An Spideal or Spiddle, the heart of the Gaeltacht. Inland is Oughterard, a long pretty village on the River Owenriff, which is very popular with anglers. Oughterard is the gateway to Connemara but a

wonderful base for a holiday or break for those who want to have easy access to Galway City. Clifden is the capital of Connemara and is laid out in a triangle. Small and compact but with wide streets and buildings perched high above the deep estuary of the River Owenglin, Clifden is renowned for its Connemara Pony Show. Many famous Irish artists, Paul Henry, Maurice MacGonigal, Jack Yeats, and Sean Keating, have immortalized Clifden in their paintings. The Alcock & Brown Memorial, which commemorates the first transatlantic flight in 1919, is worth seeing. Ten miles northeast of Clifden is Letterfrack, a 19th century Quaker village and just

northwest of that is the magnificent Renvyle peninsula, which has strong literary associations.

"A good holiday is one spent among people whose notions of time are vaguer than yours"
(J.B. Priestly)

Dan O'Hara's Farmhouse

This is a place with a real story which will strike a chord with so many people who are of Irish descent. It is also an idyllic getaway situated in the foothills of the stunning Twelve Bens, just ten minutes from Clifden village in County Galway. The namesake of this appealing Connemara country guesthouse, is Dan O'Hara, immortalised in song, a man who was evicted from his land, along with his wife and children, by his landlord in the first year of the great famine, 1845. Subsequently, they travelled on one of the infamous coffin ships in search of a new life in New York, but only the bold Dan himself survived the journey. The place is named for Dan to preserve his memory and the memory of those like him who suffered great hardship during this period, either through emigration or the cruelty of the workhouses. But fear not 21st century traveller, you shall not be exiled, but instead be given a hearty welcome by the Breathnach family who own and manage the residence.

The bedrooms are bright and cosy and the private TV -free sitting room has an old world relaxed feel – just sink back into those comfy armchairs, chill out and read. The bedrooms have en suite bathrooms, TV, tea and coffee making facilities and direct dial telephones. Internet access is also available. The bedrooms can be accessed via a lift – a great facility for wheelchair users. The long conservatory provides a suntrap with beautiful views, excellent for a lazy afternoon siesta. This guesthouse is very family friendly and babysitting services can be arranged upon request. The fact the farmhouse is on a working farm with donkeys, cattle, sheep and ponies will be of interest to the little nippers and they can even avail of the opportunity to muck in by feeding the chickens! You might even be treated to a tour of the farmhouse and surrounds by Martin complete with history and song.

The adjoining restaurant serves breakfast, carvery lunch, afternoon tea and dinner. The breakfast menu offers treats such as crisp, golden buttermilk

pancakes with bacon and syrup or steaming homemade porridge with honey, the traditional Full Irish is there too as well as a cold continental selection. Wake up to the aroma of freshly baked bread mmmm

Local amenities include golf, fishing, walking, horse riding, cycling, surfing, swimming, outdoor adventure centres and cruises on Loch Corrib, Renvyle and Killary Harbour. The Aran Islands, Inisboffin and Kylemore Abbey are worth a visit too. Packed lunched can be provided for guests going on excursions. For those of you interested in Dan's plight, guests staying at the farmhouse are given complimentary entrance into the nearby Connemara Heritage and History Centre. Galway city is only an hour away and is a nice alternative for the shopaholics among you.

Owner:	Martin & Nora Breathnach
Address:	Dan O'Hara's Farmhouse, Lettershea, Clifden, Co. Galway
Tel:	+353 (0) 95 21808
No of Rooms:	6
Price	
Double/Twin:	€76
Single:	Enquire
Family:	Enquire
Dinner:	Yes
Open:	15th March – 1st November
Credit cards:	Yes
Directions:	From Galway located on N59, 7km past Recess on the right.
Email:	danohara@eircom.net
Web:	www.lucindaosullivan.com/danoharas

Radisson SAS Hotel and Spa, Galway

The Radisson SAS Hotel and Spa, Galway, is to the Hotel Industry what the Lamborghini is to the Motor biz! Sleek in design, powerful in body, the Galway Radisson just purrs. Established in 2001, this 4 Star hotel is only five minutes walk from Eyre Square but boasts fabulous views of Lough Atalia and Galway Bay. The magnificent glass Atrium of the hotel's foyer sets the scene of lightness and clarity within. The stylish Atrium Bar and Lounge with tinkling piano opens out onto a heated terrace where you can have a drink and watch "the sun go down on Galway Bay". The rooms are pretty fab – 282 in total in various categories and with three room styles: Maritime, Scandinavian, or Classic. There are Standard, Superior, Business Class, Junior Suites, Executive Suites and Rooms catering for people with a disability. As well as that there are now 21 new Serviced Apartments. All rooms have a Power Tower, a space saving device that offers satellite television with movie channels, coffee/tea-maker, minibar, personal safe …. whilst the Executive Suites represent the world's highest technological standards. If you really want to splash out Level 5 is top drawer – where Guests are guaranteed privacy and personal service in 16 spacious luxurious executive rooms. Included in Level 5 is a Club Lounge, complimentary treats served throughout the day, soft drinks and canapés during Club Hour, secure membership only access, panoramic rooftop terrace, free use of the Business Service Centre and a separate meeting room … The stylish split level 220 seater Restaurant Marinas is a vision of blue, integrated with dark walnut, reflecting the nautical theme and, as Galway is famous for its seafood, that is the specialty – Galway Bay Oysters, Scallops, Lobster, Monkfish – but there are delicious carnivorous options too. Also new is the luxurious Veranda Lounge – perfect for lunch, afternoon tea, or cocktails and gossip – the place

to see and be seen. Chill out in the Spirit One Spa with facilities found only in the best destination Spas in the world – Sabia Med, Hammam, Rocksauna, Aroma Grotto, Tropical Rain Shower, Cold Fog Showers, Ice Drench and Heated Loungers. Ole Henriksen spa products are available here and from the spa's online store at www.spiritonespa.com. They also use Elemis and Ytsara. The Leisure Center's Swimming Pool is fab along with children's Pool, Jacuzzi, Sauna, Outdoor Canadian Hot Tub. How could you beat that – Radisson Galway is fantastic.

Owners:	Tom Flanagan (General Manager)
Address:	Lough Atalia Road, Galway.
Tel	+353 (0)91 538300
No. Of Rooms	282
Price	
Penthouse	€1500
Suites	€299
Double/Twin	€240
Single	€220
Family	€269
Dinner	Yes
Open	All Year
Credit Cards	All Major Cards
Directions	5 minutes from Eyre Square on Lough Atalia waterfront.

Email:
reservations.galway@radissonsas.com
Web:
www.lucindaosullivan.com/radissongalway

Spa NET P

Renvyle House Hotel

"My house … stands on a lake, but it stands also on the sea – waterlillies meet the golden seaweed. It is as if, in the faery land of Connemara at the extreme end of Europe, the incongruous flowed together at last, and the sweet and bitter blended. Behind me, islands and mountainous mainland share in a final reconciliation, at this, the world's end". So wrote Oliver St. John Gogarty in 1927 of his then home. Spectacularly located nestling between the blue Twelve Bens mountain range and the Shores of the Atlantic Ocean, Renvyle has a tremendous history and it has always attracted famous people from all over the world. The house has been pulled down, rebuilt, burnt to ashes, rebuilt again. It has been home to Donal O'Flaherty, Chieftan of one of the oldest and most powerful Clans of Connaught, and to Mrs. Caroline Blake who was the first to open it as a hotel way back in 1883. But, enough of the past, for Renvyle has been a hotel for all seasons and has always moved with the times and is a stylish destination which is hugely popular with the Irish public, who return again and again for blissful respite and evenings filled with fun. Situated on a 200 acre Estate, Renvyle has a lake teaming with trout, a heated outdoor pool, a 9-hole links golf course and its own beach. There is clay pigeon shooting, horse riding in season, and buckets of activities and creche facilities during holiday periods. Pets are allowed "within reason" – enquire – for that doesn't mean Pooch can sit up with his Cartier collar at the dining table! Whilst we list entry rack rates there are fabulous value packages as well as that throughout the year there are Painting Breaks, Murder Mystery Weekends,

Fly Fishing instruction, Golf Breaks and Walking Breaks. Sixty- eight bedrooms and eight suites, are spacious and very comfortable with all that even the most difficult guest could possibly desire. Excellent food is based on fresh local produce, Connemara lamb, game, fresh fish. In fact Renvyle Chef, Tim O'Sullivan, is a winner of the Moreau Chablis fish cookery competition. Classical Pianist, Derek Hoffman, accompanies dinner each evening, on Count John McCormack's Steinway Grand Piano – playing it that is! Oh, I want to get in the car and drive there again this minute … Ronnie Counihan runs a great house.

Owner:	John Coyle
	Chief Executive
	Ronnie Counihan
Address:	Renvyle,
	Connemara,
	Co. Galway.
Tel	+353(0)9543511
No. Of Rooms	68
Price	
Suites	From €200
Double/Twin	From €110
Family	€110 - €345
	(2 Adults +
	2 Children)
Dinner	Yes – Restaurant – Dinner €45 + 12.5%
Open	February – January
Credit Cards	Yes
Directions	Take N59 from Galway to Renvyle. Hotel signposted in village.
Email:	info@renvyle.com
Web:	www.lucindaosullivan.com

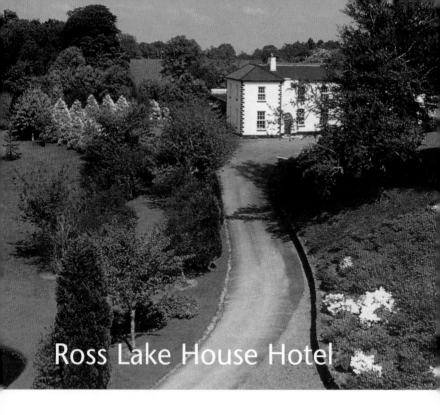

Ross Lake House Hotel

ancy waking up in a four-poster bed in a splendid Georgian house, on 6 acres of rambling woods and rolling lawns, in the magnificent wilderness of Connemara, then Henry and Elaine Reid's Ross Lake House Hotel is for you. Ross Lake House was formerly part of the Killaguile estate built by James Edward Jackson, land agent for Lord Iveagh at Ashford Castle, but renamed as a Country House Hotel because of its proximity to Ross Lake and the fishing waters of Lough Corrib. With 13 spacious guestrooms and suites, all beautifully and individually designed to reflect the charm and graciousness of the house, yet provide the modern facilities we all expect nowadays, you will be very comfortable. There are lovely classic rooms oozing with country house charm, fabulous superior rooms with period furniture and luxurious fabrics, and then, stunning suites with their own sitting area. As pretty Oughterard is only 22 km from Galway City it is ideal for visiting the vibrancy that is Galway, but choosing to leave it when you wish. There are Golf Courses all round – Oughterard, Barna, Galway Bay and Ballyconneely Links Course so if he wants to swing a club you can take off to the Antique shops. You are also ideally poised at Ross Lake for doing the rugged wilder aspects of the Connemara of "The Quiet Man". There is a cosy library bar to snuggle into and an elegant drawingroom with blazing fires to retire to after dinner and make new friends over a nightcap of the liquid variety. The dining room is gracious and the Chef concentrates on the finest fresh

produce from the Connemara hills, rivers, lakes and the Atlantic Ocean so you can expect beautiful crabmeat, wild salmon, tender lamb, scrumptious desserts and fine wines. Henry and Elaine are charming and helpful hosts and, believe me, you will really enjoy a spell at their lovely Ross Lake House.

Owners:	Henry and Elaine Reid
Address:	Rosscahill, Oughterard, Co. Galway.
Tel	+353 (0)91 550109
No. Of Rooms	13
Price	
Suite	€190 - €300
Double/Twin	€150 - €190
Single	€105 - €125
Family	€200 - €220
Dinner	Yes – Restaurant Dinner €50
Open	March 15 to October 31st
Credit Cards	All Major Cards
Directions	Follow N59 towards Clifden. Hotel signposted after Moycullen.
Email:	rosslake@iol.ie
Web:	

www.lucindaosullivan.com/rosslakehousehotel

The House Hotel

I guarantee home will never be the same once you have stayed at the new luxury Boutique House Hotel because you are going to go home and want to throw out everything you have! The House has been furnished and equipped as its name implies – like a really welcoming home away from home - with really beautifully smart contemporary furnishings that reflect and showcase the wonderfully hospitable ambiance just so well. The location is fab – right smack in the middle of the City of the Tribes – so you can just walk out for all your sightseeing and stroll the fascinating streets which abound with galleries, shops, as well as bars and restaurants.

The House is a sister hotel of AbsoluteHotel.com in Limerick and as such was developed superbly by Michael de Haast and his wife Linda. Its size and and cutting-edge design make it a true Boutique Hotel in the best sense – unlike so many others who strive to achieve that elusive feel.

At The House they want you to feel more like a houseguest rather than a visitor so there is no big ugly reception desk. To maintain its individuality and express it's soul, no two bedrooms are alike, except in the fact that they are all superbly equipped with all the de rigueur requirements of a hip boutique hotel. There are three categories of bedrooms – Comfy, Classy and Swanky – always loved that word. All rooms have LCD Flat Screen TVs, Satellite Channels, In-room laptop sized safes, High Speed Internet Access, Mini Bar loaded with your favourite goodies, Rain Dance Shower Heads and L'Occitane toiletries.

The in-house Parlour Bar & Grill is doing fab food and great cocktails. How's about a French Kiss Martini or a Cats Pyjamas to kick off? Having Siamese Cats myself I love their logo of a curled up sleeping cat – that's just how comfy you will be at the House. They do food pretty well all day – lots of Galway Bay Oysters, Crab and Salmon Cakes, Scallops, Surf n' Turf – all done with a delicious contemporary twist but classic favourites like Dauphinoise

potatoes and sauteed Savoy cabbage with Bordelaise sauce are there too. They also do a great menu for kids with real food, but real food that will appeal.

I came down for breakfast on this occasion – but you can have it in bed – and there was a great selection – porridge with maple syrup, buttermilk pancakes with crispy bacon and more sinful maple syrup, croissant stuffed with delicious scrambled eggs and smoked salmon, the full Irish of course, but I had what I always love when I see them on a menu – Eggs Benedict on a toasted muffin with cured ham and Hollandaise sauce.

This place is hot and hip.

Owner	Michael de Haast
Address	Spanish Parade, Galway.
Tel	+353 (0)91 538900
No of Rooms	40
Price	
Suites	From €250
Double/Twin	From €130
Dinner	Yes – Restaurant and Bar Food
Open	All Year – save 25th, 26th 27th December.
Credit Cards	Yes
Directions	Driving From Eyre Square go down Queen Street onto Dock Road and turn right. There are one way systems in operation.
Email	info@thehousehotel.ie
Web	

www.lucindaosullivan.com/househotel

131

County Kerry

C o. Kerry is known as "the Kingdom" and it is difficult to know where one starts to list the attractions of this amazing area. There is the world famous Killarney with its three lakes and impressive McGillycuddy Reeks looming behind them with their ever changing shades and colours. Almost as well known is the hair raising and breathtaking Ring of Kerry on the Iveragh peninsula with its sheer drops and stark coastal scenery. Coaches are required to travel anti-clockwise and leave Killarney between 10 and 11 a.m. so if you are doing it in a day, you need to be earlier or you will be behind them all day. Some books tell you to drive clockwise but it can be nerve racking if you meet a coach on a narrow pass as I have experienced. Head out to Killorglin famous for its mid-August Puck Fair where eating, drinking, dancing, singing is reigned over by the King of the Festival, a Puck Goat. From Killorglin move on taking in the beautiful Caragh Lake to Glenbeigh with

Rossbeigh's sweeping beach. On to Cahersiveen and swing out via the new bridge to Valentia island. Come back and head south to Waterville where Charlie Chaplin and family spent their summers. The final stage is Caherdaniel to Sneem and the lush subtropical richness of Parknasilla which is then about eighteen miles from

"A folk song is a song nobody ever wrote" (anon)

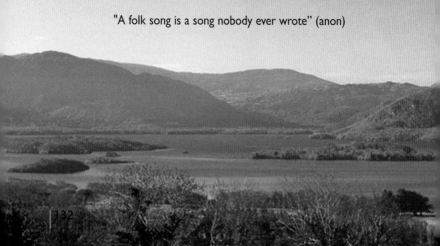

the popular town of Kenmare. North of the county is Listowel famous for its Writers Week and generally regarded as the literary capital of Ireland but also celebrates a madly popular Horse Race Week. Tralee, the principal town of the county, is a very busy commercial centre and also hosts the famous Rose of Tralee celebration. Dingle of "Ryan's Daughter" fame is stunning and has a life of its own. It also has Fungi the dolphin. Among Kerry's many famous Championship Golf Courses is Ballybunion, the favourite haunt of American golfer, Tom Watson, who was once captain of the famous Club. Kerry has an abundance of eateries at all prices and in keeping with Irish tradition is well catered for in drinking establishments, many of which provide ballads and folk songs.

Aghadoe Heights Hotel & Spa

Aghadoe Heights Hotel at Killarney is not just any ordinary Hotel, it is a unique experience. 5 star unpretentious luxury at your fingertips, just the right distance from the centre of the Town, directly overlooking the Killarney Lakes. The Aghadoe Heights is bliss and switch off time, from which you will only be disturbed by the solicitous and gentle pampering of the ever-attentive staff – they are fantastic – all of your whims just seem to be their pleasure. The public rooms are furnished with a mélange of elegant eclectic pieces from the Far East, mixed through with French antiques, a fine modern Irish art collection, and sculptures. Luxurious elegant bedrooms have balconies, whilst spacious junior suites with floor to ceiling windows have fantastic quadraphonic high tech TV's as well. A Roman style indoor swimming pool is placed to the front of the building so, as you swim, you can still see the lakes and mountains with their ever changing palette of moody colours. Right next door to the pool is a new hip cocktail bar for that cool drink or you can slip upstairs to the open plan lounge and have the

most scrumptious afternoon tea, served by white-gloved girls. Luxuriate in the fantastic new Aveda Spa. Try the Precious Stone Therapy – Aghadoe have the only Precious Stone Room in the world where you sit on a throne facing an amethyst grotto, it is blissful. In the evening you will be relaxed and ready for delicious food in Frederick's Restaurant, which is incorporated in the large first floor open plan area, where the resident pianist plays away on the grand piano. They have their own lobster tank or you might fancy the best sole on the bone, or Oysters Rockefeller, or smoked fillet of venison with fresh linguine, juniper and orange jus.... To cap it all Aghadoe now has the most fantastic two bedroomed penthouse suite, with outdoor hot tub, exquisitely furnished to include pieces by style icon Eileen Gray, as well as paintings by Maria Simmonds Gooding, and Pat Scott, and it has its own Paul Burrell – a butler who won't tell all! Chauffeur service to and from Kerry Airport available or come by helicopter. "How can you buy Killarney" were the words of the song but how can you buy Aghadoe is the real question!

Owners:	Pat & Marie Chawke (General Managers)
Address:	Aghadoe, Lakes of Killarney, Co. Kerry.
Tel	+353 (0)64 31766
No. Of Rooms	97
Price	
Penthouse	€2500
Suite	€250 - €680
Double/Twin	€250 - €680
Single	Rack Rate + €65
Family	Rack Rate + €50 per child per night
	(max 2 children under 16)
Dinner	Yes - Restaurant
Open	Mid March - End December
Credit Cards	All Major Cards
Directions	2 miles west of Killarney, signposted off N22
Email	info@aghadoeheights.com
Web	www.lucindaosullivan.com/aghadoeheightshotel

The Brook Lane Hotel

Kenmare is a fantastic town to which people gravitate in search of good food and fun and they will find it in abundance. Kenmare, or to give it its Irish name "Neidin", has lots of shops, boutiques, galleries, decent places to eat, and pubs by the score, you will never be bored in Kenmare.

THE BROOK LANE HOTEL

A very welcome addition to Kenmare is the stylish new boutique Brook Lane Hotel, which adds an urban chic dimension to the accommodation sector, having superb rooms and doing excellent modern food. The Brook Lane is very conveniently located on the corner of the road leading to, or from, Sneem and the Ring of Kerry, which means that you are very close to the centre of town. All you have to do is dump your car and stroll around "doing" the boutiques, galleries and pubs, without worrying whether you will find a parking space or not – Kenmare is a busy spot.

The Hotel has been done with immense panache – cool and contemporary – and unlike anywhere else that I can think of in Kenmare. It is

what today's traveller wants and deserves in the line of comfort and luxury without being overly expensive. The bedrooms are gorgeous, beds to get lost in, fluffy robes and heated bathroom floors to keep your toes warm. Whether your room is Superior, Deluxe or a Junior Suite, you can't go wrong. Colours are neutral with lots of big brown leather cosy chairs to settle into and the service is excellent and friendly. They have just recently added a new meeting room with multimedia projector and connection, remote control air conditioner, retractable overhead screen, plus, of course, wireless Internet access.

There is plenty of good casual food served all day in their cool Casey's Bar and Bistro, which is very attractively finished using lots of brick detail, and where you can very comfortably perch at the bar for that pint or a cocktail. Having perhaps just done the Ring of Kerry you will be hungry so for dinner you can start thinking of delicious pan-fried scallops on ginger bread, followed maybe by monkfish with a chilli and coriander cream, or roast breast of Aylesbury duck on hot and sour cabbage. In summer, Irish Nights (not every night so do enquire when booking) are organised for diners and you may well get to see a Bodhran, a traditional Irish musical instrument, being played. So at The Brook Lane you will get the very best of chic modern hospitality with a bit of tradition thrown in for good measure.

Owners	Una and Dermot Brennan
Address	Kenmare, Co. Kerry
Tel	+353 (0)64 42077
No. Of Rooms	20
Price	
Suite	€200 - €250
Double/Twin	€140 - €190
Family	€170 - €190
Single	€110
Dinner	Yes – Bar food and Restaurant
Open	All Year – Closed 23rd – 27th December
Credit Cards	Yes
Directions	On the corner at the junction of the N70/N71
Email	info@brooklanehotel.com
Web	www.brooklanehotel.com

The Butler Arms Hotel

As you drive down into Waterville, on the southern point of the Ring of Kerry, there is an air of stillness, lushness and beauty. Waterville looks out to the Atlantic but there is also an unspoken eternal sultry drama and amazing colour to the backdrop of mountains. Perhaps this is what appealed to one of the most famous movie stars of all time, Charlie Chaplin, who every summer took his large family here for their annual holidays. With undoubted good taste, they stayed at the Butler Arms Hotel spectacularly located right in the middle of Waterville with views that no set designer could ever recreate.

The Huggard family has run the Butler Arms for generations, and the present incumbents, Peter, Mary and now daughter Louise, have upgraded and maintained the hotel with the same impeccable taste that made it famous in the first place. Their enviable register reads like a roll-call of the famous including Catherine Zeta Jones, Michael Douglas, Dan Marino, as well as former US Vice President Dan Quail and, with Waterville's Championship Golf Links being a Mecca for golfers, Tiger Woods has also stayed, not to mention that the hotel was a favourite place of the late Payne Stewart.

I love everything about the Butler Arms, the beautifully restrained and impeccable bedrooms, the Charlie Chaplin lounge where I crash out and catch up on my reading, breaking for a casual lunch in the Fisherman's Bar, but saving myself somewhat for the goodies that will be available in the Fisherman's Restaurant for Dinner! The food is excellent and you can indulge yourself with lobster or wild salmon from Lough Currane or, if you are a real carnivore, there is the best of Kerry Mountain lamb … the menu is always extensive and you won't be disappointed.

So don't just whiz around the Ring of Kerry like the coach tours, make Waterville your destination and stay and enjoy its spectacular beauty and interesting spots. The home of the Emancipator, Daniel O'Connell, just six miles away at Derrynane Bay is well worth a visit and there are dozens of ancient forts and standing stones. Ballinskelligs too is nearby or you could take a boat trip to the Skelligs.

Peter, Mary and Louise, will ensure you have a wonderful time at the Butler Arms.

Owners	Louise Huggard
Address	Waterville, Co. Kerry.
Tel	+353 (0)66 9474144
No. Of Rooms	40
Price	
Junior Suite	€250 - €350
Double/Twin	€140 - €200
Single	€110 - €150
Dinner	Yes - Restaurant and Bar Food
Open	14th March to Mid December
Credit Cards	Yes
Directions.	In the centre of Waterville

Email:
reservations@butlerarms.com
Web:
www.lucindaosullivan.com/butlerarms

Cahernane House Hotel

y first introduction to the Cahernane House Hotel was over twenty years ago when my better half and I went there for a weekend. At that stage some German people owned it. I particularly remember our lovely room to the back of the house with ivy-clad walls, overlooking beautiful countryside and lawns. We decided to go for a stroll around the grounds but discovered that there was a pet fox in a wire compound and apparently he was on a diet of live rabbit, which ended our stroll rather rapidly! Since that time of course things have changed in a big way. It is now a spankingly beautiful Country House Hotel stunningly located and I have always had a great affection for it.

The former home of the Earls of Pembroke this gorgeous old historic house is at the end of the long tree-lined drive sheltered away from the world yet close to everything, just like being on one's own private estate. The Earls of Pembroke came to Ireland in 1656. One brother was given the great Muckross Estate and the other the smaller property of Currens and Cahernane, and they maintained these magnificent Estates for five generations. In 1877 the original house was considered outmoded, torn down and replaced with the beautiful house which stands today.

Located on the Kenmare road just 1.5 kms from Killarney town centre, Cahernane House has undergone a magnificent but sympathetic refurbishment providing now the ultimate in luxury, including suites and junior suites, and superb modern rooms in a new section. Do note the beautiful latticed staircase and scrumptious drawing room, they are really beautiful. Food is excellent too in their Herbert Room Restaurant. We had delicious pan-fried medallions of veal with a wild mushroom and garlic mustard cream on our visit followed by scrumptious pear and almond tart. The wine list is extensive and they also do excellent casual food in the Cellar Bar – delicious seafood chowder, white crabmeat salad and also a lovely Country House Salad of mixed leaves, smoked bacon, poached egg, and asparagus. Being run now by the Browne family, Cahernane House Hotel has the benefit of personal and dedicated attention to make your visit the best. It is a lovely romantic spot, they are charming hosts, and there is just something about Cahernane that draws you back.

The Earls of Pembroke sure knew how to pick a location!

Owners	The Browne Family
Address	Muckross Road, Killarney, Co. Kerry.
Tel	+353 (0)64 31895
No. Of Rooms	38
Price	
Suite	€290 - €380
Double/Twin	€190 - €299
Single	€150 - €255
Family	As above + €30 B&B per child
Dinner	Yes – Restaurant and Barfood
Open	1st February – 15th December
Credit Cards	Visa MC Amex Diners Laser
Directions	From Killarney Town follow the Kenmare Road for 1.5 km. Hotel entrance is on the right.
Email	info@cahernane.com
Web	www.lucindaosullivan.com/cahernane

NET H P

141

Carrig Country House

CARAGH LAKE

Caragh Lake is a lush magnificent area virtually hidden away from the Tourist be they Irish or otherwise. It has however been a popular area for many years with the Germans a number of whom bought houses in the 1960's.

CARRIG COUNTRY HOUSE

We discovered Carrig Country House, an original 19th C. hunting lodge, at Caragh Lake in 1997 quite by accident when we arrived out there disheveled, distraught and hungry, with two young boys on tow. We were staying in a dreadful B. & B. in Killorglin, which had thimbles of watery orange juice for breakfast and brown psychedelic sheets from the 1970's and we nearly cried when we realized we could have been in luxury in Carrig House had we but known of it. We couldn't find anywhere to eat and were at one another's throats when a young girl had told us about "the new house out at the lake". Off we took like the clappers, 4 miles out of Killorglin, to find there was a God, and Heaven awaited in the shape of the welcoming Frank Slattery, and his wife Mary, who had opened for business that summer. Even if we couldn't stay there on that occasion, at least we were able to have dinner in the magnificent William Morris papered diningroom overlooking the mysterious lake with its mountainous background. We did however return again and it was as blissful as we had first thought. Arthur Rose Vincent chose Carrig House in which to live after his former residence, Muckross Estate in Killarney, was made over to the Irish

State by his American father in law, following the death of his young wife. Arthur clearly had an eye for beauty. The 4 acres of gardens have 935 different species of mature trees and plants, including some very rare and exotic varieties, and are just divine. Dingly dell, mixes with rolling lawns sweeping down to the private jetty which has boats for fishing or just for guests' pleasure. Splendid new rooms have been added at Carrig including a Presidential Suite. The food is fabulous and Frank and Mary, while professional to their fingertips, are just fun. People relax and there is laughter and buzz at Carrig. We had torn ourselves reluctantly away and, as we drove out the gates, My Beloved surprisingly broke into verse "I come from haunts of coot and hern, I make a sudden sally…"

Owners	Frank & Mary Slattery,
Address	Caragh Lake, Killorglin, Co. Kerry.
Tel/Fax	+353 (0)66 976 9100
No. Of Rooms	16
Price	
Suites	€250 - €370
Double/Twin	€198 - €250
Family	Extra bed in room €40 pp
Dinner	Yes - Restaurant
Open	Early March – Early December
Credit Cards	All Major Cards
Directions.	Left after 2.5 miles on N70 Killorglin-Glenbeigh Road (Ring Of Kerry)
Email:	info@carrighouse.com
Web:	www.lucindaosullivan.com/carrighouse

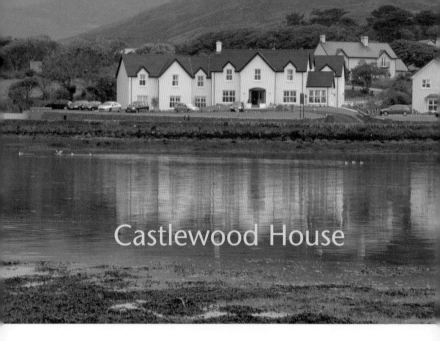

Castlewood House

DINGLE

The Dingle peninsula is so intensely shatteringly beautiful that one can almost feel its raging tempestuous undercurrent churning away. The movie "Ryan's Daughter" brought people from all over the world to Dingle and they still come in their droves including one who has remained for some time - Fungi the dolphin, who is undoubtedly Dingle's most famous resident.

CASTLEWOOD HOUSE

Brian and Helen Heaton are a young couple who have brought their wealth of style, and experience at the upper end of the hospitality industry, into their spanking brand new Castlewood House, which has to be one of the finest Guest Houses I have ever been in.

Custom built to their very discerning specifications, Castlewood offers the guest the ultimate in luxury accommodation, the equivalent of any of the finest 5 star hotels, but of course at a fraction of 5 Star Hotel prices. Castlewood curves gently demi lune style overlooking Dingle Bay and all of the bedrooms have magnificent views of the water. Each bedroom is individually themed, an Oriental room, a French room, and so on - all

equally gorgeous – for which Brian and Helen spent months buying here and abroad for all of the special little details. Each room also has a CD/DVD player, satellite TV, mini fridge, Internet access, hospitality trays, and the lovely bathrooms have whirlpool baths and power showers.

From the moment you cross the doorstep into the wide elegant hall with curved staircase and double doors to the drawingroom and diningroom you realise it is magnificently furnished with beautiful antiques and paintings. The drawingroom is splendid, the diningroom lovely, you won't want to leave here. Helen has superb taste perhaps inherited from her mother, who is a distinguished Artist and some of her work can be seen on the walls of Castlewood.

You will enjoy breakfast overlooking the water. The buffet is lavish with a beautiful selection of fruits, cereals, cheeses, charcuterie, and scrumptious breads and pastries. The pancakes with a fruit topping and maple syrup are sinful as is Helen's creamed porridge with local organic honey or Bailey's. The delicious smoked salmon omelettes are another option – don't worry for the Full Irish is there too – Brian makes sure of that as well as a Fresh Fish of the Day option.

Brian and Helen are a charming and helpful young couple and will really add to the pleasure of your holiday.

Owners	Brian and Helen Heaton
Address	The Wood, Dingle, Co. Kerry.
Tel/Fax	+353 ((0)66 9152788
No. Of Rooms	12
Price	
Suite	€190
Double/Twin	€160
Single	€110
Family	€190
Dinner	No
Open	February to December
Credit Cards	Visa MC Diners Laser
Directions	Located 500m from Dingle Town. Take main road towards Milltown, last house on right.
Email	castlewoodhouse@eircom.net
Web	www.lucindaosullivan.com/castlewoodhouse

Heaton's Guesthouse

We had intended setting off for Dingle early in the morning but we fell by the wayside. We had stayed at a house up at Caragh Lake, demurely had dinner beside an American couple without exchanging a word, walked around the house and came back in to the drawingroom to sit quietly in a bay window. Suddenly the door opened and a bright smiling blonde girl came in sat down and introduced herself as Marian. She and her husband, Nigel, were on their first trip to Ireland as their son was on a school rugby trip in Limerick. As often happens with English people who have no family connections with Ireland, it was their first trip here, and frankly they wouldn't have come unless they had to, for they usually went to exotic locations. We had a drink, and another drink before Nigel sensibly suggested they retire. Next morning at breakfast we all waved at one another, had little polite chats, and nodded to the Americans. We got our bags out to the car where the American couple were trying to map out their route. Telling us they had Restaurants in the States, I confessed to being probably their archenemy – a Restaurant Critic. With that a German car swung into the car park and came over to join in. On learning my occupation the German went to his car boot and took out a little fold up table, spread a check cloth, took out two bottles of wine from his region in Germany, some titbits, special knives and told us he had been coming to Ireland for over 30 years, using the same table, knives and equipment each year! Nigel and Marian emerged and we had the League of Nations Irish, English, Americans and Germans, having a party in a Car park in Kerry, They had never experienced anything like it and told us since it was the best trip of their lives. That's what Kerry and Ireland is really all about.

HEATON'S GUESTHOUSE

Cameron and Nuala Heaton's eponymous Guesthouse is spectacularly located on the edge of the water with magnificent views of Dingle Bay. There is something special about being close to the water that is infectious and life giving. The shimmering ripples are wonderful to sit by during the summer and stunningly dramatic viewed through a window in the depths of winter. Heaton's has 16 rooms, standard, deluxe and Junior Suites,

take your choice, but all are beautifully draped and furnished in cool clear, up to the minute, stylish colours. Each with T.V. Tea/Coffee makers, and superb bathrooms with power-showers, are spacious and have everything you could possibly want for your comfort. There is a large foyer and a lounge sittingroom area with big comfortable sofas where you can snuggle up, cosy up, or just relax. Breakfast is served in the diningroom which also makes the most of the magnificent views with big plate glass windows. This is daughter, Jackie's, area and you can chose from an amazing selection which includes juices, fruits, cereals, stewed fruits – rhubarb or apple- porridge with a dram of Drambuie, brown sugar and cream, followed by the traditional Irish, or Catch of the day, local Smoked Salmon and scrambled egg. Preserves and breads are home-made. Children over 8 welcome. Cameron and Nuala are delightful people, as is their daughter Jackie, and superb hospitality is their middle name.

Owners	Cameron & Nuala Heaton
Address	The Wood, Dingle, Co. Kerry.
Tel	+353 (0)66 915 2288
No. Of Rooms	16
Price	
Junior Suite	€138 - €190
Double/Twin	€ 94 - €138
Single	€ 58 - €102
Family	€112 - €180
Dinner	No
Open	February 6 – January 2
Credit Cards	Visa MC
Directions	Look for Marina – Heaton's is about 600m beyond it.
Email	heatons@iol.ie
Web	www.lucindaosullivan.com/heatons

147

Hotel Europe

When the 5 Star Hotel Europe opened in Killarney many years ago there was a tremenduous fuss – it really caused a countrywide stir – it was something really different – really luxurious – really special – and it still is – only even better! The first time I was ever in Killarney was with a crowd of girls for the Circuit of Ireland Car Rally – we weren't interested in the cars – more in what was driving them – and the craic. Of course at that age we couldn't afford to stay in a hotel – never mind a smart hotel – but that didn't stop us going out for a look – it stuck in my mind – we were absolutely in awe.

Times move on, and so has Hotel Europe, for whilst keeping abreast of the times all along, it has now re-opened after a major makeover and, even after all these years, this spectacular 5 Star Resort Hotel exceeds even the most discerning traveller's expectations.

The accommodation is fabulous. Lakeview bedrooms, most with balconies, have panoramic views of the magnificent McGillicuddy Reeks and Lough Lein whilst Golfside rooms, of which most also have balconies, overlook the 16th Fairway of Killarney's Mahony Point Golf Course. There are Suites, Junior Suites, as well as two Penthouse Suites which are out of this world and the suite to beat all suites - the Presidential Suite.

The décor throughout Hotel Europe is divinely elegant and chic – magnificent drapes and fabulous furnishings. We, of course, headed straight for the hip Crystal Bar for a glass of Champagne after our drive from Dublin. That got us off to a great start and a fab weekend. There are two principal dining options, the ultra hip elegant new Brasserie Restaurant, with terrace for al fresco

dining. This is open throughout the day until late evening doing light food – they also do a fab steak, flame cooked in front of you on an open grill. The Panorama Restaurant is aptly named because you have amazing views of all that Killarney is famous for. It is open for breakfast and lunch with the emphasis on fine dining highlighting Irish and International cuisine.

Now, to put the icing on the cake, Hotel Europe has a splendid new state of the art Spa with sixteen treatment rooms. You can pamper yourself on your own or with your significant other – as they say nowadays – in the couples shower or laconium. There are ice fountains, rock sauna and crystal steam rooms, vitality pools with infinity edge, air recliners. You can luxuriate away to your heart's delight and emerge totally de-stressed, which is what we all need in this ever faster world of today. There are two indoor tennis courts, indoor and outdoor children's play areas, snooker, Haflinger ponies for gentle trekking around the grounds – they are subject to availability so do check – a complimentary daily shuttle service to the centre of town. You are surrounded by Golf Courses – it is Heaven.

Hotel Europe 2008 – I am still in awe.

Owner	Michael Brennan – General Manager
Address	Fossa, Killarney, Co. Kerry.
Tel	+353 (0)64 71300
No of Rooms	188
Price	
Suites	€400 - €1750
Double/Twin	€210 - €350
Single	€170 - €300
Family	6 sets interconnecting rooms. €50 per child sharing parent's room. €180 separate children's room – up to 3 children.
Dinner	Yes - 2 Restaurants
Open	15th March – 10th December
Credit Cards	Yes
Directions	From Killarney town, take N72 towards Killorglin and Ring Of Kerry. Pass Killarney Golf & Fishing club. Hotel further on on left.
Email	hotelsales@liebherr.com
Web	www.lucindaosullivan.com/hoteleurope

149

Killarney Royal Hotel

"How can you buy Killarney?" Went the old song made famous by Bing Crosby. Well you can't of course but, if you know the right places to stay, you can buy into the best of the Killarney experience for the time you are there. It is a great town and Kerry people are just brilliant, smart, sassy, canny and fun.

Right smack in the middle of Killarney Town, very convenient for restaurants, pubs, shops and art galleries, is the Killarney Royal Hotel owned by Joe and Margaret Scally. Margaret was born into the hospitality business for in the early 60's, her parents did buy their piece of Killarney in the form of what was the Criterion, originally the old Munster Arms, built in 1900. In the mid 70s Joe and Margaret took over and, ever moving with the times, the Killarney Royal is now a superbly comfortable boutique hotel. They know what they are about for Joe and Margaret gave Cork City its first 5 Star Hotel – the fabulous Hayfield Manor. They are really hot on their staff providing the best service, without being overly intrusive or obsequious, but they give the best and they expect their people to do likewise – and they do. Joe and Margaret want you to come away from their hotels feeling you have had the very best experience and you will.

The historic building which houses the Killarney Royal lends itself to gracious rooms and each of the 24 bedrooms and 5 suites are the epitome of luxurious comfort and style furnished with lavish fabrics, antique furnishings, large marble bathrooms, twin sinks, WIFI, 24 hour room service – perfect sanctuaries after a hard day's enjoying oneself and sightseeing, and recovering from the jarvie's banter as you took your trip in the jaunting car around the legendarily beautiful Muckross Park.

Actually after the jaunting car ride would be a good time to have a jar in the bar - to steady your nerves – in fact anytime is a good time – but it is fun to recap what is probably a lifetime experience – which is what the Killarney jarvies are! The food is also excellent with a very good and reasonably priced table d'hote menu as well as a cracking a la carte. Excellent seafood is always available, including Dingle Bay lobster in season. The last time I visited I had Kenmare Bay Oysters followed by delicious sole on the bone. My better half had lovely crisp roast duck. They also do excellent sirloin or fillet steaks, pasta and fresh plaice.

Expect the best at the Killarney Royal – and be assured you will get it.

Owner	Joe and Margaret Scally
Address	College Street, Killarney, Co. Kerry.
Tel	+353 (0)64 31853
No of Rooms	29
Price	
Suites	€280
Double/Twin	€220
Single	€150
Family	€275
Dinner	Yes – Restaurant
Open	All Year – save 23rd – 27th December
Credit Cards	Yes
Directions	In Killarney Town Centre, just off the N22
Email	info@killarneyroyal.ie
Web	www.lucindaosullivan.com/killarneyroyal

151

Manor West Hotel Spa & Leisure Club

O n the outskirts of Tralee, on the Killarney Road, stands the spanking new Manor West Hotel. Custom built from the ground up, this fine addition to Tralee offers contemporary 4 star comfort and service under the eagle eye of one of the best Hoteliers in the Country, General Manager Jim Feeney, who for many years oversaw the smooth running of the Great Southern Hotel at Parknasilla.

Your arrival in the cool marble spacious lobby with its magnificent paintings and prestigious and stylish lounge area leaves you in no doubt as to the good things to come. Manor West boasts 77 rooms with all the goodies one expects of a modern day hotel and there are also 10 suites on the top floor, Master, Executive or Junior, where you can either relax, or work, in the utmost luxury.

Off the spacious lobby is the Hotel's modern restaurant, The Walnut Room. Stylishly designed and buzzing with atmosphere, right in the centre is what might be called the "inner circle" two half moon sections facing one another which would make a great set for a movie. It is a lovely room and you can expect to dine on the best of Kerry produce. If you want to eat more informally there is the option of the very casual style Mercantile Bar with its flat screen TVs and self-service food area. Manor West is ideal too for families who will love the Leisure Club facilities. There is an 18 metre swimming pool, sauna, steam room, Jacuzzi and a state of the art gymnasium. Whilst Dad is taking the kids to the pool, this is the time you can take yourself off to the Harmony Spa which has 5 treatment rooms, Laconium, Razul and Aroma Steam Room. Treat yourself to a body wrap and then take yourself off to spend his money at the nearby shopping centre! He won't know you by the time you come back!

The Hotel's easy parking and proximity to the busy commercial town of

Tralee makes it an ideal base for the businessman. While, it's central location in the beautiful Kingdom of Kerry makes it the perfect base for the tourist who wishes to explore the delights of this splendid County.

Kerry is the Kingdom.

Owners	Jim Feeney (General Manager)
Address	Killarney Road, Tralee, Co. Kerry.
Tel	+ 353 (0)66 719 4500
No. Of Rooms	77
Price	
Suites	From €295
Double/Twin	From €120
Single	From € 85
Family	From €190 (2 adults 2 children)
Dinner	Yes – 2 Restaurants and Bar food
Open	All Year
Credit Cards	Visa MC Amex Laser
Directions	Situated on the N22 – Main Limerick/Killarney Road into Tralee Town
Email	info@manorwesthotel.ie
Web	www.lucindaosullivan.com/manorwesthotel

153

Meadowlands Hotel

"Meadowlands"? Repeated the telephone enquiry operator. "Yes", I said, "its an Hotel in Tralee". "I know", she said, "I was there last night and the food is gorgeous". Now, it wasn't the "pale moon shining" nor the fabled Rose that drew me to Tralee. Word had filtered through that the owners of Meadowlands, Padraig and Peigi O'Mathuna, were in the fish business in Dingle, "had their own trawlers", and consequently the Hotel Restaurant, "An Pota Stoir" was specializing, in beautiful fresh seafood. It was true and the whisper in the breeze was right!

The first thing that struck us about the rose coloured hotel was its spaciousness and lots of parking. The corridors are wide and the bedrooms bigger than average and very nicely decorated – beautiful heavily lined beige

silk curtains, nice lamps, and furnishings and very comfortable beds. The bathrooms are very pretty, with floral painted walls, good fittings and pretty New England style doors with glass windowpanes discreetly covered with net. We came down to the Johnny Franks Bar, which is clearly very popular with local people. Modern "Traditional Irish," I suppose is how you might describe it, with a faux library at the upper level and high ceilings, lots of wood and it also does excellent barfood. The split level Pota Stoir Restaurant is casual in ethos, with lots of pine, brick, wall lights and so on, but the food and service is far from casual. There was a relaxed atmosphere as the lady pianist played away all the old favourites which lent a lovely ambience of real Ireland.

Young local man John O'Leary is the Head Chef and is clearly innovative and dedicated. You can expect to see creamy Dingle Bay seafood chowder or maybe tian of Maharees crabmeat wrapped around by a ribbon of sweet marinated cucumber and topped with shredded deep fried onion …and the scallops with Annascaul black pudding … yum … or the panfried fillets of turbot fit … for a prince.

Meadowlands is in a great location in Tralee, the gateway to Dingle, so you can take trips either up to Clare or further south around Kerry – a great central base.

Now you know where to bring your Rose for a bit of craic in Johnny Franks and good food in an Pota Stoir.....

Owners	Padraig and Peigi O'Mathuna
Address	Oakpark, Tralee, Co. Kerry
Tel/Fax	+353 (0)66 7180444
No. Of Rooms	58
Price	
Suite	€300
Double/Twin	€190
Family	€250
Dinner	Restaurant & Bar food
Open	All Year
Credit Cards	Visa MC Amex Laser
Directions.	The Hotel is situated on the N69, the Listowel Road.
Email:	info@meadowlandshotel.com
Web:	www.lucindaosullivan.com/meadowlands

Muckross Park Hotel & Cloisters Spa

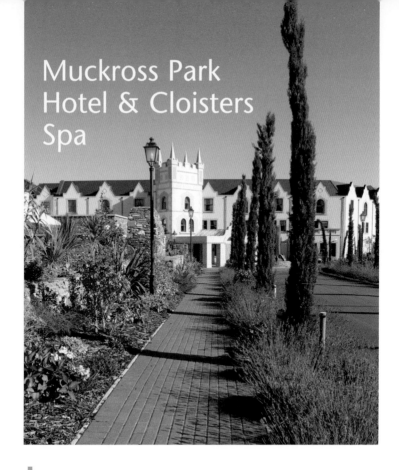

Jackie Lavin and Bill Cullen are one of Ireland's celebrity couples. Kerry born Jackie, is long recognised as one of Ireland's beauties, as well as being an astute business woman, and Dublin born Bill Cullen wrote his incredible life story, "It's a Long Way from Penny Apples", the royalties of which book, with his usual panache, Bill donated to the Irish Youth Foundation.

Some years ago Jackie and Bill bought the Muckross Park Hotel, uniquely located in the National Park on the Lakes of Killarney. A hotel since 1795, and originally part of the Muckross Estate owned by the Herbert family, it has seen visitors as diverse as Michael Collins, the Liberator Daniel O'Connell and Queen Victoria. The Muckross Park Hotel was the haunt too of great writers, it's informal Seafood Bistro "GB Shaw's" is named after George Bernard Shaw, who loved to stay with his wife, Charlotte Payne Townsend, and the new Atrium has hand painted wall inscriptions by W.B. Yeats and by the contemporary Irish poet, Brendan Kennelly.

There is a glorious olde world luxurious spaciousness to the entrance hall and gracious Country House reception rooms in the original house. The Piano Lounge – a perfect Victorian drawingroom - with its grand piano, magnificent sofas, beautiful fabrics, antiques and chandeliers is an oasis of calm.

However, the Muckross Park Hotel is not all about history, for the facilities are second to none. "Molly Darcy's" traditional Irish bar with stonewalls, wooden floors, beamed ceilings and open fires, is great craic and does excellent food virtually all day. The Blue Pool Restaurant offers a gastronomic experience. The menu is superb from Glenbeigh Oysters to Foie Gras, Sole Meuniere to Pork Belly, you will be wined and dined with the best. In 2007 the Muckross Park, with its superb Cloisters Luxury Health Spa, was awarded 5 Star Status. Throughout the year Jackie and Bill hold Gastronomic events – so do check. It is a fab and fun place - just bliss.

So, you see, the craic is mighty, the 5 Star experience second to none.

Owners	Jackie Lavin & Bill Cullen
Address	Lakes of Killarney, Co. Kerry.
Tel	+353 (0)64 23400
Price	
Suite	€350 - €1100
Double/Twin	€200 - €300
Single	€130 - €170
Dinner	Yes – 2 Restaurants + Bar Food
Open	All Year
Credit Cards	Yes
Directions	Take the Muckross Road to the National Park. Past Muckross Village on the left hand side. Adjacent to Muckross House & Gardens.
Email	info@muckrosspark.com
Web	www.lucindaosullivan.com/muckrosspark

    Spa NET P H

Muxnaw Lodge

There is a wide variety of accommodation and high prices in Kenmare so finding that something in between can sometimes be difficult but I found just the place.

Muxnaw Lodge is a lovely gabled house, a former Hunting Lodge built in 1801 ideally situated very close to the town on the Castletownbere Road. Muxnaw is a homely but understatedly classy establishment nestled on 3 acres of fine gardens, complete with its own all weather tennis court, and enjoying outstanding views of the Kenmare River and suspension bridge. Tranquil bedrooms are all different, furnished with beautiful antiques and all have tea and coffee making facilities. Its success is a credit to the wonderful hospitality of its hostess, Hannah Boland, as well as the comforts provided. Hannah knows the area like the back of her hand and delights in mapping out routes and setting her guests off on the proper track for the day. I have indeed seen her spend many an afternoon, after she has served the most delectable afternoon tea, chatting with her guests and pouring over maps and routes, planning the remainder of their holiday.

Kenmare has any number of restaurants to tickle one's taste buds and

Hannah will mark your card as to which are the best and most suitable for you. You can leave the car at Muxnaw and just stroll down the town without wondering whether you have to worry about having that second drink before you drive home. Dinner is available with advance notice and beautiful salmon cooked in the big Aga cooker is one of Hannah's specialities. There is no wine licence so you are more than welcome to bring your own. Breakfast is superb, juices, fruit, and cereals with delicious breads and followed by eggs any way you like or the Full Irish. Hannah's gentle generosity constantly shines through.

You will really feel welcome in this excellent, good value, period house in Kenmare.

Owners	Hannah Boland
Address	Castletownbere Road, Kenmare, Co. Kerry.
Tel	+353 (0)64 41252
No. Of Rooms	5
Price	
Double/Twin	€70 - €90
Dinner	Yes – book in advance
Open	All Year - Closed 24th and 25th December.
Credit Cards	Visa
Directions	On Castletownbere Road out of Kenmare
Email	muxnawlodge@eircom.net
Web	

www.lucindaosullivan.com/muxnawlodge

 P NET

The 19th Green

John and Freda Sheehan have it all wrapped up. All wrapped up in your best interests that is. They have a smashing B & B where you can lay your weary head, after you have been chasing those elusive balls around the course all day, and they also have the 19th Restaurant located at Killarney Golf and Fishing Club where you can relax, be well fed, and bemoan that short putt you missed.

The exterior is picturesque and alpine – very inviting – with wooden awning, balcony and outside benches. It's golfing theme is derived from its proximity not only to Killarney Golf and Fishing Club which offers excellent facilities to keen golfers, but also to three championship golf courses. It's location – 1km from Killarney Lakes and 3km from Killarney town make it a convenient base from which to get on par with the lush surroundings.

Breakfast is served in the on site dining room, aptly named Par 4, including the Traditional Irish with lashings of mouth-watering home-made brown bread baked by John Sheehan who is a renowned chef. For dinner at the 19th John does a delicious seafood chowder, or maybe he might also have lovely fresh crab claws. It is a compact menu but his smoked fish pie is very popular, as is the scrumptious 10 oz Irish sirloing steak with saute onions, mushrooms and fries with a cracked peppercorn sauce or garlic butter. Now that will revive you.

The antique style Wine Bar is a lovely feature of the guesthouse and houses cushy leather chairs and armchairs to sink into while nursing your aperitif or digestif. Don't forget to check out the quirky assortment of golfing images and paraphernalia here!

Bedrooms are classic, pretty and decorated in restful colours. All have en suite with shower, satellite TV, direct dial telephone services, tea and coffee making facilities and hairdryer. If you haven't grown "teed" off with golf,

having played it all day, you can flop down onto your welcoming bed and tune in to the Golfing channel.

It seems Freda and John have thought of everything – the inclusion of a drying room in the house means that guests who brave the typical Irish four-seasons-in-one-day to avail of the many local outdoor activities have somewhere to shake off the raindrops and hang out their sodden attire.

Staying in the 19th Green will facilitate an excellent golfing holiday and the staff are more than happy to assist by organising club hire, golf cart hire, lessons and transport for their guests as well as informing them of tee times.

Trust me all these details are responsible for allowing me to have a truly great stay here!

"Funny how man blames fate for all accidents, yet claims full responsibility for a hole in one".

You will sure have scored a hole in one in finding the 19th Green.

Owner	Freda and John Sheehan
Address	19th Green Guesthouse, Lackabane, Fossa, Killarney, Co. Kerry.
Tel	+353 (0) 64 32868
No of Rooms	13
Price	
Double/Twin	€70 - €120
Single	€55 - €80
Family	Yes - Enquire
Dinner	No. Restaurant nearby in Killarney Golf Club
Open	Feb 1st – Oct 31st
Credit cards	Yes
Directions	Take N72 heading for Killorglin, 500m past golf club on right.
Email	19thgreen@eircom.net
Web	www.lucindaosullivan.com/19thgreen

🐴 ▨ ▢ P NET

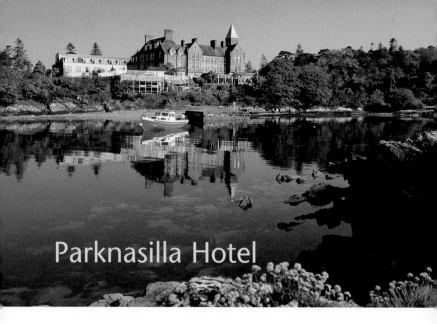

Parknasilla Hotel

PARKNASILLA

I love Parknasilla so much I always insist we set off a day early, and break the journey, because I like to make my grand entrance in top form and not lose out on a minute of my stay there. We stay reasonably close and drive then through Cahirciveen, around the Ring of Kerry, revelling in just being alive and able to enjoy that spectacular scenery. One year we stayed in Glenbeigh and, brave souls that we were, drove from Caragh Lake out over the McGillicuddy Reeks, past mountainy goats on hair-raising roads, emerging down close to Sneem. A great experience but not for the faint hearted!

PARKNASILLA HOTEL

The Parknasilla Hotel is a legend in itself. A truly original Resort Hotel, set on 500 acres of lush tropical parkland overlooking Kenmare Bay, with miles of walks between ferns and fuchsias, rock and rhododendrons, a private Golf Course, Archery and Clay Pigeon Shooting, boat rides around the bay…. A bastion of neo Gothic Victorian splendour, this was originally a Railway Hotel, owned in recent years by the Great Southern Hotel Group. In the old days guests were conveyed from Kenmare Station by pony and trap. I met one old lady, holding court by the fire in the hall after dinner one evening, who had

been coming from England for over 50 years religiously, for 19 nights with 19 different ballgowns! Everybody has been here from Princess Grace to General De Gaulle to George Bernard Shaw who described it as "part of our dream world".

The Estate was sold last year and is now part of the New Great Southern Hotel Group who have ploughed millions into Parknasilla, updating it with considerable style and panache with lavish gorgeous fabrics and furnishings. There is a fabulous Spa with 13 treatment rooms having every comfort and treatment, including a Thermal Spa incorporating a mix of wet and dry, warm, hot and cold cabins and equipment all created individually for Parknasilla.

Up the sweeping staircase, past the stained glass window takes you to the beautifully luxurious bedrooms and suites – the Princess Grace Suite being the absolute ultimate with its large private balcony overlooking the ocean.

The Pygmalion Restaurant is a magnificent room with the most splendid Victorian features and ceilings. The food is cracking using the very best of local seafood, Kerry lamb, and other delicious seasonal produce and the buzz and atmosphere in this great room is terrific before people repair to the bar for real craic and fun.

This is a place where memories are made. This was certainly true for me and my family and we treasure the summers we spent, and still spend, at Parknasilla.

It is a world of its own.

Owner	New Great Southern Hotel Group
Address	Parknasilla, Sneem, Co. Kerry.
Tel	+353 (0)64 45122
No of Rooms	92
Price	
Suites	€1500
Double/Twin	€300
Single	€250
Family	€450
Dinner	Yes – Restaurant
Open	From May 2008
Credit Cards	Yes
Directions	N70 from Kenmare – Estate entrance after Tahilla just before Sneem Village.
Email	info@parknasillahotel.ie
Web	www.lucindaosullivan.com/parknasillahotel

P NET (H) 12H Spa

The Ross

Hip Boutique Hotels have opened around the world in the past few years and this has not escaped the attention of the owners of the luxurious 5 star Killarney Park Hotel, Padraig and Janet Treacy, who have recently given Killarney a really funky hip Boutique Hotel, The Ross. We found it coming up from Dingle – four of us travelling in two cars – it was late evening – and the boys were getting impatient and hungry! I have always been of the persuasion that there is something better around the corner! We had stopped at a colourful looking guesthouse on the road out of Dingle and friend Margaret went in for a look. Quite unbelievably, she was taken out the back to the "stables" where the door was flung open to reveal a chap sitting up in the bed. "Do you come with the room?" She said. "I'll be getting out now". He replied, as cool as a breeze.

On we drove into Killarney following a sign for the Bear's Head – but it did reconditioned engines or something like that! The boys were getting fraughter and the mobile phones were going between cars. Back down into the Town centre, I circled in desperation, then I spotted The Ross. "Now that looks hot," I said, jamming on the brakes. It was and it is.

An old hotel had been taken over and given not just the kiss of life by Padraig and Janet Treacy – but they turned into a fab luxurious and cool spot - one of the hottest places in town. The Ross will appeal to the lifestyle traveller, best of everything incorporated in the bedrooms, kingsize beds, chic fabrics, Italian marble bathrooms, music system, plasma TV with full DVD library availably and toiletries by Laura Tonatto. If you are pushing the boat out on either of the two top suites, you will have wonderful views over the town of Killarney and National Park from the large bay windows.

Brendan and Mike were placated once they were ensconced in the Hotel's Lane Bar for a drink before dinner. It is a fab place, colourful and hopping. It also does casual food but we opted for dinner in the split level Cellar One Restaurant - a riot of luxurious cerise and green décor – really cool – with a stainless steel curving staircase and vaulted ceiling. Amidst the wild décor, food was cracking, using the very best of locally sourced produce. We indulged ourselves with oysters with crème fraiche and lumpfish roe; carpaccio of Kerry beef; chilled prawn salad with lemon mayonnaise and chilli jam followed by superb sole on the bone and succulent roast peppered breast of Skeghanore Duck with braised red cabbage.

I knew I'd find a winner if I kept going and I did – it's The Ross – fantastic – and by the way you can use all the leisure and spa facilities of its sister hotel, the famous 5 Star Killarney Park.

This place is hot.

Owner	Padraig and Janet Treacy
Address	Town Centre, Killarney, Co. Kerry.
Tel	+353 (0)64 31855
No of Rooms	30
Price	
Suites	€220 - €275
Double/Twin	€170 - €245
	Child Sharing €40/€45
Dinner	Yes – Restaurant and Bar Food
Open	All Year – Save 24th – 26th December.
Credit Cards	Yes
Directions	Follow signs for Kenmare Place and the cinema. The Ross is located there.
Email	info@theross.ie
Web	www.lucindaosullivan.com/theross

Sneem Hotel

S neem or, as Gaeilge, An tSnaidhm, means a "knot" and the very pretty village of Sneem, Co. Kerry, is known as The Knot in the Ring of Kerry. The village comprises two squares, north and south, joined in the middle by a real picture postcard bridge under which runs the river Sneem. A stunning location, Sneem has a number of little pubs, cafes and shops with its houses painted in vibrant colours. Bathed by the waters of the Gulf Stream, you will see the most amazing sub-tropical plants just growing all over the place.

Newly opened just last year, in a quite perfect cove, appropriately called Golden's Cove, is the new 4 Star Sneem Hotel. Just imagine waking up in the mornings and looking out at God's Own Country and Ireland's highest mountain, Carrauntouhil, as well as the calming waters of Kenmare Bay and out to the truly spectacular Ring of Kerry. No wonder it is known as The Kingdom of Kerry.

The Sneem Hotel has a variety of luxury accommodation in its 69

guestrooms and suites. The best rooms have sea views and the premium rooms have sizeable balconies which are just fantastic. So the choice is yours, depending on your pocket, but, whichever you choose, you will have a lovely view of mountains or sea because you are just in the middle of all round beauty. All of the rooms are beautifully furnished, ultra modern, in neutral tones accented with flashes of primary colours. Each room is climate-controlled and has Broadband access, multi-channel flatscreen TVs, safes and the other normal accoutrements of a decent hotel. There is also 24 hour Room Service in case you can't be torn away from the view and need sustenance!

As well as Broadband access in your room, there is WIFI in the lobby and a computer for guests if you haven't tagged along the laptop. There is also a sauna, hot tub and gym.

There is a lovely bar for relaxing after the day's driving, sightseeing, or playing of golf and you can also have something casual to eat there. They do food throughout the day, and on warm days you can eat out on the terrace. The restaurant specialises in local produce – spectacularly fresh fish and shellfish – pan-fried turbot with a spinach, black olive and lemon risotto, or black sole on the bone with dill and caper butter or maybe roast rack of Sneem lamb with braised lentils, bacon and rosemary sauce … and the prices are really good.

There is a lovely bright friendly atmosphere at Sneem Hotel and it is just the place to really switch off and enjoy the best of the Kingdom.

Don't go home without the local Sneem delicacy, a type of black pudding, cooked in slabs, fine as silk, as good as foie gras … it will put hair on your chest!!

Owner	Louis Moriarty
Address	Golden's Cove, Sneem, Co. Kerry.
Tel	+ 353 (0)64 75100
No of Rooms	69
Price	
Suites	€190 - €310
Double/Twin	€130 - €250
Single	€105 - €165
Family	Room Rate + Sharing Under 7's free. 7-12's 50%
Dinner	Yes – Restaurant and Bar Food
Open	All Year
Credit Cards	Yes
Directions	Located in Sneem Village on Ring of Kerry, on the N70, just 30 mins from Kenmare, 60 mins from Killarney.
Email	information@sneemhotel.com
Web	www.lucindaosullivan.com/sneemhotel

[icons: rocking horse | | □ | P | 🍷 | ♿ | NET | H]

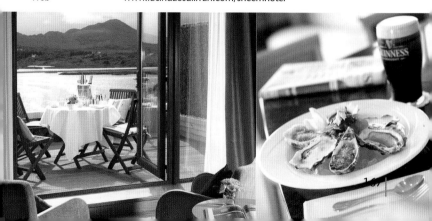

Virginia's Guesthouse

We took off, happy as sandboys, heading for Kerry with the roof rolled back on the convertible. It was a last minute trip, and as I drove along, I felt we were back in our carefree, heady, pre-nuptial days. Even His Nibs complaining that his bald patch was getting sunburned couldn't dampen our lively spirits. We sped through our favourite stretch of road, the dramatic drive between Glengarriff and Kenmare, arriving about 5 p.m. Fascinated by the interesting craft and antique shops, we strolled around for some time until, suddenly, we remembered that we had nowhere to lay our heads for the night.

It was then we discovered Virginia's Guesthouse, a rare little gem located above the popular Mulcahy's Restaurant. We were greeted like old friends by hosts Neil and Noreen Harrington. Neil was born in this house. His father was the local shoemaker and his customers had included Fred Astaire and Prince Ranier. The attraction of Virginia's is its simplicity, unpretentiousness and friendly laid back atmosphere, but with all the facilities you could require – power showers, safes, and 35 channel cable TV.

We had an excellent dinner downstairs in Mulcahy's and, what completed the perfect day, was only having to go back upstairs to bed. The greatest test of any Guesthouse or Hotel is when you decide to stay an extra night, which we did. There was never any doubt, but the breakfast was the real clincher.

168

Noreen does beautiful poached seasonal fruits in a saffron cardamom and star anise syrup served with chilled organic yoghurt. Another unusual twist in her repertoire is sliced sweet pear on toasted homemade white yeast bread smothered with melted Cashel Blue cheese, served with crispy streaky bacon and homemade apple and tomato chutney. There is also, of course, the Full Irish, scrambled eggs and Kenmare smoked salmon, porridge with whiskey cream, not to mention pancakes and maple syrup. This young couple is rapidly making a name for themselves.

As they say in Kerry " We were well sorted ".

Owners	Neil & Noreen Harrington
Address	36 Henry Street, Kenmare, Co. Kerry.
Tel:	+353 (0)64 41021
No of Rooms	8
Price	
Double/twin	€90 - €120
Single	€75-85
Family	€45-60pps
Dinner	Mulcahy's Restaurant on ground floor
Open	All Year save 21st – 25th December inc
Credit Cards	Yes
Directions	2nd building on right as you drive down Henry Street, in town centre.
Email	virginias@eircom.net
Web	www.lucindaosullivan.com/virginiasguesthouse

County Kildare

Kildare county, with its lush pastureland, is a great centre for the thoroughbred horse industry. The rolling acres of the Curragh plains are a natural training ground for racehorses and the Irish Derby, one of the biggest prize races in Europe, is held on the Curragh Racecourse each year. The National Stud, famous for the breeding of outstanding racehorses is situated in Kildare Town, on the edge of the Curragh.

The county boasts numerous fine country houses and estates, remnants of the years when British gentry had their country houses in Ireland and, believe me, they knew how to select the best places. The magnificent Castletown House in Celbridge is a prime example, designed in 1722 by Alessandro Galilei. In the 1960's the Irish Georgian Society purchased the

house and it was later transferred to the State in 1994, and guided tours are now available.

The Grand Canal, which runs through the county, boasts many pleasant walks along its towpaths, and Robertstown, where it divides into two branches, boasts the Grand Canal Hotel (no accommodation!!) which has a restaurant and an exhibition about the canal and the Hotel. Barge tours for groups can be arranged here.

Nearer Dublin, Maynooth is reachable by bus from the city. For many years the Roman Catholic Seminary at Maynooth was basically the headquarters of the Catholic Church in Ireland. While still a seminary, it is also part of the National University of Ireland.

At one end of Maynooth main street stands Carton House – a Georgian gem designed by Richard Cassels – which has now opened its doors as a Hotel and restaurant.

"I just played a horse yesterday so slow the jockety kept a diary of the trip"

(Henny Youngman)

Carton House

We have been fair deluged with Country Estate Hotels with de rigueur Spa and Golf Course. Where else can the Celtic Tigresses and Yummy Mummies show off their Convertibles, 4 x 4s, Bentley's, Botoxed, toned and tanned bodies, and tarted up little terrors. Some are good, some are terrible, and some are terrific – which leads me sleekly to the magnificent Carton House at Maynooth which hit the ground running in 2006. This place is fabulous – you can crash out in the Spa or slip off and shop 'til you drop in Grafton Street whilst he plays golf on one of the two superb courses, designed by Mark O'Meara and Colin Montgomery.

Carton and Castletown are the two Great Houses familiar to Dubliners, and oft the destination of the Sunday Drive as kids. They were inextricably linked being homes of the famous historic Fitzgerald family and the setting for the stunning BBC television series The Aristocrats. Carton House, built in 1739, is absolutely magnificent and you will be agog at the glorious reception rooms and amazing stucco work done by the Lafranchini brothers. You can almost hear the rustle of silk ballgowns and soft slippers of bewigged servants …

The sleek stylish ultra modern extension incorporates the old stonework and, in many areas, captures the wonderful serene feel of the formal gardens and great estate bringing it forward into a new era. Bedrooms are contemporary and smart with extra space allotted to the bathrooms, with both walk in shower and bath, and to the dressing area. The new foyer has a fantastic geometrically designed glass ceiling, ultra modern paintings and sofas, and to sit here at night under twinkling lights is just a delight.

In the Linden Tree Restaurant the food is seriously good and prices are very moderate for this excellence. I had a superb "Summer Salad of Fresh Lobster" followed by fab Seared Scallops circled around a tian of delicious potatoes layered with crispy pancetta. Save space for their Eton Mess. Buffet

style breakfast is brilliant with an extensive selection of pastries, cheeses, charcuterie, artisan breads, fruits, the Full Irish fixings – and lashings of it. You can also dine in the nearby Club House or have casual food in the Kitchen Bar.

Go to Carton – it's smart – it's hip.

Owner	James Tynan (General Manager)
Address	Maynooth, Co. Kildare.
Tel	+353 (0)1 505 2000
No of Rooms	165
Price	
Suite	From €330
Double/twin	From €190
Single	From €155
Dinner	Yes – Restaurant and Barfood
Open	All Year
Credit Cards	Yes
Directions	From Dublin, take N4 westbound. Exit at "Leixlip West" and follow signs to Carton House.
Email	reservations@cartonhouse.com
Web	www.lucindaosullivan.com/cartonhouse

175

Westgrove Hotel

What can I say? Beyond luxury. Swish. Super modern with a twist of antique style. The Westgrove Hotel is situated in Clane, a picturesque little town half way between Naas and Maynooth, near the rushing River Liffey, just a half hour's drive from Dublin city centre and 5km from Sallins railway station.

The large Executive Apartments will suit the long-stay guests. Suite s are individually decorated and are equipped with flat screen TVs. The Standard rooms are generously sized with a focus on modernity and simplicity in terms of decoration. Complimentary broadband services are available in all rooms.

There are two restaurants to choose from and they are both proving very popular. Kirby's boasts a divine dinner menu and an excellent A La Carte. Try the panfried brill with mussels and creamed baby leeks. The Exchange offers contemporary casual dining from an extensive and good value menu doing popular food such as seafood linguine, braised lamb shank, baby back ribs and so on. They also do traditional afternoon tea in Kirby's featuring sweets

and savouries – just one more way to spoil yourself! For the night-owls there are three bars. The Cigar Bar is perfect for that pre-dinner drink, The Oak for an animated contemporary night out and The Local for a more sedate and traditional after-dinner tipple. And as if all that wasn't enough, barfood is also available throughout the day and while you're there you must indulge in something from the full cocktail menu.

The hotel has several meeting rooms, the O'Connell and Alexandra suites provide a larger space, filled with natural light and ideal for both conferences and business lunches, while the Westport and Castlebar suites are perfect for smaller gatherings. The Boardroom and the Director's suites are also available for board meetings.

You can pamper yourself in elegant surrounds in the hotel's gorgeous spa. You can even book your own "private Spa" which is brilliant for a getaway with the girls. A minimum of 6 people are required for the mid-week spa package and a minimum of 8 for the weekends. You can choose your treatments and also have lunch from their Spa Cuisine Menu from Kirby's. For those of you who might feel more energetic, there is a swimming pool on site as part of the hotel's leisure club.

Getting married or know someone who's about to take the plunge? Look no further than the Westgrove's many sophisticated wedding packages which can be adapted to suit the couple in question.

Whether or not you can resist its many temptations, this hotel really has it all just as variety is the spice of life, it offers something for every type of guest.

Owner	Westgrove Hotel
Address	Clane, Co. Kildare
Tel	+ 353 (0) 45 989900
No of Rooms	99
Price:	
Suites	From €220
Double/Twin	From €160
Single	From €89
Family	From €180
Dinner	Yes
Open	All Year save Christmas Day
Credit cards	Yes except Diners
Directions	In Clane village
Email	info@westgrovehotel.com
Web	www.lucindaosullivan.com/westgrovehotel

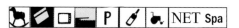

County Kilkenny

Kilkenny is a county of rich farmland, quaint villages and towns, well endowed with mediaeval ruins and friendly people who are not reluctant to talk about hurling, the very special Gaelic game at which Kilkenny people excel. Kilkenny City, on the River Nore, is a bustling busy place defined by the magnificent Kilkenny Castle, former home to the Butlers of Ormonde. The City has many hotels, guesthouses and bars and is very popular now for weekend breaks and for stag and hen parties. The surrounding county is not short on items of historical interest like Kilcree Round Tower, Jerpoint Abbey, and the ruin of Kells Priory. Go to Graiguenamanagh on the River Barrow, the home of Duiske Abbey, founded in 1204, and although much altered over the years the 13th Century interior has been lovingly preserved. Bennettsbridge, an area now home to many craft industries such as the Nicholas Mosse Pottery, is worth a visit, as is Thomastown, just north of Jerpoint, formerly a walled town of some importance, and close to the magnificent Championship Golf Course of Mount Juliet. Relax with a glass of Guinness, or whatever, in the tree lined square, or by the river, of interesting Inistiogue, which is overlooked by the ruin of the Woodstock Estate, burned down in 1922. Kilkenny is a fabulous county.

"I have made an important discovery…that alcohol, taken in sufficient quantities, produces all the effects of intoxication".
(OSCAR WILDE)

Hotel Kilkenny

Everything has changed for the better in the past few years on the accommodation and restaurant scene in Ireland, and Liam Griffin and his team at Griffin Group Hotels have forged the way, first with the Ferrycarrig Hotel in Wexford, then creating the superbly smart, seriously special, Monart Luxury Destination Spa in Enniscorthy. Those projects completed, they then turned their attentions to Hotel Kilkenny to stunning effect.

Hotel Kilkenny has, for a number of years, been one of the Marble City's most popular hotels but it has now been transformed into one of the most luxurious and hip hotels in Kilkenny. With a Kilkenny background, I have a serious love for this City and everything black and amber, so on hearing of the makeover at Hotel Kilkenny, I was off like a shot for a couple of nights break.

Uber hip and chic is the theme from the big cool airy reception lobby to the 138 bedrooms all of which are absolutely beautiful. 35 are deluxe bedrooms with pretty Italianate drawing room chairs, which would sit happily in any Interior Magazine. All of the rooms are fitted with Plasma TVs, Broadband Internet Access, all the de rigueur requirements of today's smart destinations. There are large family rooms for holiday breaks and there are 6 dedicated disabled rooms with customised showers and bathrooms.

Did anybody ever tell you before that you would feel Pure in a bar? Great name isn't it – a guilt free bar! Apart from the cool name, the Pure Bar is really hip with leather seating, sleek cocktail bar, modern music, soft lighting, black shaded chandeliers and a deadly cocktail list.

Tastes of Tuscany have been brought to the in-house restaurant Taste Italy with dishes from San Gimignano, Monterifionni, and other Tuscan villages. The menu changes regularly but think of maybe kicking off with Spaghettini Vongole – delicious little threads of pasta with clams, tomato and garlic, or Parma ham with Balsamic marinated figs, followed by gratinated seafood cannelloni or a rustic rabbit and mushroom ragout with tagllatelle and garlic spinach. When I was there I had a stunning squid tube stuffed with tiger prawns on a bed of Parmesan and garden pea risotto whilst Brendan had a succulent fillet steak with a basil crust, Barolo jus and spinach gnocchi. Absolutely delicious.

We both had a swim in the 20 metre pool in the Active Club but sneaked past the gym back to the diningroom for a hearty breakfast – more in my line!! I did, however, also avail of the beauty treatments and hair salon available in the Lilac Lodge Spa.

So what are you waiting for – Kilkenny for a break – and a touch of Italy – it couldn't get any better. Enquire too about their Special Breaks Packages.

Owner	Griffin Group
Address	College Road, Kilkenny.
Tel	+353 (0)56 776-2000
No of Rooms	138
Price	
De Luxe Rooms	€190 - €250
Double/Twin	€140 - €200
Single	€170 - €230
Family	Enquire from Hotel
Dinner	Yes – Restaurant and Bar Food
Open	All Year
Credit Cards	Yes
Directions	Located on ring road allowing easy access from N9, N10, N76.
Email	experience@hotelkilkenny.ie
Web	www.lucindaosullivan.com/hotelkilkenny

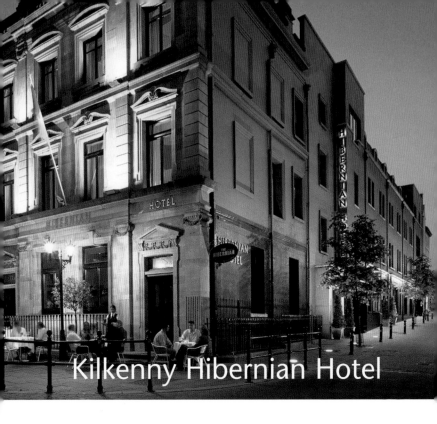

Kilkenny Hibernian Hotel

Kilkenny as a City and as a County rocks as far as I am concerned but I guess I am kind of biased as I have a Kilkenny background. Known as the Marble City, Kilkenny is filled with historic places to visit, restaurants and bars, lush hinterland, and to boot a magnificent Castle which glows goldenly over the City and its warm hearted people. I grew up on stories of the great and the good – Kilkenny Hunt, the shooting parties, the merchant princes of the City who lived in fine houses in the shadow of the Castle or on fine country estates….

One solid historic house which would have been a bastion of the "upstairs downstairs "era was No. 1 Ormonde Street, built in the mid 19th century, and lived in by the Hackett family – friends and supporters of the Liberator – Charles Stuart Parnell. In later years the building was bought by the Hibernian Bank. In 2000 it opened as a snazzy Boutique Hotel and immediately made its mark on all fronts – great rooms – great style – great restaurant – the destination of the discerning – and all under one roof. In 2007 the Hibernian has gone from strength to strength. It has been voted one of the Best Loved Hotels in the World. The bedrooms are lavishly and richly furnished and, if you really want to push out the boat, you can treat yourself to a Junior Suite or even look out over Kilkenny from the Penthouse Suite.

There are lots of restaurants in Kilkenny but Jacob's Cottage restaurant in the Hibernian is considered by many to be one of the best around. The

cuisine is modern Irish and they specialize in seafood – so you can expect maybe to feast on delicious Duncannon chowder or mussels or prawns, followed maybe by whole roast sea-bass; grilled sole on the bone and lots more. However, whilst they specialize in fish there is also plenty for the man who likes his meat – delicious fillets of Angus beef, and plenty of game in season – I love their Marinated Haunch of Wild Venison which they serve with a root vegetable mash and a redcurrant and rosemary jus. Save space for their Warm Sticky Date Pudding.... They also do bar food in their Hibernian Bar to the front of the hotel and, if you are a night owl, their fab subterranean Morrisson's Bar, which is on two floors with lots of snugs and big cozy leather sofas, will welcome you into the night with entertainment and live music. -- don't miss out.

Owners	John McNena General Manager
Address	1 Ormonde Street, Kilkenny.
Tel	+353 (0)56 777 1888
No of Rooms	46
Price	
Suite	€190 - €300
Double/twin	€130 - €240 (BBD packages also available)
Dinner	Restaurant and bar food
Open	All Year (Closed Christmas Eve to St. Stephen's Day)
Credit Cards	Yes
Directions	Follow signs for City Centre. Hotel is located right in the Centre.

Email
info@kilkennyhibernianhotel.com
Web
www.lucindaosullivan.com/
kilkennyhibernianhotel

Langton House Hotel

Kilkenny City is a hot hot destination for young and old alike. It has a zing and zest in mediaeval surroundings that are second to none. I had visiting journalists over from the U.S. during the summer and they were gobsmacked when they visited the new Langton House Hotel in Kilkenny. Their eyes were out on stalks when they saw the restaurant and the bars – "more stunning than anything in New York", they gushed.

The Langton name has always been synonymous with good food in Kilkenny. Ask anyone and they will tell you the same. In fact the "Edward Langton's Bar " won the Black & White overall Pub of the Year Award a record four times. I am mentioning this merely to tell you that Langton's have always been conscious of providing excellent service and quality but, if I said the Langton Group had moved up a notch or two, that would be putting it mildly, for they have moved up into a new stratosphere with their fabulous Langton House Hotel, their visually stunning Langton Room restaurant, and their uber cool new Carrigan's Bar, which has been designed by fashionable London based Irish designer David Collins.

Situated right at the heart of the City near the Castle, Langton's has 30 fab new oversized rooms and suites to accommodate all needs be it the Penthouse Suites, Executive Suites, Club Family Suites, Superior Garden Suites, Double/Twin Rooms … each and every one stylishly equipped for today's discerning clientele. There is cable television, mini-bars, private safes, surround sound stereo entertainment systems, 24 hour room service and wireless internet access (request at check-in).

Believe me you are never going to be bored at Langton's for in the hotel

they have the 67 Bar where throughout the week they have live entertainment through traditional music to bands and dj's. Never a dull moment. There is also Harry's Bar, the Middle Bar and the beautiful Ballroom Bar. You will never be hungry for there is food everywhere but the restaurant, now that is a stunning room and good value. Think of food like succulent melt in the mouth braised shank of lamb served on a mash with its own juices, or maybe Dublin Bay Prawns in garlic butter, or with white wine sauce, which comes with a Caesar salad or even panfried Barbary duck with Grand Marnier..... Yum. You can't do your tour of Kilkenny, never mind, your tour of Langton's emporia without visiting The Marble City Bar – its ab fab.

Owner	Eamon Langton
Address	69 John Street, Kilkenny.
Tel	+353 (0)56 776 5133
No of Rooms	30
Price	
Suites	€240
Double/twin	€200
Family	€100pps
Dinner	Yes – Restaurant and Barfood
Open	All Year save Christmas Day
Credit Cards	Yes
Directions	On N9 from Carlow at Dublin Road roundabout take 2nd exit onto Dublin Road, Turn left onto John Street. Turn left at 2nd pedestrian crossing into private carpark.
Email	reservations@langtons.ie
Web	www.lucindaosullivan.com/langtonshousehotel

Mount Juliet Conrad

Mount Juliet is a magnificent Georgian Mansion built by the Earl of Carrick, overlooking the River Nore, on 1500 acres of unspoiled woodland and meandering waters in Thomastown, South Kilkenny. Latterly, Mount Juliet was owned by the late Major Victor McCalmont and his wife Bunty, well known figures on the Irish social scene. Hunting, shootin', fishin', House Parties, were the thing along, with the Dublin Horse Show, Hacking Jackets from Callaghan's of Dame Street, antiques from Louis Wine. The lives of staff in those days revolved around the big Estate and very often went from generation to generation of minding "the Major" and previous incumbents.

Mount Juliet was then developed with great foresight and care by businessman, Tim Mahony, for even though you drive through the Jack Nicklaus designed 18 hole Championship Golf Course, past the self catering Rose Garden Lodges and Hunters Yard complex, the house is far enough away to retain the illusion of being on a private estate and still feels more

"Country House" than Hotel. Now part of the Conrad Hotel Group, you can fill your days with golf or country pursuits, chill out and be pampered at The Spa, go horseriding…do the Kilkenny Craft Trail. There are two Restaurants, the Lady Helen Diningroom, a gastronomic experience, with dishes like Beef Fillet Rossini Foie Gras and A Study of Game Birds which is Roast Wild Mallard, Confit Leg, Guinea Fowl Supreme with Pomme de Terre puree with black olives and Sauce Albufera. Albert Roux the famous French Chef comes to Mount Juliet to shoot and he cooked the Queen Mother's favourite soufflé for us on one special occasion. The other dining options are the buzzy Kendals Restaurant in the Hunters Yard and casual food in the President's Bar. The rooms in the main house are gloriously beautiful and there are fab modern rooms in the Hunters Yard. Breakfast in the Lady Helen Room overlooking the River, rolling acres and romping young cattle, is simply bliss. "Would you like to try Tiger's Breakfast"? Asked the Restaurant Manager. I was still romancing about the classy Colonial days, Indiaaah and all that, forgetting that more recent blow in, Tiger Woods, until I was enlightened. Anyway, Tiger's breakfast is stacked French toast and smoked salmon topped with poached eggs. You might fancy "The Major's breakfast" which delves into the nether regions of liver and kidneys.

Mount Juliet is an enchanting place, I could stand outside and look at the house all day! The lushness of the grounds and winding paths are a constant reminder of another life – people crave peace and space they will find it all here. Check for special rates on the website.

Owners	William Kirby (General Manager)
Address	Thomastown, Co. Kilkenny.
Tel	+353 (0)56 777-3000
No. Of Rooms	58
Price	
Double/Twin	From €199
Single	From €182
Family	From €390 – Rose Garden Lodge
Dinner	Yes – 2 Restaurants + Barfood
Open	All Year
Credit Cards	All Major Cards
Directions	Follow signs from Thomastown
Email	mountjulietinfo@conradhotels.com
Web	www.lucindaosullivan.com/mountjuliet

County Limerick

Limerick City, located at the lowest fording point of the River Shannon, is sports mad whether it be Gaelic football, hurling, horse racing, soccer or particularly rugby football which boasts that well known Limerick invention the "Garryowen":- the high kick forward which allows your team to charge after it and put the fear of God into the poor player who happens to be trying to catch it. It is also famous as the location of Frank McCourt's book *Angela's Ashes*, although some of its inhabitants find it hard to accept. From the time the

Vikings sailed up the Shannon and settled there, the place has had a troubled history but it is probably best remembered for the Williamite Siege in the late 1600's resisted by the Irish, led by Patrick Sarsfield. Probably the best-known tourist attraction in the city is the Hunt Museum, which has a collection to rival Dublin's National Gallery. In the late 1930's and early 1940's, Foynes was the terminus for the transatlantic Flying Boat service, and is home now to a Flying Boat Museum. Kilmallock and its nearby Museum is only four miles from Bruree, whose claim to fame is that it was the childhood home of Eamonn de Valera, former prominent 1916 figure, Taoiseach, and President of Ireland. The gem in the county's crown is the beautiful picturesque village of Adare which has many up market fine antique shops, friendly pubs, excellent Restaurants and art shops but also has a number of beautifully maintained thatched cottages and is regarded as the prettiest village in Ireland.

"The one duty we have to history is to re-write it"
(OSCAR WILDE)

AbsoluteHotel.com

Absolute – it's a brilliant name isn't it? It has terrific connotations. A sublimal message of enjoyment but also of excellence. The word has been used to name a vodka – and who can forget the Ab Fab duo of Patsy and Edina. AbsoluteHotel.com, however, means the ultimate in chic and hip boutique hotels for it has literally everything one could possibly want and at very reasonable prices.

AboluteHotel.com is a new brand in Irish Hotels owned and founded by South African Michael de Haast and his wife Laura. Michael's family were in the hotel business so you could say he was born into it, before he moved out on his own managing a chain of boutique hotels in South Africa coming then to Europe with the Rezidor SAS Hotel Group - ending up in Galway and then Limerick. Michael has an innate sense of what people want in a Hotel nowadays. We all travel so much both for fun and for business that we want and expect all the facilities we have at home with the fun of being away in a

cool spot – and that is what AbsoluteHotel.com is – Absolutely on the nose for today's discerning guest.

Being located in the centre of Limerick City, a vision of glass and contemporary design, close to the Hunt Museum, means that you can walk to the best shopping areas, and then you can come back and pamper yourself in one of the six treatment rooms in – you've got it – the Absolute Spa with its thermal suite, Vitality Pool and relaxation lounge – Patsy and Edina would love it!

There are three levels of bedrooms – Comfy, Cosy, and Chic – the difference in the first two choices being basically the size for they both have absolutely everything – 32" Plasma TVs with Satellite Channels, Spacious Rain Dance Power Showers, TV Internet with wireless keyboard, Airconditioning, Laptop size in-room safes, Writing Desk, Air Conditioniong et al. Then there are Chic Suites and Business Suites with all of before only more and more…

We had done the Hunt Museum from top to bottom and were more than ready for a stiff Cosmopolitan in the Hotel's Riverbank Bar and Grill, with its stunning location and terraces overlooking the Abbey river. The food is excellent – modern and contemporary using the best of local and seasonal produce.

I love the whole modern openess of AbsoluteHotel Limerick – the colours, the vibrancy, textures and artwork. It was just what this famous City needed – an Absolutely Fabulously brilliant hotel.

Owner	Michael de Haast
Address	Sir Harry's Mall, Limerick.
Tel	+353 (0)61 463600
No of Rooms	
Price	
Suites	€209 - (€189 Room Only)
Double/Twin	€115 - €125 (From €105 Room Only)
Single Occ	€105 - (€95 Room Only)
Dinner	Yes - Restaurant and Cafe
Open	All Year
Credit Cards	Yes
Directions	Just off N7 on Dublin side of Limerick City
Email	info@absolutehotel.com
Web	www.lucindaosullivan.com/absolutehotel

Dunraven Arms Hotel

Every November I look forward to an Invitation from my Horsey friends to The Hunt Ball in Adare. Whilst a night of Tallyho with The Equine Fraternity of Limerick has its own special appeal, the real appeal for His Nibs and myself is to escape to Irelands prettiest village and stay in The Dunraven Arms, which never disappoints. This year was no exception and, even though it was a bleak mid winter day when we descended on Adare, the village looked stunning with its many thatched cottages, up market restaurants, funky art galleries, and serious Antique Shops. The Dunraven Arms with its richly painted walls and limestone trims stands out like a beacon of light and welcome in Adare Built in 1792, The Dunraven Arms is wonderfully stylish and one is always assured of a warm welcome, as well as all the advantages of modern creature comforts and modern technology. There is complimentary WIFI access throughout the hotel which is brilliant nowadays. We arrived in the early afternoon in time for a swim in the leisure centre and for me a facial. Our rooms were beautifully furnished and filled with every creature comfort, Bliss. Suites and Junior Suites are superb with ample seating areas and dressing rooms. I have had many an encounter

with shoddy service delivered by souls that possess what I call "The After the Party Look", not so in Dunraven Arms. There was an abundance of extremely well groomed, well trained and very helpful staff to cater to our every whim. On the morning after, when we trundled down to breakfast, many of us bearing the aforementioned "After The Party Look" there was a feast of freshly squeezed juices of all types, platters of fruit, bowls of cereals, steaming hot silver pots of tea, and lovely breads but, best of all, hidden under a silver dome was the most delicious baked ham which is their Sunday morning speciality. From all my friends who have stayed in the Dunraven Arms I have never heard anything but high praise and, I can guarantee you that I would walk barefoot on broken glass back to The Dunraven Arms just for a sliver of that honey baked ham. The food is wonderful, the service is excellent, and the location is stunning. Golly gosh old boy, an all round corker!

Owners	Louis Murphy
Address	Adare, Co. Limerick.
Tel	+353 (0)61 605900
No. Of Rooms	86 Bedrooms inc 30 Suites
Price	Suite/Junior Suite €335 upwards
Double/Twin	€155 - €195
Family	€230
Dinner	Yes – 2 Restaurants
Open	All Year
Credit Cards	All Major Cards
Directions	On right as you enter Adare Village from N21 from Limerick direction.
Email	reservations@dunravenhotel.com
Web	www.lucindaosullivan.com/dunravenarms

County Longford

Bordered by Ireland's greatest river, the Shannon in the west and counties Westmeath and Cavan in the east, Longford is a quiet peaceful midland county with pleasant rolling countryside. It is reckoned that Pallas, 10 miles north of Glasson, is the birthplace of Oliver Goldsmith, author of "She Stoops to Conquer" and "The Vicar of Wakefield".

Longford Town is a large busy rambling place and home of St. Mel's Cathedral – and a pleasant restful spot. For the tourist interested in archaeology a visit to Corlea Trackway Visitor Centre (April – September), nine miles south of Longford is well worthwhile.

Three miles northeast of the Town is Carriglass Manor with its gardens and Costume Museum, open to the public from May to September. Carriglass was built in 1837, by Thomas Lefroy, who was probably the model for Mr. Darcy in "Pride and Prejudice" as, at one stage, he and Jane Austen were romantically involved. The house is still owned by the Lefroy family.

"The very essence of romance is uncertainty. If ever I get married, I'll certainly try to forget the fact."
(OSCAR WILDE)

Viewmount House

Viewmount House is a beautiful Georgian house built in 1740 by the Cuffe family. Viewmount was inherited by Thomas Packenham (first Baron of Longford) when he married Elizabeth Cuffe, for the "what's yours is mine" rule was in force when a man took a wife in those days.

Viewmount has had various distinguished residents and in the late 19th Century was occupied by Harry McCann, a famed gardener who set the tone for future generations. Beryl and James Kearney have continued the gardening tradition, for the house today sits on four acres of magnificent gardens. It is an absolute oasis on the edge of Longford town where you can escape from the hurly burly of the real world and amble amongst the large old trees and orchard, the knot garden, herbaceous borders, Japanese or white garden. From the splendid red hall with open fire, you can't but marvel at the fine elegant staircase which spirals up to big beautiful bedrooms and the drawingroom, very stylishly decorated and furnished with antiques. In the past year Viewmount has seen the addition of 7 new spacious, divine, airy suites. Another happening for 2008 at Viewmount is their new Restaurant, which was about to open as this book was going to print. Beryl and James will be sourcing the very finest local and seasonal produce to titillate the palates of their guests and bring something really new to the Longford dining scene – and just imagine you won't have to drive anywhere so you can quaff to your heart's delight from James' cellar!

Breakfast is cracking, served in the fabulous vaulted diningroom and includes fruits and muesli, pancakes with maple syrup and pecan nuts, or scrambled eggs with smoked salmon … After you have fortified yourself you

can visit the exquisite Belvedere House where Robert Rochfort imprisoned his wife Mary Molesworth for 31 years, and also see Ireland's largest man made folly – The Jealous Wall. Nearby too is the beautiful Strokestown House with its famine museum. This is a perfect spot too for fisherfolk with Lough Gowna, Lough Ree and the River Shannon and it is right next door to Longford Golf Club.

Viewmount is a delightful house to visit for a break or ideal for stopping over on the way to Donegal or the far West. James and Beryl are very friendly with a great sense of humour … you will enjoy the place.

Owners	James and Beryl Kearney
Address	Dublin Road, Longford, Co. Longford.
Tel	+353 (0)43 41919
No. Of Rooms	13
Price	
Suite	€130 - €160
Double/Twin	€110 - €130
Single	€65 - €75
Family	€130 - €150
Dinner	Yes – Restaurant – Dinner €55
Open	All Year
Credit Cards	Yes
Directions	On Dublin Road out of Longford
Email	info@viewmounthouse.com
Web	www.lucindaosullivan.com/viewmount

County Louth

County Louth, the smallest county in Ireland, is on the main Dublin to Belfast road. The saying that there are "good goods in small parcels" is very true of Louth. The county is steeped in history and mythology from the famous Battle of the Boyne to the legendary Cuchulain and the "Cattle Raid of Cooley".

Drogheda is the principal town and straddles the Boyne River, site of the famous Battle where the Protestant forces of William of Orange defeated those of Catholic, King James, in 1690AD. Drogheda also had a visit from Oliver Cromwell in 1640 when his army breached the walls of the town and massacred its Royalist garrison.

County Louth, however, has more to it than mayhem and bloodshed. Drogheda itself has enough sites of interest and sources of entertainment to make a visit worthwhile. Millmount Hill is a good place to start exploring the area, as it offers an unimpeded view of the whole terrain. The Martello Tower on the hill was badly damaged during the 1922 Civil War but the mount on which it sits has always been a strategic military site. It was first recognised as such by the Anglo Normans in the 12th C and later a castle was built there which remained until 1808, when it was replaced by the present tower and military barracks. Also close by is the Millmount Museum, one of Ireland's finest town museums. Close to Drogheda is the glorious Baltray Golf Links which spawned so many of Ireland's top golfers.

North of Drogheda are the two historical sites of Mellifont and Monasterboice Monasteries. In fact the Boyne Valley is home to the most important cluster of megalithic monuments in the country. Further north along the main Dublin Belfast road is the busy border town of Dundalk with its reputation of uncompromising republicanism. Dundalk also boasts St. Patrick's Cathedral with its embellished towers, turrets, and crenallated walls, and Kelly's Tower, a four storey Franciscan Bell Tower, is the oldest building in Dundalk, dating from the 13thC.

For those who like to take things easy, there is the coast road from Drogheda through Termonfeckin and Clogherhead, back to the main road at Castlebellingham which makes a very pleasant diversion.

Also north of Dundalk, turn right around the Cooley Peninsula to the coast of Carlingford Lough as far as Omeath, just short of the border separating the Republic from Northern Ireland.

By the way, Drogheda was one of Ireland's leading manufacturers of alchoholic drinks – at one time the town had 16 Distilleries and 14 Breweries.

"Abstence is a good thing, but it should always be practised in moderation."
(ANON)

The d hotel

DROGHEDA

My father was a scratch golfer but it didn't ever end there – there was always the 19th hole. He disappeared early on a Saturday morning and didn't arrive home until the late hours which, I suppose back in those days, left a very long empty day for my mother. She took a great fancy to going on bus tours and the one that stuck most memorably in my mind was to Drogheda, where we visited St Peter's Church which had on display the skull of Saint Oliver Plunkett. I suppose when you are about 10 years old – it is going to stick in your memory.

Drogheda is one of Ireland's oldest and most historic towns. It is only 28 miles from Dublin and very handy from both Dublin and Belfast. It is a fantastically interesting area and so many people want to visit the site of the Battle of the Boyne, Newgrange, Slane Castle, all the very interesting spots.

THE D HOTEL

Drogheda has been buzzing in recent years which brings me to the addition of the fantastic new hip hotel – the **d** hotel – located on the waterfront area overlooking the famous Boyne river. As in many of our cities, the waterfront areas are now the fashionable rejuvenated areas and the **d's** new bar and restaurant on the ground floor has a cosmopolitan creative urban feel. Part of the Monogram Hotel Group which also owns the **g** hotel in Galway, the **d** adds a new dimension to sophisticated sleek accommodation not just in Drogheda but in the north east and County Louth area.

Bedrooms are just so cool. They offer different levels and price ranges from rooms with superior river views, to rooms with balconies or penthouse suites. All have the de rigueur accoutrements of sleek hotels of today such as plasma screen TV - mini bar - 24 hour in room dining facility – in room safes – Broadband internet access and so on. But to get away from the serious stuff, you will really enjoy the **d** bar followed by dinner in the contemporary restaurant, which opens onto the riverside terraces. They are serious about their food at the **d**. The food is eclectic modern european and we had luscious roasted crab claws with coriander and chilli butter and aioli as well as a lovely goats cheese and red pepper tart with rocket and toasted pine nuts. To follow I had delicious pan fried fillet of seabass with pepper, onion, tomato and white bean stew with basil oil whilst my better half had a whacking great 12 oz Louth sirloin steak with hand cut chips, onion rings and peppercorn sauce.

After succulent fresh Drogheda strawberries and a bottle of champagne, we looked out at the sun going down over the Boyne river and thought, this is what life is all about.

Rock on....

Owner	Rory Scott
	General Manager
Address	The d hotel, Scotch Hall, Drogheda, Co. Louth.
Tel	+353 (0)41 987-7700
No of Rooms	104
Price	
Suites	€500
Double/Twin	€160
Single	€140
Family	€220
Dinner	Yes - Restaurant
Open	All Year – save 23rd – 29th December.
Credit Cards	Yes
Directions	Follow signs for Drogheda town centre. Go on down Dublin Road. Turn right for St. Mary's Bridge, take a sharp right before the bridge (Gunne Auctioneers), carry on down the Marsh Road. Hotel is c. 300 meters left.
Email	thed@monogramhotels.ie
Web	

www.lucindaosullivan.com/thedhotel

County Mayo

Mayo is a beautiful county with a landscape of high cliffs, lonely mountains and fuchsia hedges and is renowned as the home of Grace O'Malley, the notorious female pirate, rustler, and rebel whose story is a book in itself. Grace's stronghold was at Clew Bay, which is close to the Pilgrim Mountain of Croagh Patrick, the highest mountain in the area. It is from this spot that Ireland's patron Saint is said to have rid the country of snakes. Off to the east, situated snugly between Lough Conn and Lough Cullin is Pontoon, an ideal base for exploring the shores of the lakes or for casting a fishing line. Further east is Knock, well known for its shrine and apparition but now also known for the International Airport at Charlestown nearby. In the south is Cong, site of the ruined 12th Century

Cong Abbey, and where the mountains of Connemara give way to the fertile farmland of east Mayo. Probably the best-known centre in Mayo is the Georgian town of Westport, a popular playground for travelers who wish to get away from the wild western countryside. During the summer the town is very popular with visitors from all over Europe and the United States who return annually to enjoy once again its many charms and also to take in its Art Festival.

"No great artist ever see things as they really are, if he did, he would cease to be an artist."
(OSCAR WILDE)

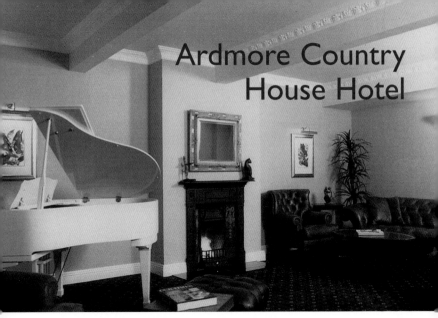

Ardmore Country House Hotel

WESTPORT

Having travelled the length and breath of Ireland, I know only too well that wherever you stay can literally make or break your visit and leave an indelible memory. Unfortunately, my first visit to Westport was destroyed by rude receptionists, a stained bed, a dirty room, and bad food and I won't even go into the after effects of that visit but it took six months to recover. Now, if we had only known of the wonderful Ardmore Country House Hotel we could have spared ourselves that disaster.

Westport is a busy tourist orientated Town, very pretty, lying on the water, within the shadows of a Great House - the famous 18th C. Westport House belonging to the Altamont family. Just 3 kms from the centre of the town is Pat and Noreen Hoban's Ardmore Country House. Stunningly located overlooking Clew Bay, Ardmore House is in the shadow of Croagh Patrick, enjoying breathtaking sunsets, and is within walking distance of the gates of Westport House. The 13 very large and spacious bedrooms are dramatically and stylishly furnished with luxurious fabrics, wonderful colours, and have all the little extras, one expects nowadays in top hotels, including a turndown service, power shower and good toiletries. Bedroom prices vary depending on whether they are to the front of the house with those spectacular sea views, or have a rural outlook to the rear. Open fires and a tinkling grand piano are what you can expect to enjoy at Ardmore after you have enjoyed a lovely meal in the Restaurant – it's a grown up place and not suitable for children under 12. Pat Hoban is a fine chef so you can expect to enjoy spanking fresh seafood from Clew Bay, including scallops, and lobster when available. Carnivores are not ignored because prime Irish beef, lamb and wild foul feature too. Organic vegetables and herbs come from local producers along with an extensive selection of

Irish farmhouse cheeses. There is an extensive wine list with affordable, as well as fine, wines from all the de rigueur Chateaux for the discerning connoisseur. Pat and Noreen are warm and friendly hosts who will only want to ensure that you enjoy your stay with them and see to your every comfort. Following Ardmore's inclusion in the first edition of my Little Black Book of Great Places to Stay, one visitor wrote in the Ardmore guest book "Lucinda O'Sullivan has it just right". Go and find out for yourself.

Owners	Pat Hoban
Address	The Quay, Westport, Co. Mayo.
Tel	+353 (0)98 25994
No. Of Rooms	13
Price	
Double/Twin	€170 - €220
Single	€100 - €160
Dinner	Yes - Restaurant
Open	March - December
Credit Cards	Yes
Directions	Leave Westport on R335 Louisburg/Coast road for 3 km, watch for sign.
Email	ardmorehotel@eircom.net
Web	www.lucindaosullivan.com/ardmorehousehotel

☐ ✎ ▭ NET P

Ashford Castle

The former country home of the Guinness family, Ashford Castle is on 350 acres of the most beautiful grounds, walks and lakes, and is incredibly romantic and evocative. It was founded in the 13th C and through the centuries had had various additions, the most signaficant being a French Chateau section in 1715. The guest book reads like a roll call of the world's most famous people – Princess Grace, Tony Blair, John Ford, John Wayne, Bob Hope, Ronald Reagan, Fred Astaire, and George V of England. Pierce Brosnan and his wife Keely chose it for their wedding. However, you do not have to have your name in lights or be mega rich to enjoy Ashford Castle for they also do wonderful special breaks at certain times of the year. There is so much to do within the estate – a 9 hole golf course, fishing, clay pigeon shooting, horseriding, health spa and beauty centre and the school of falconry is an incredible experience, not to be missed. Walks through the woods with these birds will bring you straight back to Lancelot and Guinevere. This too is "Quiet Man" country and "Squire Danagher's" house is on the estate.

The magnificent oak panelled halls lead to a central drawingroom, the social hub of the castle. On our first evening there, we dined in the Connaught Room, considered the finest room, with its fairytale inglenook fireplace and glorious ceiling holding the most exquisite chandelier. If you want a special treat, an experience you will remember, this is it. The sublime degustation menu is prepared by Michelin starred chef, Stefan Matz, and you will be waited on with grace and style as you sit romantically facing out to the lake.

There are three other dining options at Ashford, the King George V room which is also fabulous with the most luxurious food – poached foie

gras with melted figs and sauterne jellies, scallops and black pudding on creamed potatoes, and seared monkfish with Connemara lobster claw are but a few. They also have an extensive menu for kids. More casual food is served in the Drawing Room and in their latest addition "Cullens at the Cottage which does delicious bistro food very reasonably priced. The staff are fantastic and do everything possible to make your stay perfect.

Ashford is a special experience.

Owners	Niall Rochford (General Manager)
Address	Cong, Co. Mayo.
Tel	+353 (0)94 9546003
No of Rooms	83
Price	
Suite	From €747
Double/twin	From €244
Single	On Request
Family	From €540 Deluxe Queen Rooms
Breakfast	Full Irish €25 plus 15%
Dinner	3 Restaurants plus drawingroom menu
Open	All Year
Credit Cards	Yes
Directions	From Galway take Castlebar/Headford Road N84. Continue on through Headford and on to the village of Cross. In Cross turn left at the Church for Cong. As you drive into Cong the Castle is on your left.
Email	reservations@ashford.ie
Web	www.lucindaosullivan.com/ashfordcastle

 NET 9H Spa H P

JJ Gannons

BALLINROBE

Ballinrobe is a thriving town in what is known as the Lake District of County Mayo so as you can gather that means it has an abundance of fishing lakes and rivers.

JJ Gannon's was one of the best kept secrets in Ireland but word has been getting out in the past year! Incredibly, however, JJ Gannon's has been thriving at the heart of the little old town of Ballinrobe since 1837 and is now being run by third generation John Joseph Gannon and his lovely wife Niki and oh boy have they added their stamp to the place.

Jay and Niki are determined to put JJ Gannon's on the map and they are succeeding for they are getting bouquets and praise from all quarters. They have developed and extended very rapidly into a sleek, modern, eco friendly, operation providing excellent food, accommodation and hospitality for today's discerning guests.

The bedrooms are superb. They have family rooms, junior suites and deluxe rooms equipped with superking beds, the finest cotton sheets, fluffy towels, velour bathrobes, internet access, satellite TV, and private balconies where you can sit and sip champagne while soaking in the beautiful lakes and mountains of Connemara and Tourmakeady.

On the ground floor is a super contemporary cafe bar with wooden floors, stonewalls, leather bucket style chairs and cool cubes. In the bar is where you will first encounter Jay and Niki for they are always on hand to take care of their guests and customers. You won't actually ever go hungry at Gannon's because in the bar and the lovely Red Room they do terrific Gastropub style food.

The menu changes daily on sourcing local produce and their organic poultry and meat. Their suppliers are named on the menu, fresh fish is delivered daily, breads, jams and desserts are all made in their kitchen. The food is innovative and you can look forward to trying maybe Bluebell Falls goat's cheese terrine with marinated vegetables, red onion jam and cumin toast, followed by perhaps delicious big bangers and mash, Irish Stew, belly of pork. They have a well thought out wine list and a great selection of wines and champagne by the glass.

Enjoy!

Owners	Jay and Niki Gannon
Address	Main Street, Ballinrobe, Co. Mayo.
Tel:	+353 (0)94 954 1008
No of Rooms	10
Price	
Suite	€150 - €200
Double/twin	€150
Family	€200
Dinner	Yes – Gastropub
Open	All Year save Good Friday
Credit Cards	Yes
Directions	On N84. 40 mins from Galway, 25 mins from Westport or Castlebar. Knock 40 mins.
Email	info@jjgannons.com
Web	www.lucindaosullivan.com/jjgannons

Kelly's Gateway Hotel

Recently revamped, this boutique style Hotel is situated in Swinford town, which is nestled between Charlestown and Castlebar on the N5. Just 8 km from Knock airport, 10km from Foxford railway station and only a stone's throw from Mayo's many natural and cultural amenities, the Gateway is aptly named. The locality is a haven for those of you desiring a fishing or golfing break. The river Moy, famed for its salmon stocks, flows close to the town and Lakes Conn and Cullin are within a short driving distance from Swinford and are brimming with brown trout, eel and grilse. The Brabazon 9 Hole Golf Course is a mere five minutes away, on the grounds of the estate once owned by the Brabazons, a family of landed gentry who are credited with establishing Swinford town in the 1700s. For the culture vultures, Swinford offers walking tours of various heritage and Famine sites in the town and The Museum of Irish Country Life is a about a 20 mile spin, east of Castlebar.

The foyer and lounge areas of this family-run establishment are appealingly bright and airy, with modern leather furnishings and a welcoming fire. The staff are friendly, attentive and more than obliging in catering to your requests. The dining areas combine classic traditional and contemporary décor with blends of light and dark woods for the furniture and floors, exuding an open and relaxed ambience. You can choose from the Winery Bistro which offers an A La Carte menu in the evenings specialising in succulent local fish and meat, or the Old Barracks Restaurant, which is suitable for private parties of up to 35 people. Breakfast provides a generous, ample selection. Carvery lunch is available Monday to Saturday and on Sundays runs until 5 p.m. There is also a Sandwich bar, which operates to the same time table, which offers a selection of baps, wraps and

paninis. If you fancy a lively evening's musical entertainment or somewhere quiet to relax with a drink, the Flying Docs Bar & Lounge and the Jack Feeney Lounge are on site for these respective purposes.

The bedrooms continue the classic/modern feel, with the warm dark wood off-setting the paler walls. Smoking and non-smoking rooms are available on request. Rooms have flat screen TVs, 6ft beds, Broadband internet access and room service – all the necessities the modern traveller requires. For those staying for business rather than pleasure, Kelly's has a well-equipped conference room named the Brabazon suite.

Kelly's Gateway Hotel is a convenient and luxurious spring board for exploring our country's West and North West regions and would be an excellent place to stay, in the heart of the town, during the annual street festival, Siamsa Sraide Swinford, one of Ireland's oldest street festivals, held on the August Bank Holiday.

Owner:	Cathal Kelly
Address:	Main Street, Swinford, Co. Mayo
Tel:	+353 (0) 94 9252156
No of Rooms:	22
Price:	
Double/Twin:	€90 - €130
Single:	€50 - €70
Family:	€90 - €130 (Children Under 12 sharing Accom FOC, Under 16s 50% discount).
Dinner:	Yes - Restaurant and Bar Food
Open:	All year except Christmas Day.
Credit cards:	Yes
Directions:	On Main Street in Swinford town
Email:	info@gatewayswinford.com
Web:	www.lucindaosullivan.com/kellysgatewayhotel

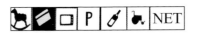

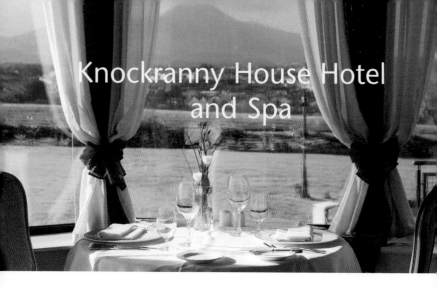

Knockranny House Hotel and Spa

"I can resist anything but temptation" quotes Knockranny House Hotel of Oscar Wilde. He also said "only dull people are brilliant at breakfast". At Knockranny House Hotel in Westport you are going to yield to every temptation put before you and you are going to be dull as hell at breakfast having had a 'wilde' night before in their gorgeous La Fougere Restaurant and Brehon Bar.

Knockranny House Hotel opened in 1997 and steadily since then they have been upgrading and adding to this very successful operation. Built in classic Victorian style, the interior is lavishly furnished, with numerous antiques and cosy log fires to create a very warm welcoming atmosphere. The bedrooms and suites are beautiful, serene and calming with lovely soft furnishings. A classy ambience. It is the sort of place that one could settle in to very comfortably and drift into a state of total relaxation. I went down with my son Ian, who likes to climb Croagh Patrick each year - in the traditional fashion - which means bare feet!

He didn't get this stamina from his ever loving Mama because I much prefer to be soaking my bare feet in Knockranny's Spa Salveo, which suitably enough in Latin means "to heal". I had an Exotic Lime and Ginger Salt Glow which sure sorted me out leaving my skin silky and smooth whilst Ian went off to play nine holes of golf at Mulranny, only thirty minutes away.

On both nights I am afraid we hit the Brehon Bar and, after a cracking Cosmo for me and a Coke for him, we had the most scrumptious dinner in the hotel's restaurant - La Fougere. It is a spectacular room with columns and is a little bit remeniscent of a 1920's ballroom in Paris. This year too they have opened a new section with an exclusive wine cellar and panoramic views of Croagh Patrick and

Clew Bay. I had the most delicious warm smoked haddock, asparagus and dill tart with mixed leaves and a balsamic reduction, followed by superb roast loin of venison on a ragout of wild mushrooms and purple potato, whilst Ian had Jerusalem artichoke and Parmesan soup followed by roasted Atlantic halibut which was on parsnip puree, saffron roasted courgettes, asparagus and red pepper cream. And the puds … warm chocolate molten with white chocolate icecream – by two of course! Like mother, like son.

Next morning before departure we hit the Connoisseur's Corner shop in the hotel and departed for Dublin with delicious breads and locally smoked salmon.

I don't think we let dear Oscar down – in fact we did him proud!!!

Owners	Adrian and Geraldine Noonan
Address	Westport, Co. Mayo.
Tel:	+353 (0)98 28600
No of Rooms	97
Price	
Suite	€310
Double/twin	€210
Single	€140
Family	Yes – Sharing Under 3's free . U12's €35BB. 12-16's 35% reduction on adult rate.
Dinner	Yes – Restaurant
Open	All year apart from two days over Christmas
Credit Cards	Yes
Directions	Situated just off main N5 main Dublin/Castlebar/Westport road entering Westport town.
Email	info@khh.ie
Web	www.lucindaosullivan.com/knockrannyhousehotel

The Ice House

You only have to look at the cool romantic picture of The Ice House to know that it is a special place in a special location. You only have to know too, that with the dedicated expert duo of Ray Byrne and Jane English behind the newest development in the North West, this is not just an Ice House but an Ice Cool place to be, for they are the couple behind the superb Wineport in Athlone and Lisloughrey Lodge at Cong. Like their other two Hotels, The Ice House Hotel & Spa is beside the water, the salmon rich River Moy, and set on a particularly picturesque stretch at The Quay lending spectacular serene views of the rippling water.

The Ice House, a protected structure built in 1859, was originally the Moy Fishery Manager's House and cold store for salmon exports. Empty for a number of years it was wonderful to see it being brought back to life again – vibrant and joyful - decorated and designed from head to toe in a style that complements the historic building but brings it into the 21st Century. It is a joy to see it shimmer again with happiness as it takes on a new life.

So individualistic, The Ice House defines what a luxury retreat has to offer. A perfect getaway from the stresses of modern life. There are 28

bedrooms and 7 suites located between the main house and the architecturally dazzling contemporary wings. They have been luxuriously and individually designed with floor to ceiling windows, superking pillow top beds with goose down duvets, and equipped with the latest technology - everything that is required by today's discerning guest. The bathrooms have underfloor heating, extra soft towels, and gorgeous toiletries by L'Occitane en Provence.

The Spa is superb and offers all the high end range of treatments. You might have a SeaCreation Infinite Facial which works to the deepest layers of the skin using Jacob's Shells which will leave you looking radiant and refreshed or maybe a HSR Anti-Ageing Power Lift – well that's for me anyway!! There are all sorts of wonderful treatments for you and your better half and all sorts of Spa Packages and Ice House Breaks. Ask about the Ice House Weekend Escape or the Ice House Sunday Recovery.

The fab 80-seater Pier Restaurant and cocktail bar starts in the high vaulted rooms of the Ice House and leans right out into the River Moy within a spectacular glass box. Food is contemporary with a lavish array of seafood, Irish beef and lamb, and local game in season. Superb food is matched by the genuinely friendly and attentive service by the staff and you will have a really good fun time.

Pristine, pure, like no place on earth. The Ice House will be one of the hottest destinations in the country.

Owner	Ray Byrne and Jane English
Address	The Quay, Ballina, Co. Mayo.
Tel	+353 (0)96 23500
No of Rooms	32
Price	
Suites	€295 - €495
Double/Twin	€165 - €220
Dinner	Yes - Restaurant
Open	All Year
Credit Cards	Yes
Directions	Take the N4/M4 to Sligo until turn off for N59 to Ballina. On entering at traffic lights at the bridge. Take a Right. Follow road along the river. Hotel on left up this road Quay Village.
Email	chill@theicehouse.ie
Web	www.lucindaosullivan.com/icehouse

NET Spa

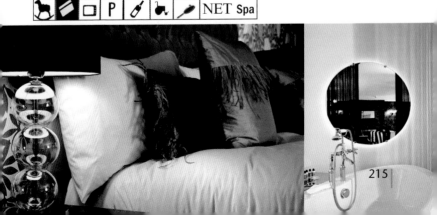

Lisloughrey Lodge

Obviously Jane Byrne and I have a lot in common - a love of water and cats being two things - I don't know in which order. Following my visit to her and husband Ray's well known and fabulous Wineport Lodge on the shores of Lough Ree at Glasson some years ago, where there were lots of "catty" bits and memorabilia in the bar, Jane sent me a Black Cat figure for luck – which I still have. I also live near the sea and always like to be close to the water, not that I ever even dip my toe in it but I just find it immensely soothing and revitalising.

So, for Ray and Jane's second Hotel venture, they have also chosen a waterside, location, this time by the stunning Lough Corrib at Cong with their beautiful new hip country house hotel, Lisloughrey Lodge. Ray and Jane had been thinking for a while about a second project and when Lisloughrey Lodge, on ten acres overlooking the stunning Lough Corrib in the heart of Quiet Man country, came up, they pounced!

They have done a stunning job on the Lodge, transforming it from old style country house into hip country house with all modern comforts and technology that today's discerning guest requires. No more squeaky floors and draughts of the 1970's glossed over as the remnants of auld dacency and country house living! Lisloughrey is comfort and style, worthy of all the best Interior Décor magazines where, no doubt, it will be featuring. There are 28 bedrooms and 22 suites, some in the old house, and others in a beautiful courtyard setting linked to the house. Bedrooms and Suites are individually stylishly decorated with super king beds, deep piled carpets, the latest flat screen technology and bathrooms have underfloor heating so your little tootsies won't get cold. Oh yes, and they bring a touch of Provence to their bathrooms with the wonderful aromas of toiletries by L'Occitane.

The entire first floor of the house has been given over to their new uber smart red and black Salt Restaurant, overlooking Lisloughrey Quay, and with a spectacular view of Lough Corrib. Jane and Ray have built their reputation on superb food and wine at the Wineport and the same attention to detail has been brought to their table at Lisloughrey. The Head Chef is ex Four Seasons so, you can be sure you will be dining on the best of locally caught fish and shellfish, game, viandes, and the desserts ... after which you can retire to the Malt Bar for the proverbial Ball of.... Or if you are like us you will have been in there before dinner too!!

Cong is a fantastic village and the craic is only mighty – the atmosphere unbeatable. There are so many golf courses close by and of course there is the fishing! Himself might like to try the fishing and you can take yourself to Lisoughrey's resident beauty therapist for a bit of pampering with Comfort Zone treatments – do book in advance though.

There is a buzz to Lisloughrey Lodge and it is a place we will be hearing a lot of in the future.

Owners	Ray Byrne and Jane English
Address	The Quay, Cong, Co. Mayo.
Tel	+353 (0)94 9545 400
No of Rooms	50
Price	
Lakeview Suites	€300 - €400
Duplex Suites	€250 - €350
Quay Suites	€250 - €350
Courtyard	€200 - €300
Dinner	Yes - Restaurant
Open	All Year
Credit Cards	Yes
Directions	On The Quay in Cong
Email	lodge@lisloughrey.ie
Web	

www.lucindaosullivan.com/lisloughrey

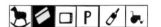

The Mount Falcon Hotel & Estate

One of the great romantic stories of the 19th Century was that of Elizabeth Empress of Austria, better known as Sissi, the Princess Diana of her day. Three movies were made of her life story starring Romy Schneider. I must have seen them 50 times when I was a teenager. Like Diana, Sissi was a troubled body who travelled all the time and was a frequent visitor to Ireland for the Hunting, and great House Parties of the time. No doubt she would have felt very much at home on The Mount Falcon Estate, itself resulting from another true love story.

In 1872 Ultred Knox commissioned architect James Franklin Fuller, who also designed the Guinness family homes of Ashford Castle and Farmleigh, as well as Kylemore Abbey, to construct a palatial home for his beautiful bride Miss Nina Knox-Gore of Belleek Manor. And so was born the stunning Mount Falcon 2,200 acre Estate on the west bank of the River Moy.

In more recent years it became a Country House open to visitors including Vivien Leigh and Peter Sellers. In 2002 the estate was bought by the current owners who hail from the area and have, with great love and attention to detail, restored Mount Falcon to its former glory.

The Mount Falcon Estate re-opened in 2006 and now comprises the most magnificent 4 Star Country House Hotel, Fisheries, and a small number of luxury self catering suites located in lakeside, woodland and courtyard settings, around the 100 acre Estate. It is an ideal destination for golfers to enjoy the numerous nearby Golf Courses and there is unprecedented access to the most prolific salmon river in Ireland, the River Moy. Mount Falcon has already attracted Tiger Woods, Mark O'Meara and Nick Faldo as guests.

Bedrooms are stunning. Suites and de-luxe rooms are on the top floor of the original house with all the old features intact – high ceilings, original marble fireplaces, cornices, and a bell to summon the servants. Superior rooms, too, are glorious with superking beds, custom designed free standing

furniture. There is a fabulous 17 metre swimming pool, steam room, treatment rooms and so on – everything to enable you relax and enjoy.

Before dinner we ensconced ourselves in the Boathole Bar. The food is fabulous as is the really cool Kitchen Restaurant transformed from the original kitchen and pantry. French Chef Phillippe Farineau - cooks Irish food with a French heart – lobster, veal, salmon – and if you don't enjoy his food there is something wrong with you. We had delicious Seared Clew Bay Scallops with celeriac and Black Truffle puree, celeriac chips, and Black Truffle Cappuccino, followed by Mayo Rack of Lamb with Black Eye Beans Cassoulet, Dauphinoise Potato, Mint Crumbled and Goat Cheese Jus. Phillippe is wonderful with chocolate – he even does Sunday Lunch with a Chocolate Buffet – so look out too for the Petit Four Trolley.

Mount Falcon is pretty irresistible.

Owner	Alan Maloney
	Eamonn Elliott – General Manager
Address	Foxford Road, Ballina, Co. Mayo.
Tel	+ 353 (0)96 74472
No of Rooms	32
Price	
Suites	€500
Deluxe Dble/Twin	From €250
Superior Dble/Twin	From €180
Family	On Enquiry – Some interconnecting rooms
Dinner	Yes
Open	February - December
Credit Cards	Yes
Directions	On N26 Foxford/Ballina Road – 3 miles south of Ballina.
Email	info@mountfalcon.com
Web	www.lucindaosullivan.com/mountfalcon

County Meath

Meath, with its sweeping fertile pastures, is one of the richest farming areas in the country. However, it is not for the farming that the county is of such interest to the tourist, but to its wealth of interesting historical areas and remains. The famous Hill of Tara in County Meath was the seat of High Kings of Ireland for many years. Trim can boast the Ango-Norman Trim Castle, which featured prominently in the Mel Gibson movie, Braveheart. Meath is bisected by the River Boyne which gave its name to the famous battle between William of Orange with his Protestant supporters and the deposed English King, James 11, and his Catholic armies. Duchas, the Irish Heritage service, run a 30 minute tour of the battle area.

Slane Castle, although built from 1785 onwards, is probably more famous now for its massive open air Rock Concerts featuring some of the world's top stars. The nearby Hill of Slane is where the patron saint of Ireland, Patrick, lit his paschal fire at Easter 433 AD to proclaim the arrival of Christianity in Ireland. Navan, which is the main town of the county, and a busy commercial centre, is situated where the River Blackwater meets the

Boyne which was very important in the days when waterways were the chief means of transport. If you follow the River Blackwater, upstream from Navan, you come to Kells. While it is a place of monastic antiquities, it is most famous for the beautifully illuminated Book of Kells which is now on show in Trinity College in Dublin.

Probably the most interesting site in the county is Newgrange, possibly the most important Stone Age site in Europe. Built around 3000 BC, it is older than the Egyptian Pyramids and has fascinated historians and astronomers for years as to its original purpose, but was most probably an ancient burial ground with astronomical connections.

Meath, one must also record, is one of the leading Gaelic football counties in the country. This reminds me of the story of the football coach trying to exhort his players to greater efforts with roars from the sidelines "Come on Murphy, wake up, its time you got ferocious". "What number is he wearing", came Murphy's reply!

"History is too serious to be left to historians"
(Ian MacLeod, House of Commons)

Dunboyne Castle Hotel & Spa

DUNBOYNE

Dunboyne is a very pretty village in Co. Meath where we used to go many a year ago beagling with the Goldbourne Beagles. Beagling is a form of hunting on foot – in fact that is where I caught my better half! Dunboyne is now part of the commuter belt but it still retains its rural and village charm. It is a super place for a weekend break and it is also convenient for Newgrange Megalithic Passage Tomb.

DUNBOYNE CASTLE HOTEL & SPA

Dunboyne Castle Hotel & Seoid Spa made a stunning entrance onto the upmarket hotel arena in Ireland in 2006. Home to the historic aristocratic Butler family, the present castle was built in 1700's and completed in 1764 with wonderful stucco plasterwork by the famous Lafrancini Brothers. With 21 acres of grounds and formal gardens in which to relax, the whole ambience is of contemporary elegance and style. The Seoid Spa, which spans three floors, is amazing – so book yourself in for a fab weekend. The Terrace lounge overlooking the gardens is where you can enjoy afternoon tea or an aperitif before dinner, or indeed in the main Sadlier Bar. There is even a Cellar Bar where you can enjoy the craic and the singalong after dinner – or you can give them all a whirl!!

Bedrooms are state of the art scrumptious luxury – mostly set back slightly in the new wing – which in no way overshadows the beauty of the original house. This was planning and design carefully and ecologically carried out – would that it be the same everywhere. Stand outside the main entrance of the hotel and, if you close yours eyes slightly and cast your imagination,

you can visualize 18thC aristocracy strolling around the parklands.

Now to the superb food in the Ivy Brasserie. Think along the lines of a Torchon of Marinated Foie Gras with red onion marmalade, or maybe Swedish style Gravalax of Marinated Salmon with new potato and mustard salad. You might follow up with Seared Pave of Turbot with a light bouillabaisse with cockles and mussels, or being out with the County Set you might fancy oven Roast Squab Pigeon with roasted shallots. All delicious. Puddings are scrumptious …warm chocolate fondant …. It goes on.

Dunboyne Castle is very special – you will love it.

Owners	The Fylan Group
	Peter Borralnan - (General Manager)
Address	Dunboyne, Co. Meath.
Tel	+353 (0)1 801 3500
No of Rooms	145
Price	
Suites	€580 Single/€640 Double
Double/twin	From €150
Single	From €130
Dinner	Yes – The Ivy Brasserie
Open	All Year
Credit Cards	Yes
Directions	Take N3 exit off M50. Continue and take exit for Clonee/Dunboyne. Go through Clonee and this will bring you to Dunboyne. Drive through village and take a left at lights for Maynooth. Hotel is on your left hand side.
Email	reservations@dunboynecastlehotel.com
Web	www.lucindaosullivan.com/dunboynecastle.com

228

Tankardstown House

I had heard a report of Tankardstown House and consumed with curiosity I decided to check out whether or not its charms were exaggerated. On arriving, we skipped up the gleaming limestone steps to the open doors of this restored mansion and estate were warmly greeted by Patricia and Bryan Conroy who are natural hosts.

This forward thinking couple have spared no expense in the impeccable restoration work of the main house and seven stylish cottages with patios which are located in the U shaped courtyard. These are no ordinary cottages but sanctuaries of comfort, furnished with the finest antiques, state of the art appliance and bathroom fittings, ever forgiving mirrors, grandmother clocks, even the most trivial details are attended to. These houses offer luxury and style and I could just visualise Pearce Brosnan settling in next door while making a movie in his home territory.

That night we wined and dined and partied in the great house to the sounds of a string quartet. As the fires roared in the main hall, drawingroom and diningroom, we languished on the decadent sofas, admired the sumptuous furnishings and rich rugs on the highly polished floors and we felt maybe we had passed through the pearly gates without realising it.

More of the finest champagne, great wines from an interesting list, and course after course of sumptuous food cooked and served by Patricia and her four charming daughters, Georgina, Roisin, Laureen, and Amber. Bryan regaled us with stories of his recent trip climbing Mount Kilimanjaro. Later we

all retired to our respective cottages and slept like babies on specially imported V1 mattresses. A fresh breakfast hamper was delivered to our door in the morning by Georgina. The guests dispersed for their various destinations – Tattersall's Sales, Newgrange, Hill of Tara, Dundalk and Drogheda – whilst we enjoyed a spell in the gym and a massage in the Treatment Room.

Later I curled up in front of the fire in my fairyland cottage and helped myself to the generous mini-bar and, on answering the gentle tap on the door, there stood Georgina again with a basket bearing a sumptuous Tankdardstown supper. This is a one of a kind special events venue. It offers total privacy, discretion, and gracious estate living to the discerning guest – all tailored to suit you. If you want to have that really drop dead sophisticated party – this is the place – they have a Party Room which accommodates 50 for dinner or 75 Conference style.

Tankardstown is different – a world of stylish luxury

Owners	Bryan and Patricia Conroy
Address	Tankardstown House, Rathkenny Road, Slane, Co. Meath.
Tel	+353 (0)41 9824621
No of Rooms	7 Cottages
Price	
1 bed Cottage	€160 per night Sleeps 2 (enq re weekly rates)
2 bed Cottage	€320 per night Sleeps 4 (enq re weekly rates)
Dinner	Yes – in Main House (24 hours notice required.
Open	All Year
Directions	Take Slane exit off M1 Motorway. Take N51 to Slane. Take Navan Road out of Slane; at Castle gates turn right to Kells. Go past Slane Farm Hostel (on right). At fork, keep left, Tankardstown 2 miles on, on right.
Email	trish@tankardstown.ie
Web	www.lucindaosullivan.com/tankardstown

County Offaly

County Offaly, a midland county is bounded by the Shannon River to the northwest and the Slieve Bloom Mountains in south. The old Grand Canal connects the Shannon and the Barrow rivers and passes through Tullamore, the principal county town. The Tullamore name is well known because it was the original home of the distillery that made Tullamore Dew, one of the better brands of Irish Whiskey. West, along the Shannon, is one of the earliest Celtic monasteries and probably the most important one in the country, Clonmacnoise. Continuing south on the River Shannon brings you to Shannonbridge. This is the meeting point of the counties Offaly, Roscommon and Galway, and was once considered to be strategically important, hence the large artillery fortification dating from the Napoleonic era. A visit to County Offaly would not be complete without a visit to Birr with its famous Castle. Home of the Earls of Rosse, the Castle is also the home of the Rosse Telescope built in 1845 by the 3rd Earl and for three quarters of a century it remained the largest telescope in the World. It has been restored and is operational to this day.

County Arms Hotel
& Leisure Club

We were in Birr at a Jazz weekend when we discovered not only what a brilliant place it was for an interesting weekend but it was the first time we stayed at the County Arms Hotel, a fine imposing Georgian House set back from the road in grounds and gardens.

We stayed in a very pretty room with a bay window overlooking their wonderful historic walled gardens – it has stuck in my mind to this day – I thought it was lovely.

Since my first visit way back then, things have got even better, for the Country Arms has been completely upgraded and has now been awarded 4 Star status by Failte Ireland. The main house, which was built in 1809, has been restored to its original Georgian splendour and there has been an addition of 62 new bedrooms. There are suites, executive suites, deluxe family rooms, interconnecting rooms – everything you could possibly want plus a fabulous new Leisure Club – The Springs – with Wellness Suites for all the rejuvenation and pampering you will want on your stay. Elemis products are used and whether you have an Aroma Spa Ocean Wrap or an Exotic Lime & Ginger Salt Glow you will have expert therapists looking after you. I am a great believer in time for oneself – so send him to the Leisure Centre with the kids!

After all the beautifying and relaxing you will just be in form to visit their new Trilogy Brasserie Restaurant and terrace, which now overlooks the beautiful walled gardens. Having these wonderful gardens and greenhouses means you can be really sure that they are using local produce. Their Chef has travelled the world bringing back the benefit of his Australian and Asian experiences so the food will always be interesting. Locally sourced beef is just delicious, as is the slow roasted lamb shank – falling off the bone … and the confit of duck leg likewise. They have a superb wine list that I am sure even the good Earl in his Castle would approve. They have special package rates available throughout the year – there are Seasonal Murder Mystery Weekends, Monthly World Food Evenings as well as Tullamore Fleadh Ceoil and Birr Vintage week in August and, if you are a walker, you will be interested in the May Slieve Bloom Walking Festival. Now you have no excuse for not combining genteel culture with good food, state of the art facilities, and health benefits. Oh yes, there is now a new visitor attraction – Macregol's Gospels – The Book of Birr (820AD) – 300 yards from the hotel.

Most importantly, The County Arms is still a family run hotel and the very professional Loughnane family know how to look after their guests.

Owners	The Loughnane Family
Address	Moorpark, Birr, Co. Offaly.
Tel	+ 353 (0)57 912 0791
No of Rooms	70
Price	
Suites	From €300
Double/twin	From €140 - €200
Single	From €100
Family	From €180 - €240
Dinner	Yes – Restaurant and Bar Food
Open	All Year
Credit Cards	Yes
Directions	Approach Birr from either N52 or N62. Hotel is on edge of town on N62.

Email
info@countyarmshotel.com
Web
www.lucindaosullivan.com/countyarms

229

Dooly's Hotel

Birr is a town I know very well having spent quite a lot of time there over the years both for the craic at their annual Vintage Car week and Birr Jazz Festival. Birr Castle and its magnificent gardens were another separate trip for us as a family, for my boys loved to visit not just the Giant Telescope but the fantastic Historic Science Centre with its photography, engineering and amazing astronomy displays. Whilst my boys and better half spent hours and hours examining everything, I have had a great time in the Castle Shop and looking at the beautiful specimen plants and shrubs, some of which were brought back from the Himilayas by former Earls. So you see, Birr has something to attract all ages and interests.

There is no other town in Ireland quite like Georgian Birr with its beautiful terraces, squares, and buildings, and right in the heart of this stunning complete Georgian Town, in Emmett Square, is what is probably the oldest Coaching Inn in Ireland, Dooly's Hotel. A perfect upright and beautiful Georgian gem, Dooly's dates back to 1747. I have always found these Inns very interesting partly because my mother's old home in County Kilkenny was originally a Coaching Inn dating back to Cromwellian times – indeed burnt down by his soldiers and re-built – but sadly, while it still stands today, it is lying forlorn and empty.

Dooly's is what one might call a Georgian Boutique Hotel for it has just 18 bedrooms but nonetheless full of character with all facilities, en suite, direct dial phones, TV, and is perfect for those who want to soak in the olde worlde atmosphere on their trip. It is family run and the staff, too, are very helpful and friendly – imagine what they would give for a real 18th C Inn like this in America – you just couldn't buy the experience. Dooly's is very much the lifeblood of the town for their Coach House Lounge is a hot favourite with locals and visitors alike. They now also have a contemporary

bar specialising in cocktails and beers of the world – this is called The Nebula Bar. Their coffee shop opens from 8.30 a.m. and does everything from a hearty mixed grill to a cappuccino for the girly chat and the indulgence of irresistible home made scones.

Dooly's is perfectly placed for doing Birr on foot – the best way to absorb its splendours – but then you can come back – refresh yourself in either the bars or the shower – or hopefully both – and have a delicious dinner in the Emmet Room Restaurant.

Owner	Sharon Grant
Address	Emmet Square, Birr, Co. Offaly
Tel	+ 353 (0)57 91 20032
No of Rooms	18
Price	
Double/Twin	€140
Single	€75
Family	€140 + under 5's free. Children over 5 sharing - €15 per child.
Dinner	Yes – Restaurant and Bar Food
Open	All Year – Save 25th/26th December.
Credit Cards	Yes
Directions	Approach Birr from either N52 or N62. Dooly's Hotel in centre of town.
Email	info@doolyhotel.ie
Web	www.lucindaosullivan.com/doolyshotel

County Sligo

This is a county of scenic beauty and historical interested loaded with magical names like Coney Island, Dead Man's Point, and Inishfree, which is closely associated with famous Irish names such as W.B. Yeats, Countess Markiewicz, and Eva Gore Booth.

Sligo town is one of the busiest and fastest growing towns in the West and manages to be relaxed and busy at the same time. It boasts an Arts Festival in May, Summer Festival late July, Yeat's Summer School in August and Choral Festival in November.

Rosses Point, about five miles from Sligo town is an ideal spot for a day at the beach with a beautiful Atlantic view with the outline of Coney Island and its neighbour Oyster Island on the horizon. If your interest is in something more energetic, Strandhill's magnificent beach with its huge Atlantic breakers is a popular venue for surfers. At Strandhill you can try your hand and your body at the seaweed baths which are claimed to relieve stress, rheumatism and arthritis- and leave the skin beautiful too. Not very far away, are the ruins of Carrowmore Megalithic cemetary. This is said to be the largest such cemetary in Europe and possibly the oldest. On top of the nearby Knocknarea Mountain is Medb's Cairn which some say is the tomb of the legendary Queen Medb of Connacht whom they say was buried upright so she could keep an eye on the enemy!

Further west is the village of Aughris, home to an early monastic site, and a promontary fort. Continue west towards Easkey where two Martello Towers were defensive positions during the Napoleonic era. Easkey is also popular for surfing.

Just close to Sligo town is the lovely village of Ballintogher on the banks of Lough Gill, known as the Town of the Causeway. Further south is Ballisodare with the remains of a 7th century monastery. On to Collooney, or the nearby village of Riverstown, home of Sligo Folk Park. Further south the market town of Ballymote boasts the 14th C castle built by Richard de Burgo (Red Earl of Ulster). If you are into traditional music, Gurteen is a popular and thriving centre for it. For me probably the most peaceful and atmospheric place in the county is the small austere cemetary and church at Drumcliffe under the shadow of nearby Ben Bulben mountain where the poet W.B. Yeats and his wife are buried under a headstone inscribed "Cast a cold eye on life. On death. Horseman pass by."

"Writing free verse is like playing tennis with the net down."
(ROBERT FROST)

The Glasshouse

The first time I stayed in Sligo was only a dozen years or so ago when we took our boys to visit Yeat's country. It seemed our overnighting options were not terribly exciting at the time and we ended up in a damp B & B near Ben Bulben which looked as if it had been furnished with a job lot of Dutch furniture. Breakfast in the morning was served on a sideplate … and they wonder why many B & Bs are closing down … if only we'd had….

It is easy to see why The Glasshouse caused such a stir when it opened at Swan Point in Sligo, for the fact of the matter is that it is absolutely stunning. It shines like a glittering star beckoning people inwards to its magnetic colourful interior, full of life and fun, and it totally changed the level of accommodation and dining available in Sligo. Stunningly located on the banks of the Garavogue river, the Glasshouse is within metres of Sligo's main O'Connell Street – it has underground parking – so you have nothing to worry about just walk out and shop 'til you drop.

The Glasshouse has pushed out the boundaries both in design and décor, every turn you take leads you to a new brilliant area, and to top it all, prices for such high quality are extremely reasonable. All of the bedrooms, spread over five floors, are beacons of light and colour in sunshine and citrus colours with floor to ceiling windows and gossamer light curtains. They are what I call "happy rooms". There are four levels from standard through superior, deluxe and junior suites. All rooms are soundproofed, have Broadband access points, climate control and 26" LCD TVs with a full entertainment menu, a selection of movies from the movie library and remote onscreen internet access. There are also rooms with reduced mobility facilites.

We'd had a long drive up from Dublin and once we settled in we went down to the View Bar, which is literally that – wonderful views over the weir on the river and out over the ever more vibrant Sligo. We progressed into The Kitchen Restaurant which has an innovative menu – they have been winning awards already. We liked their combinations and pairings of food – confit of duck was with a mango salsa and coriander dressing, pan seared scallops with a spring onion and Thai green curry sauce with a roasted salad, horseradish – which I love – used with Atlantic crab meat in a gratin, and panfried medallions of venison on sauerkraut with grilled apple and wild berry jus. Oh, and leave room for the puds, they do a deadly deep-fried chocolate cake in a chilli batter.

Breakfast, too, is served in The Kitchen and did we have The Healthy Option? No, of course we didn't, I could never do anything sensible – although I did have an orange and banana smoothie before I had the bacon and onion potato cake topped with fried egg. Brendan was more restrained, he had delicious freshly scrambled egg with oak smoked salmon on brown bread.

The Glasshouse Glitters....

Owner	Roisin Buckley General Manager
Address	The Glasshouse, Swan Point, Sligo.
Tel	+353 (0)71 9194300
No of Rooms	116
Price	
Suites	€210
Double/Twin	€160
Single Occupancy	€120
Dinner	Yes - Restaurant
Open	All Year – save Christmas Day
Credit Cards	Yes
Directions	N4 into Sligo Town. From Lord Edward Street, continue onto Wine Street. Hotel on left on Hyde Bridge.
Email	info@theglasshouse.ie
Web	www.lucindaosullivan.com/theglasshouse

County Tipperary

Tipperary is the largest of Ireland's inland counties. Situated in the rich fertile lands of the Golden Vale it is also a very wealthy county. Without a doubt, the most outstanding of its many attractions is the Rock of Cashel, rising sharply to over 200 feet and topped by mediaeval walls and buildings. Not far from Cashel is the peaceful town of Cahir on the River Suir with its wonderful Castle dating back to the 13th and the 15th centuries, an Anglo Norman stronghold of the Butlers, the Earls of Ormond. North of Cashel the River Suir passes through the towns of Thurles, not far from Holy Cross Abbey, and is the birthplace of the G.A.A., the ruling body for our National Games. Templemore is like Westpoint on flat feet, being the training headquarters of the Irish Police Force, the Garda Siochana. The area around Nenagh and Lough Derg – Terryglass, Coolbaun, Puckaun – is very popular now with many people having holiday homes near the Lake. Nenagh also boasts a colossal round Castle Keep with walls 20 feet thick and a height of 100 feet topped with 19th century castellations. Clonmel is probably Tipperary's prettiest centre. It was the principal base for Bianconi, the most successful coach company in the 1800's in this country. Clonmel also boasts the 19th century St. Mary's Roman Catholic Church, the 19th century West Gate and the Greek Revival style Wesleyan Church and more. The county has many peaceful and pleasant villages to appeal to visitors such as Bansha, not far from Cahir and backed by the Glen of Aherlow and the Galtee Mountains, or Ballyporeen whose claim to fame is that U.S. President Ronald Regan's grandfather hailed from there.

"An actor's a guy who, if you ain't talking about him,
ain't listening"
(MARLON BRANDO)

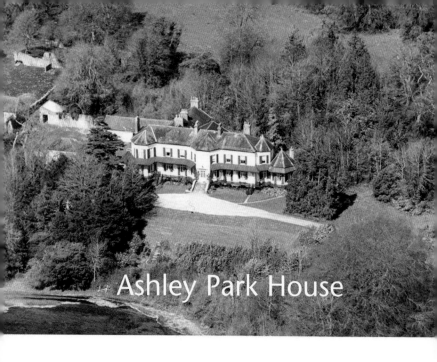

Ashley Park House

The first time I saw Ashley Park House I took a deep intake of breath and thought I had entered the film set of Gone With the Wind or Raintree County. It is a most dramatic and unusual house for this part of the world which would do Savannah proud. An 18th Century house, a white vision with elaborate green painted verandahs, overlooking the sultry Lake Ourne, with hanging weeping trees. Ashley Park House is on 76 acres of beechwood and formal gardens, with strolling peacocks and ancient walled gardens, and is quite spellbinding. Friend Carmel and I had whirled up in my little blue MGF open topped car . Sean Mounsey, the family patriarch complete with cap, who is one of the greatest characters you are ever likely to meet said, "I want you to be happy here Ma'am". I felt like Princess Margaret. Sean took us up to the "Bishop's room" where he had put up a small temporary bed beside the half tester as the house was full and, looking puzzled, said half to himself, "I wasn't expecting two such fine strapping women as yourselves – now if one of you were smaller". Tears streamed down our faces we laughed so much, and as Carmel collapsed over the dressing table in a heap, Sean Mounsey beat a hasty retreat….

Ashley Park House has some of the finest rooms you will ever come across, and you can live out all of your Scarlett O'Hara fantasies in this house. The front bedrooms at either end of the house are vast, splendid and romantic. The house is magnificently furnished with impeccable taste by Sean's daughter Margaret. Relax in the impressive drawingroom with a drink in front of the fire or chill out in the beautiful octagonal Chinese reading room off it. Explore the old walled garden which they are restoring. Dine in the magnificent diningroom. Go to Ashley Park quickly you might not find Rhett Butler but you will find Sean Mounsey, and his beautiful daughter Margaret, and they are much more interesting altogether. Children are welcome. It is incredible value and an equally incredible experience.

Owners	Margaret and P.J. Mounsey
Address	Ashley Park, Ardcroney, Nenagh, Co. Tipperary.
Tel	+353 (0)67 38223/38013
No. Of Rooms	5
Price	
Double/Twin	€100 - €130
Single	€55 - €60
Family	€110/€130 + (Children sharing 50% over 2 years)
Dinner	Yes - €40 (Book by 2 p.m.)
Open	All Year
Credit Cards	Visa MC Diners Amex
Directions	From Nenagh, turn right on the N52 for 3 miles. Ashley Park is the large white house on the opposite side of lake.
Email	margaret@ashleypark.com
Web	www.lucindaosullivan.com/ashleyparkhouse

Bailey's Hotel

Bailey's Hotel is a mélange of the best of the old and the new. The original very fine old house, which fronts onto the main street of Cashel was built in 1703 by The Wesley Family, so is just over 300 years old, and has a great history.

Dermot and Phil Delaney are your very hospitable and friendly hosts here. They have transformed what was a very successful Guest House into a lovely family run hotel. Phil's impeccable taste is evident from the moment you set foot on the black and white tiled floor of the Hall of the main house, with its lovely historic Farrow & Ball colours. The bedrooms are beautifully furnished, both in the old house with its high ceilings, and the new. With Bailey's morphing into a hotel, there is now a fab new swimming pool and leisure centre. The addition of their cracking new contemporary restaurant No 42, doing really good modern food, has meant that even more so, Bailey's is now the focal point for Cashel's discerning diners. Their atmospheric Cellar Bar is where you will meet the locals, have a jar and enjoy the chat, and they also serve delicious casual bar food there. Being so well located in the town, you can just leave the car and walk around and do the shops and sights, returning for a casual lunch or to the drawing room to relax. Phil herself is a natural cook and a generous one to boot. She is the type of Chef who bakes two types of Bread for Sunday Lunch crusty white soda bread and a dark brown bread.

Bailey's is a superb place to stay when visiting Ireland's most famous monument, the famous Rock of Cashel. It is also a great spot for a short break – there are lots of golf clubs and pubs and places to see such as the Cashel folk village, Cahir Castle, the picture postcard Swiss Cottage at Cahir and much much more. Oh if you want a bit of ceoil and rince there are sesiuns in the Bru Boru Heritage Centre from June to September.

Owners	Dermot & Phil Delaney
Address	Main Street, Cashel, Co. Tipperary.
Tel	+353 (0)62 61937
No of Rooms	33
Price	
Suite	€325
Double/twin	€180
Family	€220
Dinner	Yes – Restaurant and Bar Food
Open	All Year
Credit Cards	Yes
Directions	In Cashel Town Centre

Email
info@baileys-ireland.com
Web
www.lucindaosullivan.com/
baileyshotel

Bansha Castle

I got a tall order from an English PR agency representing the head of a large Legal Firm. "The Boss" was suffering Hip Hotel Fatigue and looking for something different. He wanted to rent a big Country House where he could entertain his best customers for a week. If it was that simple I would, as they say in Tipperary, be away on a hack, but no, he wanted more and a lot more. He wanted a house where he could self cater and indulge his passion for cooking some nights, and have dinner provided other nights. Still simple you may say but he also wanted a place where he and his friends could hunt, shoot and fish and be within walking distance of the local pub Well you will be delighted to know that I found the perfect retreat at the 18th C. Bansha Castle. As I travelled the road from Cashel to Bansha, it reminded me a little of Beverly Hills without the traffic for it definitely had the mansions, secure Stud Farms and prime beef units. This is 4-wheel drive territory so I knew when I arrived at Bansha Castle that I had backed a winner for Mr. Lawyer. Teresa and John Russell are welcoming hosts and there is a great casual welcoming feel to the whole house. You just know where you can throw your riding jacket on the hall stand, and leave your riding boots at the bottom of the stairs, without fear of reprimand. Teresa will organize the Huntin', Shootin', Fishin' and she can also organize a

beautician to come if you want to pamper yourself. The Drawing room is an impressive room with a large full size Snooker Table just off. Perfect for someone with a wasted childhood in Pool Halls or for a visiting member of the Mafia.

Teresa has organized the House so well that you can rent the entire place and have a private kitchen and dining room at your disposal, or she will cook breakfast and dinner for you at times to suit you. If the Castle is not let then you will have the opportunity to stay on a B & B basis, and also be able to enjoy a dinner at one of her beautifully laid tables in the large Dining Room where she serves up good unpretentious home cooking. This arrangement also suits people celebrating special occasions, even divorces, and you can bring your own booze.

Owners	John & Teresa Russell
Address	Bansha, Co. Tipperary.
Tel	+353 (0)62 54187
No. Of Rooms	6 (for self catering sleeps 12/17)
Price	
Double/Twin	€100
Single	€65

The Castle is available for self-catering. It sleeps 12/17 Price on application.

Dinner	Yes – Has to be pre-booked.
Open	All Year
Credit Cards	None
Directions	Located just outside village of Bansha

Email	teresa@banshacastle.com
Web	www.lucindaosullivan.com/banshacastle

 P

Coolbawn Quay Lakeshore Spa

Twenty years ago if you said you were going to a Spa people would have thought you weren't well but, oh boy, once we copped on to the joys of Spas did we ever take to them like ducks to the proverbial waters. Spas are for you, for me – not just a Leisure Centre where you are "working" watching the kids splash around, or a Health Farm where you go and pay for the joy of starving. Finally there is a place where we can go, be pampered, forget all our worries, have delicious healthy food and just crash out and rejuvenate.

Coolbawn Quay is a unique private village nestling on the shores of Lough Derg, complete with magnificent marina. Understated and elegant, accommodation is in a series of snug village rooms, larger lakeshore suites, or in luxury cottages with French doors to a private decking area. I watched a legendary movie star being interviewed on T.V. and he was asked what was the secret of his long marriage - "separate bathrooms", he replied. At Coolbawn Quay they obviously realise this so, their luxurious cottages have a choice of 2, 3 or 4 bathrooms. Here you will receive full hotel style service and, indeed, you may also dine in your cottage. Alternatively, cottages can also be taken on a self-catering basis.

The Aqua Spa Suite comprises a counter-current pool, sauna and steam room, as well as a relaxation room overlooking the lake. There are all sorts of

body wrap treatments, Algimud Body Masks, Deep Sea Black Mud envelopment and facials using the holistic Dr. Hauschka and Rene Guinot products. I had the Algae Seaweed Body wrap which was fabulous leaving my skin exfoliated and feeling like silk. Facials for men are superb too, designed to rejuvenate tired skin.

Owners Jay and Kevin Brophy are also in to food, they once owned a top Dublin restaurant, so you are going to enjoy the very best of delicious fare, using fresh local and organic produce, beautifully prepared by their Chef and served in a the candlelit diningroom. Oh there is a bar too, where you can also imbibe and/or have lunch. Coolbawn is on my agenda for regular de-stress visits.

Get the girls together, you deserve it, or take Himself – maybe he deserves it too – it's the sort of Lough Derg you can both really enjoy! There are all sorts of packages – click on our website.

Owners	Jay & Kevin Brophy
Address	Coolbawn, Lough Derg, Co. Tipperary.
Tel	+353 (0)67 28158
No. Of Rooms	48
Price	
Suite	From €280
Double/Twin	From €180
Single	From €125
Dinner	Yes – Restaurant
Open	January to December (Closed Christmas)
Credit Cards	Visa MC Amex Diners Laser
Directions	From Nenagh N52 to Borrisokane for approx 1Mile, turn left opp AIBP factory, on to Lake Drive Route. Pass through villages of Puckane and Coolbawn Entrance exactly 2 miles past Coolbawn Village on left.
Email	reservations@coolbawnquay.com
Web	www.lucindaosullivan.com/coolbawnquay

NET Spa H P

Inch House

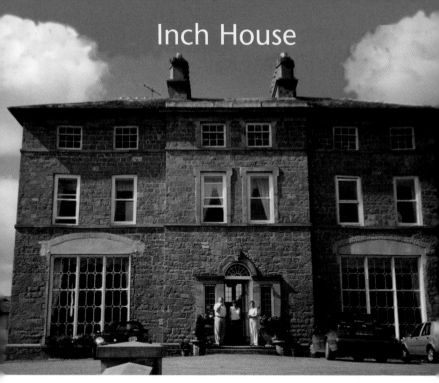

Eamonn de Valera was President when I was a child. A very old man at that stage, he was almost blind and was an austere and forbidding figure sitting up in the back of the old State Car wearing a black hat. To me he was a terrifying sight and I didn't like him at all. Well, whatever I thought about the man, he got his own back because when I got married I was in a fairly pressurised job and when we moved into our new house the timing of the move, arranged three months in advance, was down to seconds. The carpet layers were coming first along with the plumbers. De Valera upped and died and the Nation went into mourning. His funeral was on the day of the move, the carpet layers went out in sympathy, whilst the furniture removers from the old house didn't, hence the furniture arrived first and the carpet layers arrived after dark much the worse for the wear....

John and Nora Egan's Inch House in Thurles sits proud in the middle of lush farmland with a drive up to the stately front door. The first thing you notice about Inch, is the meticulous care given to the pot plants outside the door – perfectly cared for but the second thing I noticed was the portrait of Dev over my bedroom door! Get John Egan talking about politics and you could have the fun of your life – he is gregarious and brilliant all in one. Nora laughs quietly in the background at the good of it all while she overseas this meticulous well cared for house. Their daughter Mairin, who has wide experience in the hospitality industry, has now also returned to base to help run this great house. Have a drink in the beautiful William Morris papered blue, white and gilt, drawingroom and listen to the local stories. The Restaurant attracts people from all over the place for the ample cracking five

course dinners served by wonderful ladies who will look after you like a mother. The House was the former home of the Ryan family for hundred years– a great Tipperary name- and in fact shortly after I wrote about Inch House I had an email from the Ryans in New Zealand where they have now made there home. Have a look at the stained glass Ryan coat of arms on the staircase the family motto was "Death Before Dishonour". The bedrooms are peaceful and comfortable and you will recline on the finest linen in a Prince Albert bed before coming down to a lavish breakfast in the magnificent diningroom again. It is a beautiful house on wonderful grounds and I can't wait to get back there again. Please note this is a non-smoking house.

Owners	Nora Egan and Family
Address	Thurles, Co. Tipperary.
Tel	+353 (0)504 51348
No. Of Rooms	5
Price	
Double/Twin	€140
Single	€ 75
Family	€130 (U 10's free sharing parent's room. Under 15's 50% sharing parent's room
Dinner	Yes – Restaurant -5 Course €55. Closed Sun & Monday Nights.
Open	All Year – Save Christmas, New Year and Easter.
Credit Cards	Yes
Directions	From Thurles take Nenagh road for 6 kms past The Ragg. House is on the left.
Email	mairin@inchhouse.ie
Web	www.lucindaosullivan.com/inchhouse

County Waterford

A walled city of Viking origin, Waterford is the oldest city in Ireland and even today it retains much of its medieval character. It is the home of Waterford Crystal, the world-famous handcrafted, cut glass product. The parameters of the 10th century settlement can be clearly identified in The Viking Triangle. Reginald's Tower is the most historic urban medieval monument in Ireland while the elegant Chamber of Commerce building, the City Hall and the Bishop's Palace are prime examples of beautiful 18th century architecture. Waterford has a long theatrical and musical tradition, which centres on the historic Theatre Royal, which hosts the Waterford International Festival of Light Opera each year. East of the city is the pretty village of Passage East with its ferry service to Ballyhack in Co. Wexford. Stay on the coast road south to the long sandy beach, flanked by woodland, at Woodstown ideal for a quiet stroll or gentle dip in the sea. Go further south to the popular holiday village of Dunmore East which is largely undiscovered by tourists, or go west to the honky tonk family holiday town of Tramore. Further west is the busy commercial town of Dungarvan but swing inland to the beautiful hidden stretch of the River Blackwater around Cappoquin within three miles of Lismore and its ecclesiastical past and most dramatic castle in the country, Lismore Castle, owned by the Duchess of Devonshire. It is a fabulous area and also largely undiscovered by tourists. If you want to learn a few words of the native tongue drive back south to the Irish speaking area of Ring where the language thrives as do other traditions such as music and set dancing.

"Never drink black coffee at lunch, it will keep you awake all afternoon"
(JILLY COOPER attrib)

Athenaeum House Hotel

"I watched the Tall Ships sail gracefully by from here – it was absolute heaven", I said to friend Miranda. We were sipping champagne on the terrace of Zak's Restaurant at the Athenaeum, a chic new boutique hotel on ten acres, with views down over the river Suir and marina at Waterford Harbour. The best of modern classical taste and design has gone into the Athenaeum – not a frill in sight – just clean lines and stunning colours. From the Grand Piano in the elegant anti-room to the beautiful side chairs in the hall, the Athenaeum is different. Cardinal purple carpets lead down to the bedrooms, which are understated and elegant, but with funky chairs, flat screen television, modem connections, fridge, and anything else today's discerning traveller might want.

Stan Power and his wife Mailo own the Athenaeum and they cannot do

250

enough for you. Stan is so cool, professional and helpful, I would imagine if he had been captaining the Titanic it would have made it to New York. Mailo is an Interior Decorator and is responsible for the slick beautiful cool décor with its clean architectural lines and modern classical atmosphere, which has been wowing the who's who of Irish society, who have been beating a path to their door.

Zak's Restaurant, which is one of the most attractive dining rooms in the country, runs across the back of the hotel. Long and conservatory style, with those great views, you won't however be too distracted from what is on your plate, which is just delicious and also very well priced. Do have dinner and think Tartare of diced salmon, onion, capers and chives, wrapped in a saffron cream and salmon pearls, or lightly sautéed foie gras on brioche served with duck liver pate with caramelised apple chutney followed, maybe, by the pinkest rack of lamb with aubergine Provencal or Dover Sole. You can look forward to a lovely breakfast too – try their muesli complete with cardamom seeds – they could sell that by the stone weight and make a fortune.

This lovely boutique Hotel on the banks of the River Suir is a real find.

Owners	Stan & Mailo Power
Address	Christendom, Waterford City, Co. Waterford.
Tel	+353 (0)51 833999
No. of Rooms	29
Price	
Suite	€280
Double/Twin	€120 - €180
Single	€100
Dinner	Yes – Restaurant
Open	All Year
Credit Cards	Visa MC Amex Laser
Directions	From roundabout at Railway Station take N25 in direction of Wexford. After traffic lights take first right on to Abbey Road, then first right after hump back bridge.
Email	info@athenaeumhousehotel.com
Web:	www.lucindaosullivan.com/athenaeum

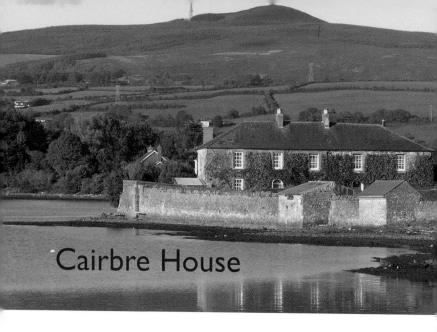

Cairbre House

As you drive out of Dungarvan towards Dublin, you will see on the estuary to the left, a beautiful ivy clad Georgian house sitting virtually on the water. I had looked at this house and wondered for years what it was all about. One day I took the bull by the horns, turned off the main road, and drove up for a closer look. Stepping gingerly through the gates I suddenly found I was in a world that reminded me of Jane Austen, for behind the big boundary walls was a very beautiful olde world garden of roses and herbaceous borders. It just seemed like heaven and, to cap it all, who strode around the corner but Mr Wickham! Brian Wickham, quite unfazed by this nosey person at his door, welcomed me warmly and took me through his lovely home, which has been in his family for over 100 years.

Cairbre House was built by the Duke of Devonshire in 1819 and it is sitting on the Colligan River Estuary sheltered and protected with a backdrop of Cruchan and the Comeragh Mountains. It is quite stunning, understated, and a gardener's paradise. The walls surrounding the property were built at the same time as the house. Made of limestone they give protection to the amazing gardens, which enjoy a microclimate, allowing a large number of

rare and unusual Mediterranean, South African, Australian and other sub tropical plants to be grown successfully.

The house has beautiful features. There is a very comfortable drawing room for guests use with a blazing fire. The bedrooms are comfortable and pretty and it is amazing to wake up in this lovely historic atmosphere – but with all modern comforts! Brian's breakfasts are super. You can have the traditional Irish Breakfast but at Cairbre it will be with free range eggs and potato bread plus herbs from the garden, or kick the morning off with succulent local Helvick smoked salmon on brown bread with scrambled egg and a garden salad decorated with fresh herbs and flowers. He also does a lovely hot vegetarian special with tomatoes, courgettes, mushrooms, peppers and chives sautéed in a light olive oil with fresh herbs, topping it off with edam cheese and grilling it for a few minutes – and you can have Earl Grey tea if you ask nicely. Jane Austen would approve of Mr. Wickham.

Owner	Brian Wickham
Address	Strandside North, Abbeyside, Dungarvan, Co. Waterford.
Tel	+353 (0)58 42338
No of Rooms	4
Price	
Double/twin	€80 - €90
Single	€45 - €55
Family	€40 - €45pps + 50% reduction children under 12. If under 3 years free sharing with parents.
Dinner	No
Open	February - November
Credit Cards	Yes
Directions	From Waterford approaching Dungarvan remain on N25. Take right hand exit off 2nd roundabout
Email	cairbrehouse@eircom.net
Web	www.lucindaosullivan.com/cairbrehouse

 NET P

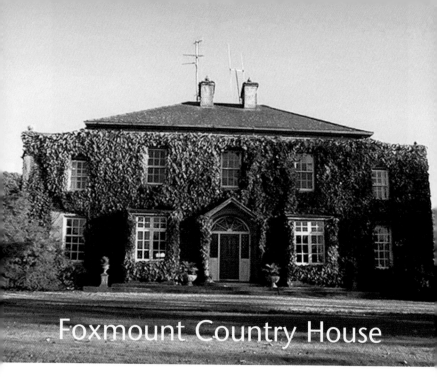

Foxmount Country House

Our French visitors, Michelle and Zandra, had expressed a definite interest in visiting the Waterford Glass Factory so, the decision was taken, to drive down and overnight in Waterford. We drove down through Wicklow, the Garden of Ireland, and Wexford and duly did the tour of the Waterford Glass Factory. Living in Paris, the idea of an Irish farm appealed and I had one up my sleeve. They took a sharp intake of breath when the ivy clad Foxmount House came into view. "Oh, this beautiful", they exclaimed of its impeccably kept lawns, glorious flower beds and gravel paths, that looked as if they had been fine combed. Inside, too, they were delighted with a blazing fire in the drawingroom, as they admired the family silver, antiques, and general good taste of Margaret and David Kent who, with their son and daughter, run this lovely house and dairy farm to perfection. Michelle and Zandra were anxious to explore the farm so David took them under his wing and showed them around. Some time later I looked out my lovely bedroom window and was surprised to see the pair of them belting a ball back and forth out on the tennis court, but what struck me most when I gazed out the window was being able to see into Margaret Kent's kitchen where perched on the windowsill was a perfectly arranged bowl of soft and dewy pink roses. For me, that said it all. Foxmount House is perfection, from the sign on the main road, right through to the hidden sections of the kitchen. Breakfast was beautifully presented with little bowls of floating flowers and leaves. Delicious breads and scones with homemade preserves sit on beautiful plates followed by a delicious cooked breakfast. I couldn't resist picking up all of the plates and looking underneath to see who made them! One of the brilliant things about Foxmount too is its location. It is a farm on the edge of Waterford City so you are in to the centre by taxi or car in literally ten minutes, yet you have the joy of being close to the sea, you are on the road down to the little ferry in picturesque Passage East and very close to any number of golf courses.

Owners	David & Margaret Kent
Address	Passage East Road, Waterford.
Tel	+353 (0)51 874308
No. Of Rooms	4
Price	
Double/Twin	€130
Family	€65pps
Single	On Enquiry
Dinner	No
Open	Mid March – End October
Credit Cards	No
Directions	Take Dunmore East Road from Waterford City, then take Passage East Road for one mile. Sign on right for house.
Email	info@foxmountcountryhouse.com
Web	www.lucindaosullivan.com/foxmount

Glasha Farmhouse

You know that great Irish welcome that we all boast about and very often don't find – well you can be sure of it at Olive and Paddy O'Gorman's lovely Glasha Farmhouse set in the beautiful Nire Valley. It is a large white house impeccably maintained and, as you drive in and get out of your car with your bags and baggage, you are suddenly swept up in the enthusiastic warm welcome that Olive bestows on everyone – no wonder she was the first B & B to win the Failte Ireland Warm Welcome Award. Before you know where you are, you are ensconced on comfortable sofas being plied with tea and apple tart while Olive talks a dime a dozen. Paddy is delightful, a gentle smiling farmer, who knows and is proud of what Olive has achieved and her enthusiasm for visitors and tourists. Olive has thought of everything for the very comfortable bedrooms, with all sorts of extras like electric blankets, hairdryers and nick nacks often lacking in good hotels – and some rooms have Jacuzzi baths. The Nire Valley is very popular with walkers and anglers but you can drive around like me if you wish!! These are the real hidden places of Ireland very often not found by Tourists as they beat a track for the West. The river Nire runs beside Glasha and fishing permits are available locally. Have a delicious dinner – maybe Rack of Comeragh Lamb or Poached Monkfish and, if you are good, Olive and Paddy will show you the back gate, which slips out onto a little windy road where at the foot of the hill is one of the dinkiest old pubs I have ever been in. It is like something out of a movie – absolutely wonderful and a perfect

way to end the day before strolling back up to Glasha for a wonderfully peaceful sleep in the stillness of Ballymacarbry. Come down next morning and you are in for one of the best breakfasts in Ireland – what a spread Olive puts out – you will have the camera out – it is one of the best I have ever seen. Houses like Glasha are the real hidden places of Ireland very often not found by the tourist. You are in for a treat.

Owners	Patrick & Olive O'Gorman
Address	Glasha, Ballymacarbry, via Clonmel, Co. Waterford.
Tel	+353 (0)52 36108
No. Of Rooms	8
Price	
Double/Twin	€100 - €120
Single	€60 - €70
Family	€140
Dinner	Yes
Open	All Year except Christmas
Credit Cards	Visa MC
Directions	Signposted on Clonmel to Dungarvan Road
Email	glasha@eircom.net
Web	www.lucindaosullivan.com/glasha

 NET P

Lismore House Hotel

When Prince Charles introduced Camilla Parker Bowles as his fiancee onto the world stage, the first place he brought her was to visit was his friend the Duke of Devonshire at Lismore Castle, Co. Waterford. I can't actually say whether he took her down to the local pub for a glass of Guinness, but I do know they took in the local sights in this heritage town with its distinctly colonial feel. Lismore Castle is one of the few places that makes you stop and take in a really deep breath for it is mesmerising. Truly stunning. Lismore is also a colourful place because this too is where Adele Astaire, sister of the legendary Fred Astaire, lived for many years after she married into the aristocratic Devonshire family.

What Lismore did lack was somewhere decent to stay – if you weren't invited to stay in the Castle of course! This has now been rectified since Michael Foley and Richard Evans bought over the beautiful old Lismore House Hotel at the heart of the town, making it the perfect destination for any visiting Princes, Rajahs, Hollywood stars, who come to visit His Grace, not to mention you and I!

Lismore House Hotel was built in 1797 by the then Duke of Devonshire and was Ireland's oldest purpose built hotel. It has now been extended, restored and refurbished, brought up to date but retains the glory of it's Georgian old world style and charm. It thoroughly reflects the heritage of Lismore Castle and it's surrounds.

Bedrooms are deliciously comfortable, luxurious fabrics, duck down quilts, deluxe carpets, Plasma TVs, Broadband Connection, and anything you could possibly want. There is a fab new bar – The Malt – with a touch of the colonial atmosphere and, apart from a decent ball of malt at the mahogany bar counter, you can also enjoy afternoon tea or casual food both at lunch time and in the evening. There is also WIFI in this area if you can't get away from the laptop.

The Riverbank Restaurant in truly Georgian style offers a serene elegant ambiance and overlooks the town's Millennium Park. The food is a combination of new and old country recipes with an emphasis on the very best of local, seasonal produce given a new twist. Kick off maybe with a fulsome Seafood Chowder or Gravlax of Salmon with an unusal twist, marinated in Seville oranges, grain mustard and Oak Aged Whiskey, served with a horseradish cream. Think then of Pan-fried Whole Black Sole with an Almond and lemon butter or Canon of Lamb with a mustard and herb crust or a great fillet of beef on gallette potato with glazed shallots and Bearnaise sauce.

So practice your dance steps and skip up to Lismore … you never know … you might meet a Duke.

Owner	Michael Foley and Richard Evans
Address	Main Street, Lismore, Co. Waterford.
Tel	+353 (0)58 72966
No of Rooms	29
Price	
Suites	€240 - €380
Double/Twin	€130 - €270
Single	€ 65 - €135
Family	(Under 4's Sharing Parent's room free. 4-12 Sharing €30 each)
Dinner	Yes – Restaurant and Bar Food
Open	All Year – Save Christmas Day
Credit Cards	Yes
Directions	On Main Street
Email	info@lismorehousehotel.com
Web	www.lucindaosullivan.com/lismorehousehotel

Waterford Castle

S omebody said to me one time "Waterford Castle is decorated just the way a Castle should be". Rich and regal with lavish antiques, ornate plaster ceilings, and all the elegance of the original features preserved, it is just perfect. They should see it now because it has had a major revamp for 2008 – utterly tasteful in keeping with tradition with superb furnishings and fabrics - which no doubt will be featuring in all the Style magazines. From the moment you pass through the carved granite arch and the studded oak door into the amazing hall, dominated by a beautiful Elizabethan stone cavernous fireplace and magnificent tapestries from generations of yore, you are in another world. You will notice on the chimneybreast, raised proud from the stone, like some giant ornate jewel, the carved Fitzgerald coat of arms. Likewise the crested carpet on the floor, for Waterford Castle, built in the 15th Century, and the Norman Keep before that, was in the hands of the Fitzgerald family for 800 years. Fabulously located on its own private 310 acre island estate on the River Suir, yet just 2 miles out of the hustle and bustle of Waterford City, the Castle is surrounded by woodlands and an 18 hole Championship Golf Course.

Getting to the island adds to the experience. You just nip out the Dunmore East Road, turn left at the sign, and head down to the private ferry which transports you across the little channel into another world of luxurious retreat, sanctuary and seclusion. Over a thousand years ago the first inhabitants cut a rough track to their secure settlement but this is now a tree lined driveway, lush, with ever changing colours and ahead stands the stunning Castle, picturesque and enchanting.

The splendid guest rooms and suites are bright and airy with magnificent

views of the surrounding estate and golf course. Guests get the feeling, for this is the way that they are received, that they are residents rather than "hotel guests". Dinner in the beautiful Munster Dining Room, with its original oak panelled walls and ornate ceilings, is a memorable occasion and has been wowing all the food critics. You might be indulging in panfried Dublin Bay Prawns with potato rosti, toasted almonds and a lobster cream followed by Brill with green beans, oven dried tomato and wholegrain mustard sauce … and the puds….

Go and be a part of this Fairy Tale lifestyle.

Owners	Gillian Butler (General Manager)
Address	The Island, Ballinakill, Waterford.
Tel	+353 (0)51 878203
No. Of Rooms	19
Price	
Suite	From €375
Double/Twin	From €200
Family Suite	From €375
Dinner	Yes - Restaurant
Open	Open All Year save 24th 25th 26th Dec and month of January.
Credit Cards	All Major Cards
Directions	Look out for sign to left off Dunmore East Road.
Email	info@waterfordcastle.com
Web	www.lucindaosullivan.com/waterfordcastle

County Westmeath

A county rich in fertile farmland and an important producer of beef with a wide area for dairy farming. Mullingar, the central town, is no sleepy town but a busy commercial trading centre with its own traffic congestion problems. One of the town's claim to fame is that in 1951 it hosted a music festival which became an annual celebration of traditional music, An Fleadh Ceoil, which now moves about the country to a different town each year.

Westmeath has many attractions including its lakes in the northern part of the county around Castlepollard and well worth visiting. Close to Castlepollard is Lough Derravaragh, which is famous for the legend of the Children of Lir. Lir, King of Connacht, whose second wife, jealous of Lir's love for the children of his first wife, turned them into swans condemned to remain so for 900 years. Many people visit this area for its fishing – mainly roach, pike and trout.

If something a bit stronger than water is needed, a trip to Kilbeggan and Lock's Distillery Museum, could fill the bill. The entrance fee includes a free sample which certainly enhances the tour. In the west of the county is Athlone town, the traditional centre of Ireland. Situated where east meets west, and north meets south, on the River Shannon, it is an ideal spot from which to visit the islands and shores of Lough Ree to the north and historical ruins at Clonmacnoise to the south.

"A farm is an irregular patch of nettles, bounded by short term notes, containing a fool and his wife who didn't know enough to stay in the city."

(S.J. Perelman)

Mullingar is the town in the heart of the midlands whose name can be translated from Gaelic to mean "the Wry Mill". Rest assured, though, if you choose The Mullingar Park Hotel for a short stay or business meeting venue, nothing should go awry.

This four star hotel on the Dublin side of Mullingar town is equipped with 95 bedrooms, a fitness suite and extensive conference and banqueting facilities. (That's 1000 and 700 capacity respectively to you and me). Perfect for purposes of business or leisure in the Midlands. It houses the gorgeous Azure Leisure and Beauty Treatment Rooms with a refreshing 20 metre swimming pool, scintillating sauna, hydrotherapy pool, children's pool, sizzling steam room, aerobics studio and various pampering beauty treatments all available on site. An a la carte menu is available at the Terrace Restaurant. Carvery lunch is served at the stylishly modern Horse Shoe Bar, decorated in a surprisingly pleasant combination of pink and purple hues with wood and brick mix, and afternoon coffee and snacks can be consumed at Café Revive. If you haven't had your fill sampling the delights of this day to evening variety of eateries, 24 hour room service is offered to guests.

Nearby places of interest include the Mullingar Pewter Factory, Lough Derravaragh, the lake where the mythical Children of Lir were said to have spent hundreds of years as swans, and of course, the famous Belevedere House and Gardens. You can partake in angling and horse riding in the area. Don't forget the head honcho of Ryanair resides in the town, so if you're at a loose end after browsing through the shops, you could always drop in and complain about that one-time delayed flight of yours ... or maybe you'd be more likely to run into him at Mullingar Golf Club.

Complimentary wireless Internet access is available to conference

delegates and guests. You can even have your clothes laundered and dry-cleaned for you - no need to lift a finger. Executive and Luxury bedrooms are in existence for guests with more particular needs. Comfort and style are really emphasised here – the standard bedrooms are spacious and modern and have direct dial phones, flat screen TVs and ironing facilities.

You will dine well, sleep well, be pampered, have lots of fun, what more could you ask?

Owner	Matt O'Conner
Address	Dublin Rd., Mullingar, Co. Westmeath
Tel	+353 (0) 44 9337500
No of Rooms	95
Price	
Suites	€300
Double/Twin	€250
Single	€150
Family	€300
Dinner	Yes – Restaurant and Bar Food
Open	Open all year save 24th – 26th Dec
Credit cards	Yes
Directions	N4 exit number 9, hotel on N52
Email	info@mullingarparkhotel.com
Web	www.lucindaosullivan.com/mullingarparkhotel

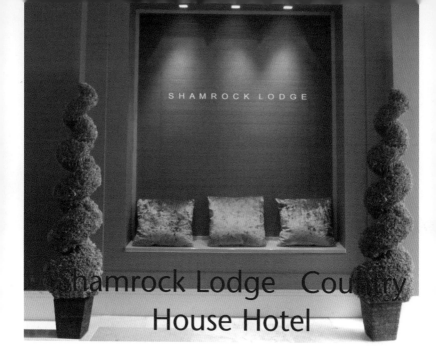

Shamrock Lodge Country House Hotel

Athlone is a busy bustling lively place spanning the mighty River Shannon. It is a halfway house for the pleasure boats that negotiate the river from north of Carrick-on-Shannon to Limerick in the south. It is also an ideal central place from which to tour and investigate the many places of interest in midland Ireland. Steeped in history, the town walls were built by the Normans in 1257. Part of these walls are still in evidence and the 13th C Castle stands proud on the west bank of the River Shannon. Another great attraction is the nearby medieval site of Clonmacnoise founded in 548AD. As a monastic city, it flourished under the patronage of the kings, including the last High King of Ireland, Rory O'Connor, whose remains were buried there. (1198AD). Athlone boasts numerous excellent recreational facilites, not least being Athlone Golf Club at Hodson Bay, a short distance outside the town, which must be one of the finest inland courses in the country.

To enjoy a visit to any town depends on finding somewhere pleasant, comfortable and enjoyable, to stay and the Shamrock Lodge Country House Hotel has all the necessities to provide these pleasures. The Hotel was beautifully refurbished in 1991 with all modern luxuries while still retaining the Country House atmosphere. A new additional development was opened in 2005 which transformed the Shamrock Lodge of yore into a hip cool destination.

From the moment you enter the elegant reception area, you feel the friendly and luxurious ambience. Go to your room and enjoy the comfort and ease that only beautiful décor and facilities can provide. Visit the fab Iona Bar, overlooking the gardens where friendly and courteous service and good drink will put even the most depressed into good humour. Their An Luain restaurant

produces excellent cuisine sourcing only fresh and local produce – so you can expect to enjoy the best of Irish Angus beef fillet maybe on a bed of pepper relish or delicious panfried seabass with tomato caper and olive salsa but whatever is on the menu you can be sure you wont be hungry.

The Shamrock Lodge is also ideal for small parties, or large parties, or even a romantic tryst for just two – you can bring pooch too but check first.

If the standard of an hotel is the people who stay there then a list of former guests includes Princess Grace, Queen Salote of Tonga and President Mary Robinson.

Owners	Paddy McCaul
Address	Clonown Road, Athlone, Co. Westmeath.
Tel:	+353 (0)906 492601
No of Rooms	52
Price	
Suite	€295
Double/twin	€150
Family Suite	€295
Dinner	Yes - Restaurant
Open	All year save Christmas 24th – 27th inc
Credit Cards	Yes
Directions	From Town Centre - go over the Town Bridge and veer left around by Athlone Castle. Follow one-way system to Battery roundabout (Walsh's pub on left). Drive straight and take immediate turn left after Battery Bridge. Hotel entrance further on, on the right.
Email	info@shamrocklodgehotel.ie
Web	www.lucindaosullivan.com/shamrocklodgehotel

County Wexford

The Vikings have a lot to answer for when you think of the number of Irish Towns they have founded. Wexford in the southeast, the sunniest part of the Country, is another example of their handiwork. It's very narrow streets are now teeming with thriving shops and businesses and, along the quayside, on the Slaney estuary stands a statue to Commadore John Barry, the Wexford man who founded the U.S. Navy during their War of Independence. This lively town is host to the ever popular and important Wexford Opera Festival every year. South of the town, almost on the extreme southeast corner of the country is Rosslare Strand with its magnificent beach and two 18 hole golf courses. Rosslare Strand is very popular with Irish people but very often missed by tourists who disembark from the ferry at Rosslare Harbour and drive madly out of the area. Going north the county has many towns with historic connections and none more so than Enniscorthy. Enjoy its period atmosphere and its connection with the 1798 Rebellion with its backdrop of Vinegar Hill site of a famous battle of the same name. Also worth seeing is the Pugin designed St. Aidan's Cathedral. Of more recent interest are the sandy beaches at Curracloe where Steven Speilberg shot those realistic battle scenes for his movie "Saving Private Ryan". In the south west of the county, on the banks of the Barrow Estuary in the quaint village of Arthurstown close to Dunbrody Abbey and less than a mile from Ballyhack from whence the ferry runs to Passage East in County Waterford.

Aldridge Lodge

A great attraction of France are the little restaurants with rooms where you will dine on superb rustic food at reasonable prices and not have to worry about driving afterwards.

Well, I found a real little gem in Ireland called Aldridge Lodge in Duncannon, Co. Wexford, Duncannon is right down on the coast, a world apart, and definitely worth a detour. Driving past Aldridge Lodge you would just think it was any modern dormer style brick house, but behind this "Wisteria Lane" suburban façade is an ultra modern restaurant with a few simple but charming bedrooms upstairs for guests. Seriously talented Chef Billy Whitty, whose father is a local fisherman, met his partner, Dublin girl, Joanne Harding, whilst working in another Country House. They are a lovely pair and have created this smashing restaurant, on two levels, with cool white walls, modern paintings and girls in long black bistro aprons in attendance.

This is seriously good food, beautifully cooked and presented, at bargain basement prices. Dinner is €35 and if you want to indulge in lobster it will cost you maybe a fiver or a tenner more – can you believe it? Even at those prices we were brought an amuse bouche of brown crabmeat and little Mediterranean vegetables – olives, peppers and breadsticks. We kicked off with panfried fillet of John Dory with buttered asparagus and a brace of succulent seared Kilmore Quay scallops served in an intense pool of Hook Head Lobster bisque, perfectly judged and quite sublime. We followed up respectively with pan-fried fillet of hake with chorizo sausage, scallop, and a pepper orange and lemon butter, and a baked whole lobster on an enormous white plate topped with a fluff of deep fried noodles

As for puds – try the Tasting Plate for Two which had beautiful little morsels of sticky toffee pudding, warm apple puff pasty lattice, Wexford strawberries, Peach Schnapps parfait, chocolate hazelnut caramel torte with chocolate fudge sauce.... get the drift!

We weren't feeling any pain when we fell upstairs to bed!! By the way they do a cracking Sunday lunch too.

You should be salivating and rearing to go – if not there is something wrong with you!

Owners	Billy Whitty and Joanne Harding
Address	Aldridge Lodge, Duncannon, Co. Wexford.
Tel	+ 353 (0)51 389116
No of Rooms	3
Price	
Junior Suite	€100/€110
Double/twin	€100/€110
Dinner	Yes – Restaurant – Dinner €38.50 – 4 Course Menu
Open	February - December
Credit Cards	Yes
Directions	From Duncannon village follow directions for The Hook Lighthouse. House located 1 km on this road on the left.
Email	info@aldridgelodge.com
Web	Aldridge Lodgewww.lucindaosullivan.com/aldridgelodge

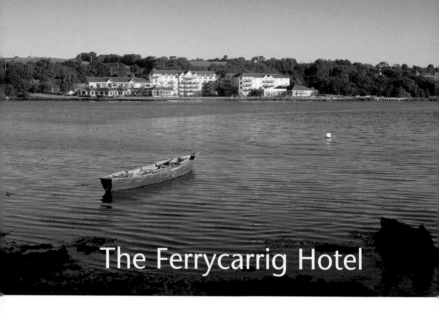

The Ferrycarrig Hotel

If ever there was a winner it is the Ferrycarrig Hotel, but then "winners" are the name of the game for Liam Griffin and his Griffin Group Hotels. which includes not only the Ferrycarrig but Hotel Kilkenny and the superb Monart Destination Spa. As most people in Ireland would know, Liam Griffin is a very well known figure in Irish life being not only a celebrated entrepreneur and hotelier but, even more importantly, former Wexford County Hurling Manager bringing his team to victory in 1996. Liam Griffin is an inspirational figure with tremenduous drive and foresight – he expects the best of his team and he delivers the best.

Ferrycarrig is an area just on the edge of Wexford Town, on the estuary of the Slaney River, of great natural beauty and wildlife, where some years ago Liam Griffin recognised the potential and developed an old hotel into the superb 4 Star hotel of today. On my first visit some years ago, before the major renovations, I made a crack about the quirky lift and, with considerable panache and humour, Liam Griffin invited me down to open their new all singing and dancing lift!

I have had great times in the Ferrycarrig Hotel for it is an all round dynamo of a Hotel that appeals to all ages. The location is fabulous, set down low right on the waters edge, serene and calming, bullrushes and

lapping water, native river birds providing a gentle wake up call, and all of its 102 sleek bedrooms have fabulous views out over the Slaney estuary – you couldn't buy better anywhere in the world.

The interior of the hotel, too, is full of atmosphere, there are parts of it which remind me almost of Morrocco. There is an on-site beauty lodge and hairdressing salon where you can indulge yourself – whilst the kids are enjoying themselves in the 20m pool – kids under 14 must have parental supervision unless they are taking part in an organised and supervised Active Club Class. During School Holidays and on Saturdays and Sundays during the year – the Crazy Clubbers club kicks into action for 4-12 year olds – so that is absolutely brilliant. My kids just adored the Ferrycarrig.

Food too is cracking – casual or formal. A steakhouse menu is served all day in the Dry Dock Bar and you can eat out on deck by the river – the Texan Steak Sandwich and Warm Hazlenut Chocolate Fondant are to die for. For the formal dining experience there is the beautiful creamy and subtle Reed Restaurant – you could almost imagine the steamboat gliding by. The food is really innovative and Reed's is really popular with non-residents and residents alike. They are very serious about sourcing local produce naming all the artisan producers, such as: "Tom Cleary's rocket, Turkish Figs, Walnut and Quail's egg with Balsamic and orange dressing" – South East Asian Seafood Bouillabaisse – red mullet, calamari, prawn, haddock with Kim Chee in a shellfish broth, Wild Boar ham, Kilmore monkfish, Roast Wild Mallard…. Do book your table in advance!!!

Owner	Griffin Group Hotels
Address	Ferrycarrig, Wexford.
Tel	+353 (0)53 912-0999
No of Rooms	102
Price	
Suites	From €300
Double/Twin	From €209
Single	From €209
Family	From €259
Dinner	Yes – Restaurant and Bar Food
Open	All Year
Credit Cards	Yes
Directions	4 kms north of Wexford Town. On N4.
Email	info@ferrycarrighotel.com
Web	www.lucindaosullivan.com/ferrycarrighotel

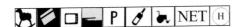

Glendine Country House

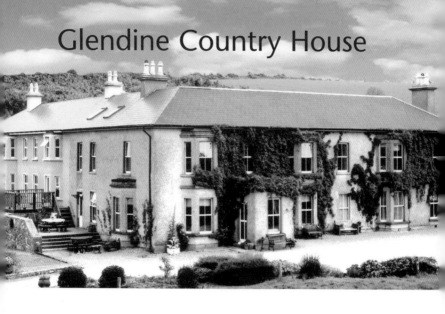

ARTHURSTOWN AND BALLYHACK

From whichever side you approach Arthurstown and Ballyhack on the Hook peninsula, there is a positive feel of never neverland. Coming from either Dublin or from Rosslare, the Duncannon roundabout outside Wexford is where you change worlds. Sit back and head straight out towards Ballyhack, trundling through hedgerows, along miles of straight road downward towards the sea, taking you little by little back into history to this totally undeveloped area. From the Waterford side, you take the car ferry at Passage East, it only takes a few minutes but the scene is set and as you approach Ballyhack and its 16th Century Castle you are almost exhilarated. Have a pint of the black stuff in the local pub you deserve it after that five minute voyage!

GLENDINE COUNTRY HOUSE

Tom and Ann Crosbie's fine Georgian Country House sits on 50 acres of beautifully landscaped gardens and paddocks, which hold their Highland cows, Jacob sheep (the ones with the curly horns) and deer. A Dower house to the Dunbrody Estate it was first occupied by the Chichester family and later by land agents until one of them absconded with the Nursery Nurse causing a great scandal. Glendine retains many of its original 1830 features, and, overlooking the Barrow Estuary, all of the rooms are stylishly beautiful and all have magnificent sea views. Beautifully decorated, using soft historic Farrow & Ball colours, the original large en suite bedrooms have Victorian beds, pitch pine floors, crisp cotton sheets, original wooden shutters. In the past year a wing of new bedrooms has been added and these too are absolutely beautiful, large and spacious. All rooms have T.V. and all mod cons. The lovely yellow drawingroom with fine fireplace, antiques and works of art, is comfortable and welcoming. Breakfasts are hearty and wholesome, where possible using organic produce. Help yourself to a fine range of fresh fruits, cereals, porridge, yoghurts and juices followed by delicious cooked breakfast with lashings of wholemeal toast or homemade brown bread. Two cosy 4 star self catering cottages are available in the courtyard, converted from the original 1830 stone buildings, and these sleep five people comfortably. Dinner is available for a minimum of 10 people and soup and open brown bread sandwiches are happily provided at all times. There are very nice Restaurants close by and excellent pub grub. Glendine has a wine license but you can bring your own. This is a gorgeous house, Tosh and Annie are charming hosts, and you couldn't find a finer place to stay.

Owners	Tom & Ann Crosbie
Address	Arthurstown, Co. Wexford
Tel	+353 (0)51 389500
No. Of Rooms	6
Price	
Suite	€140
Double/Twin	€110 - €120
Single	€65 (supp €25 July + August)
Family	€140 (2 Ad + 1 Ch) €160 (2 Ad + 2 Ch)
Dinner	Dinner available min 10 people. €35 each. Book.
Open	All Year except Christmas
Credit Cards	Yes
Directions	From New Ross turn right at Brandon House Hotel. Pass JFK Arboretum, Arthurstown is signposted.
Email	glendinehouse@eircom.net
Web	www.lucindaosullivan.com/glendine

Kelly's Resort Hotel

Since 1895 four successive generations of the Kelly family have each added their own stamp to Kelly's Resort Hotel. Bill Kelly and his wife, Isabelle, have, in turn, enlarged and added a whole new cool modern dimension in the last few years culminating in the addition of the fabulous new SeaSpa incorporating eleven treatment rooms, seawater vitality pool, rainforest shower, rock sauna, lanconium, steam room, mud chamber and seaweed bath, which has been their biggest project ever.

Being right on the beach there is that upmarket sandy resort ethos and atmosphere, for, as soon as you swish up and park, you will see people strolling around in bathrobes between Spa, Leisure, Beauty Centre, Hairdresser or Hot Tub – it is just switch off time. I know people who drive down to Kelly's, park their car, and don't move it again until they are leaving Rosslare Strand. Why would they, everything one could possibly want is encompassed within the Hotel. When one mentions Kelly's Hotel, people generally say – "Oh, the food is fabulous, and one eats so much". That's true. It's like a cruise ship, non-stop wonderful food all included in your rate.

Breakfast and lunch are available buffet style in the Ivy Room or with formal service in the gorgeous Beaches Restaurant, which had over a €1m spent on it alone not so long ago. Likewise with lunch, not forgetting afternoon tea and all day availability of free coffee. In the evening people gather for drinks before dinner - which is always superb – oysters, foie gras terrine, game, fish, just as much of anything you could want and Kelly's import their wine direct from France, where Isabelle's family are in the wine business in the Chateauneuf-du-Pape region, resulting in excellent very well priced wines. Dancing follows dinner so join in the fun. Bedrooms are lovely – some with doors opening out onto your own mini terrace or else have balconies. There is also the La Marine Restaurant (not included in the "all in" rate) and Bar which is popular with visitors to Rosslare. Kelly's Irish Art Collection is famed and in this regard it is opportune to mention that throughout the year there are different breaks revolving around Art, Cookery,

Wine, Antiques, Gardening, Ballroom Dancing and of course golf. Kelly's mainly operates on an all-inclusive package, anything from two days to a week and, for what is included, it is superb value. Sometimes, midweek only, they do a room and breakfast rate if that is what you want and you can dine in either Beaches or La Marine. I don't think it is possible for Bill & Isabelle to carry out any further improvements!

Owner	Bill Kelly
Address	Rosslare Strand, Co. Wexford.
Tel	+353 (0)53 913 2114
No. Of Rooms	118
Price	
Suite	From €352 + 10% Service Charge
Double/Twin	€198 + 10% Service Charge
	Spring and Autumn inclusive rates from €280pps + 10% (for 2 days upwards)
Dinner	Yes – 2 Restaurants
Open	16th February to 9th December
Credit Cards	Visa MC Amex
Directions	On Rosslare Strand
Email	info@kellys.ie
Web	www.lucindaosullivan.com/kellyshotel

Monart Destination Spa

Monart is the jewel in the crown of the Griffin Group Hotels. Liam Griffin spotted the beautiful 18th Centure Monart House near Enniscorthy when it came up for sale about five years ago and realised he could create something really different here, something that wasn't already in Ireland, a stand alone Destination Spa for adults only.

He restored the original Monart house and it now acts as a gateway to this stunning 21st Century Spa experience designed with the emphasis on the 3 Rs – not the ones you learned in school – but Rest, Relaxation and Renewal. Nothing has been spared and this whole place is a hymn to design – really gorgeous.

In a world that has become increasingly concerned with being eco-friendly and monitoring our carbon footprint impact, this purpose-built spa offers accommodation in beautiful, chalet-style wooden residences that blend in with the timber surrounds, embracing the lush outdoors. It's restful from first glance, inspired by the restorative powers of nature and incorporating lots of natural light through large windows. Once inside, you can avail of the tools of relaxation which man-kind has harnessed and developed.

All rooms boast either woodland or lake view, with balcony or terrace. If, like me, you've always fantasised about sinking into a gorgeous four-poster bed, why not book yourself into one of the suites? Rooms are decorated in calm, muted colours and are furnished with the most luxurious bedding imaginable – all you need to do after your rigorous treatments or lazy lounging is to reserve enough energy to tuck yourself in!

Monart offers the most comprehensive and cutting edge range of Spa facilities and treatments, and has an exclusive partnership with the top American Spa product line Pevonia Botanica. In its vast 2400 square metres, the Spa area contains 14 neutral gender treatment rooms, sanarium, outdoor Swedish log sauna with ice shower grotto, cadarium, aroma cave, salt grotto, traditional Hamam, mud chamber and hydrotherapy pools to name but a few. So think along the lines of luxuriating in a Full Detox Seaweed Thalasso Wrap for the poor old body and achieve inch loss as well. Another good one is the Green Coffee

Body wrap for the breakdown of cellulite and fat, which also helps transform fat into energy. The Elasto-firm facemask treatment, cited as a non-surgical face-lift, is also popular.

Fine dining is available at the Spa's restaurant – guests can select healthy/detox options or go for something a little more sinful - depending on the particular persuasion of the devil/angel on your shoulder that day! As a Food Critic I don't have to tell you what is always on my shoulder!! The restaurant prides itself on preparing and serving local produce and there is a big emphasis on providing fresh home-made fare including breads, dressings and preserves. A lighter, bistro style menu is available for guests and non-residents, as is afternoon tea which is served every day in the Garden Lounge. There is also a café on site which is open to residents and day-guests.

Just about 90 minutes from Dublin's big smoke, this is THE ideal place to get away from it all and start tree hugging!

Monart is where it is at!

Owner	The Griffin Group
Address	The Still, Enniscorthy, Co. Wexford.
Tel	+353 (0)53 923-8999
No of Rooms	68
Price	
Suites	€695 - €1295
Double/Twin	€280 - €600
Single	€182 - €342
Dinner	Yes – Restaurant and Cafe
Open	January – 23 December
Credit Cards	Yes
Directions	Approaching Enniscorthy on N11, turn right onto N80, take 1st turn to left and follow directional signs.
Email	info@monart.ie
Web	www.lucindaosullivan.com/monartspa

Seafield Hotel

BALLYMONEY

Driving from Gorey to Ballymoney, Co. Wexford, you soon realise you are in a different world. The windy roads with lush, thick, tropical greenery always remind me of scenes from Jurrasic Park – not that you can expect any galloping dinosaurs to cross your path – but there is a feeling of being away from it all – escape from the real world.

My first visit to Ballymoney was as a young child on a day out at the seaside from my aunt's farm in Tullow, Co. Carlow. I never forgot the joy of romping on the beach, in and out of coves, and coming home convinced that I had seen a real live mine with spikes stuck in the rocks – well I had a vivid imagination!

The wonderful thing about Ballymoney is its simplicity. It is located on the Courtown to Castletown road and the village itself is very simple – and this is what appeals. There are wonderful golf courses, pitch and putt, craft shops and pubs nearby, plus that great beach. There were many shipwrecks off the Ballymoney coast including the famous "Orphan Girl", the nautical memorabilia of which are in the local pub.

SEAFIELD HOTEL

Now there is a super new hotel in the midst of this rural seaside bliss – appropriately called the Seafield Hotel on 160 acres of lush parkland – with a fab Oceo Spa which has 14 treatment rooms, a Hydrotherapy pool, Vitality outdoor pool, Hammamtable, Ice Grotto… You will be really thrilled with the Spa and your better half will be equally thrilled with the 18 hole Golf Course designed by Peter McEvoy. In fact you can both play a

round of golf and, if you have a day in the rough, jointly recover in the Spa's Couple's Suite.

The whole ethos of the 4 Star Seafield is ultra contemporary with every luxury and facility and it was designed by Italian Architect Francesco Beia, who has maximised the natural elements of this great location. Bright and airy, ultra hip, accommodation is in luxurious bedrooms, beautifully furnished and fitted out, with some having an open terrace. There are also two and three bedroomed suites in the courtyard which are brilliant for families.

The bar could be in New York or Milan. You will be sipping your cocktails under Roberto Cavali lights with Mooi furniture, marble counter tops and walnut floors. Then you will be dining in the most spectacular restaurant where limestone and black Venetian plaster walls meet lofty ceilings. The emphasis on food in Seafield is to create contemporary dishes. Think maybe of Diver Sea Scallops, pumpkin and apple puree, with a Calvados sauce or maybe Jumbo Lump Crab Cake followed up by delicious Pan Roasted Sea Bass with crab mashed potatoes and lemon butter sauce.

Food is also available in the bar as well as the Club House.

Seafield is a great place for a holiday, short break, a weekend of pampering in the Spa with the girls and wonderful too for families.

Owner	David Stone – General Manager
Address	Ballymoney, Gorey, Co. Wexford.
Tel	+353 (0)53 942-4000
No of Rooms	102
Price	
Suites	From €495
Double/Twin	From €150
Single	From €105
Courtyard Family Suites	From €200
Dinner	Yes – Restaurant
Open	All Year
Credit Cards	Yes
Directions	From Dublin take N11 South for 80kms. Exit at Junction 23 signed Courtown. At r'abt take 1st exit signed Courtown. Straight after 2nd r'abt take left until T Junct. Turn left. Hotel 1 mile on right.
Email	sales@seafieldhotel.com
Web	www.lucindaosullivan.com/seafieldhotel

P   NET   18h   H   Spa

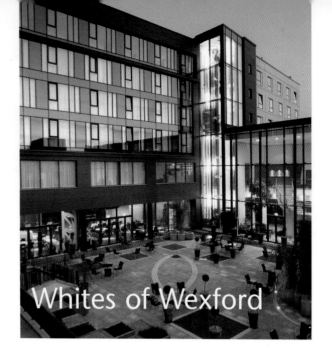

Whites of Wexford

We got married in St. Mullin's in South Carlow and spent our first night in White's Hotel. The funniest part of the whole event was that the Bridesmaid got a double bed, the Best Man got a double bed, the other couple with us got a double bed, but even though a bottle of champagne had been sent to the Bridal Couple's room we got two single beds and we were too embarrassed to ask for a double!! That is all a very long time ago, needless to say, but White's Hotel is still a part of pivotal life in Wexford, but it is not the White's of yesteryear for it has been completely reconstructed. We went back for a look at the metamorphosis and were absolutely wowed by it all.

The new hotel now features a fabulous Tranquility Spa & Wellness Centre with a hydropool and thermal suite – that is apart from the Leisure Centre with 20m pool. In addition, they also have the first Cryotherapy Clinic in Ireland. It can be used for all sorts of medical conditions. So you won't have to go to Switzerland or America you can have a fabulous break combined and try the latest therapy.

The bedrooms are superb, furnished to 4 Star standard, big beds, crisp sleek and modern, plasma screen televisions, Broadband, minibar, iron and ironing board, in room safes, in house movie and satellite channels. They also have a very large number of family rooms – so bring the kids folks – they will love it.

Being a food critic, I suppose I tend to always come back around to the restaurant and bar facilities and at Whites of Wexford they are superb. There are two bars, the Lobby Bar or the fashionable La Speranza Café Bar – you can have food throughout the day in both places. Their main Restaurant overlooks the Courtyard – where you can also sit out and enjoy a glass or ten of champagne or dine alfresco. Think along the lines of having crisp crab and prawn spring rolls

with sesame noodles, baby bok choy, avocado puree and lime vinaigrette followed maybe by grilled fillet of brill with braised fennel, spicy chorizo, crushed potatoes and sauce vierge or maybe roast loin of venison with a smoked cheese and caramelized onion rosti, root vegetable puree and a light juniper and port reduction.

The boys of Wexford are being well looked after at Whites.

Owners	Peter Wilson (General Manager)
Address	Abbey Street, Wexford.
Tel	+353 (0)53 91 22311
No of Rooms	157
Price	
Suite	From €250
Double/twin	From €136
Family	From €136 + €25 BB per child.
Dinner	Yes – Restaurant and Bars
Open	All Year
Credit Cards	Yes
Directions	In centre of Wexford.
Email	info@whitesofwexford.ie
Web	www.lucindaosullivan.com/whitesofwexford

 Spa | NET | P

County Wicklow

Truly the Garden of Ireland, County Wicklow, is rich in mountains, valleys, gorse, heather, and bracken, and as any hiker, cyclist and motorist will undoubtedly agree, it more than deserves its title. Less than an hour's drive from Dublin City, the county quickly portrays the two dominant traditions in Irish history, Glendalough with its Monastic background and the magnificent Anglo Irish Powerscourt Estate at Enniskerry. Glendalough set in a remote valley is a mediaeval Monastic site with its period cemetery, round tower, remains of a monastic chapel and its two lakes, is a very popular haunt for tourists. The area is surrounded by a number of pleasant welcoming villages, Kiltegan, Knockree, Roundwood, Laragh, Rathdrum and, of course, Avoca whose name was made famous by the poet Thomas Moore, and the peaceful village of Aughrim. Enniskerry in the foothills of the Wicklow Mountains is a very popular summer weekend destination for tourists, who trudge uphill from buses to the Powerscourt Estate and its beautiful gardens. Powerscourt also boasts two 18-hole golf courses. The impressive Powerscourt House designed by Richard Cassels was destroyed by fire in 1974, it has now been restored to house a number of shops and a restaurant. The famous Powerscourt Waterfall is almost three miles away from the main house but is still within the Estate's extensive grounds. On the coast to the south is Greystones a pretty somnambulant town where many of the inhabitants commute to Dublin daily and is close to the town in Ireland with the longest name, Newtownmountkennedy. Further south is Wicklow town, which enjoys a fine setting on the coast, and proudly proclaims its restored historic jail. On south past the beautiful sandy beach at Brittas Bay brings you to Arklow town a chiefly commercial centre well known as a boat building and fishing port and immortalized by Van Morrison in his "Streets of Arklow".

"It takes a lot of experience for a girl to kiss like a beginner."
(LADIES HOME JOURNAL, 1948)

Marriott Druids Glen Hotel & Country Club

I thought I had lost him. He thought he was in Heaven. We were in the 5 Star Marriott Druids Glen Hotel & Country Club on a 400 acre estate in the Garden of Ireland which has not just one, but two Championship Golf Courses – Druids Glen and Druids Heath. Golfers can view both Golf Courses, hole by hole, on their website. Known as the Augusta of Europe, Druids Glen Golf Resort has been host to 4 Irish Opens, the Seve Trophy Golf Tournament. It has been voted European Golf Resort of the Year, and is a magnet for Ryder Cup stars. There is a Golf Academy – a golfer's dream resort in other words!

Druids Glen was originally the Woodstock Estate, dating back to 1600 when it formed part of Sir Thomas Wentworth's landholdings. Woodstock House, the beautiful clubhouse at Druids Glen, was built in 1770.

We could, in fact, have stayed in the Marriott Druids Glen Hotel forever and just met up for dinner in the evenings because, while he was on the Golf Courses, I was indulging myself in the fab Elemis Spa. There is an 18 metre indoor swimming pool, Whirlpool, Solarium, Sauna, Fun Shower and Mist Grotto, Aroma Steam Room and 'Hydrotheraphy Room along with a Fitness Suite, which overlooks the pool area. I am afraid I am a total pleasure girl so indulged in the relaxing massages and beauty treatments. There is also Teambuilding on site. It is only 35 minutes from Dublin City so ideal for combining both sightseeing and shopping. It is also very close to Powerscourt and all the little southside village upmarket boutiques.

Druids Glen Hotel was the first Marriott Hotel in Ireland and has settled into being a serious resort destination for those who enjoy an all round good time. The décor is modern with Celtic twists and superbly comfortable. The

bedrooms are enormous, all at least 38 sq m, with King size or two Queen size beds, plus minibars, room safes, individual climate control, all luxury facilities expected of a good 5 Star Hotel. On top of that, if you want to take the sprogs with you, believe it or not you can have two under 16s share your room free of charge – and if they are under 13 they don't even have to pay for breakfast – now that is fantastic!!

Food is excellent. There is Flynn's Restaurant – an upmarket American style steakhouse doing really good Irish beef, seasonal game and freshwater fish, and the popular Druids Brasserie doing excellent popular Irish food including a delcious Traditional Irish Stew with soda bread; Traditional Guinness battered fish, green peas and chips, steaks, and daily specials including a Sunday favourite of Slow Roast Rib of Beef with a rich jus and horseradish cream. If you want casual food during the day it is available in the Thirteenth Bar

What are you waiting for?

Owner	Richard Collins – General Manager
Address	Newtownmountkennedy, Co. Wicklow.
Tel	+353 (0)1 287-0800
No of Rooms	145
Price	
Suites	From €240
Double/Twin	From €180
Single	From €155
Dinner	Yes – 2 Restaurants and Barfood
Open	All Year
Credit Cards	Yes
Directions	20 miles south of Dublin on N11 look for signs.
Email	mhrs.dubgs.reservations@marriotthotels.com
Web	www.lucindaosullivan.com/marriottdruidsglenhotel

Houses in alphabetical order

Slow down

Enjoying Ireland is not about tearing down a motorway at 90 miles an hour, for doing it that way you will miss the whole ethos of the country. Tourists planning their trip in advance from America and other distant places tend to look at our little green, bear shaped, island in the Atlantic on the edge of Europe and think "we'll see it all in 3 days" – believe me you won't have even "done" West Cork properly in that time. You may have seen the views but you won't have experienced anything except a sore backside from sitting in the driving seat!

Take time out, get to know your hosts, it makes such a difference. They can give you all the local lore and recommendations. Go down to the local pub – you won't be long on your own – because the Irish love to talk. Every time I arrive at a destination, my first stop is the nearest hairdressers, which absolutely delights Brendan, for he then has an hour to find the best pub and in no time at all, the locals will have found out his seed, breed and generation, and he will have been rewarded with the best local information.

In the immortal words of Simon and Garfunkel – "Slow Down You Move to Fast..."

Unless otherwise stated room prices include breakfast. Apart from Hotels we suggest that you make arrangements for dinner on the night of your arrival at the same time as you book your accommodation as most houses would like 24 hours notice.

L'instant

TAITTINGER

Wine is constant proof that God loves us and loves to see us happy.

Benjamin Franklin.

At Febvre & Company we're strong admirers of Benjamin's line of thought. Seeing our customers happy is at the heart of everything we do. We understand the importance of reputation and we want our customers to be sure that every time they serve a Febvre wine, the care with which we select our growers shines through.

Febvre and Company Limited,
Highfield House, Burton Hall Road,
Sandyford Industrial Estate,
Sandyford, Dublin 18, Ireland.

Tel.   +353 1 216 1400
Fax.   +353 1 295 9036
Web.   www.febvre.ie
Email. info@febvre.ie

FEBVRE
Original thinking in wine

NOTES